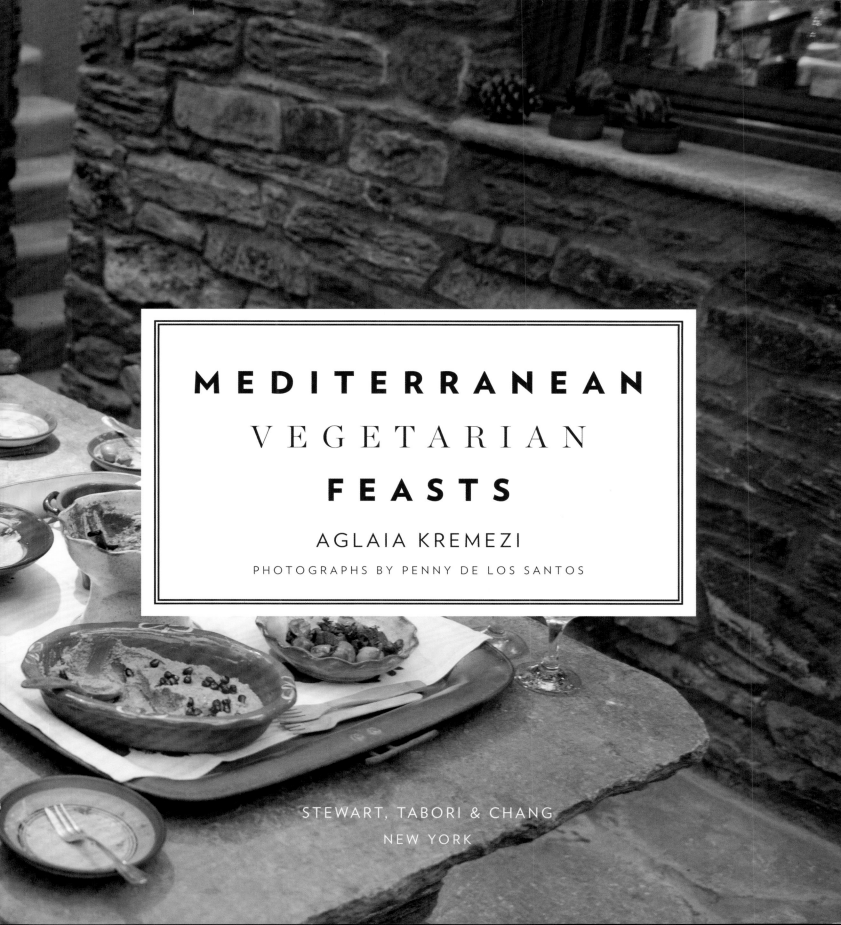

MEDITERRANEAN
VEGETARIAN
FEASTS

AGLAIA KREMEZI

PHOTOGRAPHS BY PENNY DE LOS SANTOS

STEWART, TABORI & CHANG

NEW YORK

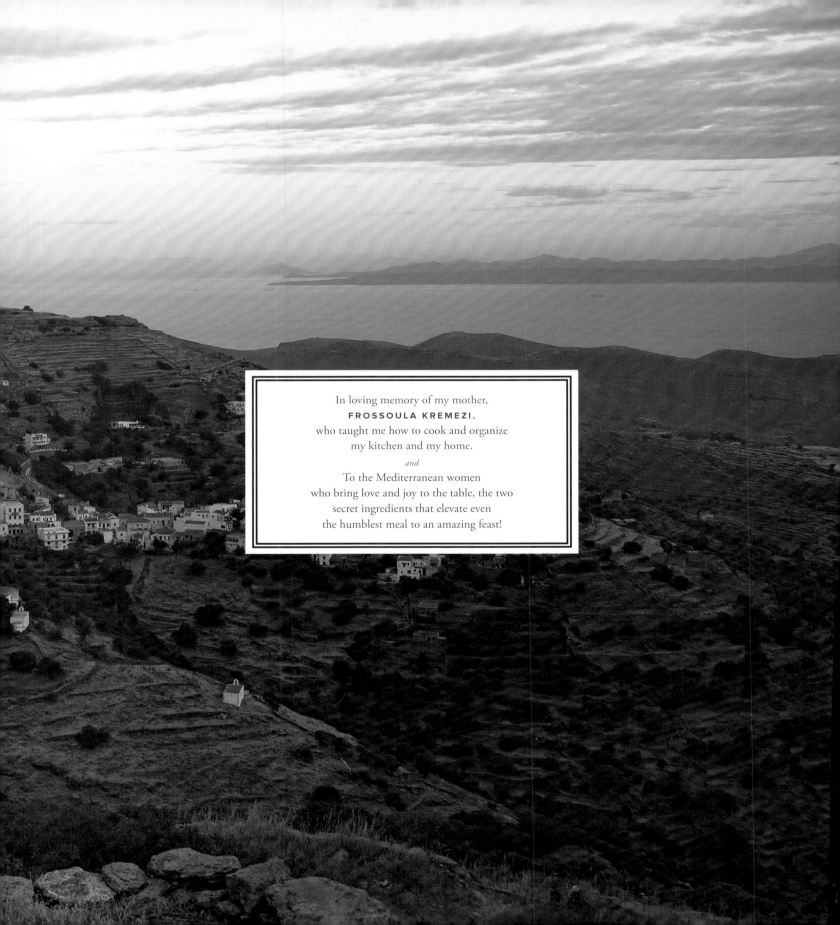

In loving memory of my mother,
FROSSOULA KREMEZI,
who taught me how to cook and organize
my kitchen and my home.
and
To the Mediterranean women
who bring love and joy to the table, the two
secret ingredients that elevate even
the humblest meal to an amazing feast!

CONTENTS

FOREWORD

Although I don't consider myself a vegetarian, for as long as I can remember I have predominantly cooked and eaten vegetables and greens. Like Molière's *bourgeois gentilhomme*, who exclaims, "I have been speaking prose without knowing it for more than forty years," I recently realized that I have been mostly vegetarian, without knowing it, all my life!

This early-fall morning I grilled the sweet red peppers that Costas, my husband, brought from the garden. As I was dressing their charred skins and tender, full-bodied flesh with olive oil, vinegar, crushed coriander seeds, and a little garlic—quite a simple preparation—it occurred to me that these intensely flavored heirloom peppers illustrate the deep, multilayered story of mostly vegetarian Mediterranean cooking. Like tomatoes, the small, fiery-hot peppers from America were gradually incorporated into the Mediterranean kitchen. Stubborn peasant cooking does not change or move forward easily—it does not know the word "fusion"—but it does evolve. The strong attachment to tradition, with small openings for change and incorporation of new ingredients and techniques, is the lifeblood of our cuisine. *Siga siga,* we say often in Greece: "Slowly slowly." But, in time, we embrace products and techniques from faraway places. The dialogue between old and new shows how Mediterranean cooks reflect deeply upon, and constantly improve, their traditional plant-based diet.

Tomato paste—the Mediterranean equivalent of soy sauce—is such an indispensable year-round flavoring that it is easy to forget its modern Italian origins in the mid-nineteenth century. Can you imagine a Mediterranean cuisine without tomatoes? I think not. Both peppers and tomatoes earned their places in the Mediterranean pantheon of cooking because they so perfectly complement the flavor of olive oil

and the Mediterranean summer crops. Other ingredients—such as tofu—have failed to gain traction in our kitchens because they simply don't mesh with the basic principles of Mediterranean cooking explored in this book.

Going through thousands of my photos the other day—old Kodachromes and digital photos alike—I could barely find any meat dishes to include in a slideshow. Vegetables are more photogenic, colorful, and sexy, so obviously they were the "Lolitas" of the camera lens. And yet, if I had prepared meat more often over the years, I would certainly have more than a few decent pictures to show for it.

My cooking, I realized, is mostly vegetarian and often vegan, with the occasional use of fish or small amounts of meat as flavoring. Though I have embraced spices and flavorings from my travels throughout the world, my approach to cooking remains much in the tradition of my mother and grandmother. There is a big difference, though, between my kitchen and theirs: Widespread, quotidian consumption of meat is a relatively new phenomenon in this part of the world. I have options previous generations did not have. I could eat meat every day if I chose to, like most people I know. But I choose not to. Frankly, I find vegetable cooking and eating so much more exciting and wonderfully delicious. In this sense I remain with my feet firmly grounded in the traditions of the past, but with a constant eye on the trends of the present and the future. Slowly and carefully, I choose what new elements to bring into my repertoire. Some of the dishes I cook would be heretical in my mother's eyes. But I firmly believe that tradition must evolve in order to remain true to itself. This book adheres to the old ways and incorporates the benefits of the new. Is that not the essence of a healthy, living tradition?

PREVIOUS SPREAD: *Late spring vegetables and greens from our garden.*
OPPOSITE: *Rosemary (top) and* za'atar, *the particular kind of thyme indigenous to Syria and Lebanon (see page 56), from our herb garden.*

COOK CREATIVELY: A METHODOLOGY OF MEDITERRANEAN COOKING

This book is designed to make you a better chef and a smarter shopper. It will help you to choose the best of the most tempting seasonal produce in your local markets. But there are a few simple, essential steps you must take to get the most out of the recipes that follow and to save yourself hours of daily preparation. A small investment of your time now will reap huge rewards every time you cook.

Before you head to the market, consult the Flavor Arsenal (page 50) to stock up and mix your spices. Then go through the lists in Essential Ingredients (page 16) to see what you should have at all times.

IN YOUR PANTRY: olive oil, flour, rice or bulgur, tomato paste, tahini, garlic, onions.

IN THE REFRIGERATOR: lemons, cheese, yogurt.

See also what I suggest you have **IN THE FREEZER** (precooked chickpeas, beans, and other legumes and grains) and plan and shop accordingly.

Go to the farmers' market without preconceived ideas. Ask yourself: What are the freshest vegetables at the market today? Then buy them. Every day the answer will be different, and your ingredients will be at your mercy, not vice versa.

Choose plentifully so that you can make a few different dishes for the week's meals.

Shop when you will have extra time upon returning home. Once home, *don't just stuff everything in the fridge.* This is the first step toward spoiling your excellent purchases.

Go to Basic Preparations & Techniques (page 23) to see how you can store, prepare, and organize your produce. Then look up recipes and plan the stages that will help you cook easy yet fabulous dishes to showcase the season's best vegetables!

For more inspiration, see the Seasonal Menu Suggestions (page 21).

INTRODUCTION

I grew up eating mostly vegetarian food. In the mountainous, rocky Greek countryside, it is not possible to pasture large herds of animals, so a steady supply of meat was never certain. Until the 1960s, when commercial meat distribution started to touch all corners of the country, Greeks (like most southern Europeans) were mainly, if somewhat unwillingly, vegetarians by necessity. Since ancient times meat was a rare and expensive commodity consumed on Sundays, at Easter, at Christmas, and during important family feasts. Our traditional, well-balanced diet is based on garden vegetables and leafy greens called *horta*, which are either foraged from the hills and fields or cultivated. Garden vegetables, along with greens, are the basic components for countless diverse dishes served every day at Mediterranean tables. Beans of all kinds—chickpeas, lentils, dried fava beans, split peas, and black-eyed peas—as well as nuts and grains, mainly in the form of bread, are our dry staples. They are complemented by and enriched with good, fruity olive oil, olives, capers, local cheeses, yogurt, and occasionally fresh or cured fish, especially anchovies and fresh or salted sardines—the delicious fare of poor fishermen.

A Rich, Frugal, Vegetarian Legacy

Each morning, as I plan lunch—our main meal—and consider the produce from our garden, I feel that I can rely upon a tremendously rich legacy to guide me. The dishes I grew up eating were created and perfected over centuries by resourceful female cooks from all over the Mediterranean. They had to invent myriad ways to use the overabundance of *horta*—various kinds of dandelion, chicory, mustard greens, and, of course, spinach, chard, and summer *vlita* (amaranth shoots). In the winter we have squash, by spring lots of tender zucchini; for months, these are the only vegetables we get from our garden, but the cornucopia in a limited range inspires me, as it did

cooks before me, to combine such produce with any number of staples. Consider the irresistible batter-fried zucchini slices in *Fritto Misto* (page 68); the hearty rice-and-herb-stuffed zucchini, often cooked together with dolmades (stuffed grape leaves, page 164) that share the same stuffing; zucchini fritters (page 77); the caramelized mix of roasted zucchini, eggplants, and peppers, flavored with garlic and oregano (page 147); and the mouth-watering crustless zucchini pie (page 141). They look and taste so different, yet they all share the same basic ingredient: zucchini!

In the winter and spring, I briefly sauté my garden's kale, cabbage, chard, spinach, artichokes, and fresh fava in olive oil, then braise the vegetables in white wine and finish the dish with a generous squeeze of fresh lemon, chopped dill, and fennel. I always serve slices of crusty homemade bread (page 198) alongside to soak up the vibrant sauce. Often I roll cabbage, chard, and other large leafy greens around a stuffing of rice, vegetables, and herbs (page 162); squash can be hollowed out and filled with a similar stuffing. Sometimes I serve them drizzled with creamy *avgolemono* (egg-and-lemon sauce). I regularly make a pilaf with rice, toasted bulgur, wheat berries or orzo pasta and flavor it with a jumble of colorful seasonal vegetables and herbs. At times I cook the grains and vegetables together with beans—my husband's favorite—or with chickpeas or lentils. My everyday dishes are almost all vegetarian, I now realize—my language in the kitchen is much like the prose of Molière's hero! And this is not the result of an effort to follow a healthy diet in today's medical sense. We eat this plant-based diet because we love and enjoy the bright, bold flavors of vegetables!

"Nose-to-Tail" Vegetarian

I strongly believe that the practice of "nose-to-tail eating" should not be restricted to meat, but should include all vegetables, greens, herbs, and fruit. Although today most people don't have to be as frugal as my poor ancestors, throwing away less and making the most of what we have is better for the environment. Besides, cutting down on waste forces the cook to invent new and exciting dishes. Thrown-out parts of vegetables have hidden qualities: The fragrant green part of scallions are ideal for all kinds of stuffing or pie fillings, while the pink roots and bottom stems of spinach make a delicious salad or side dish—briefly blanched, their crunchy texture and sweet, earthy taste is quite addictive, distinct from the taste of tender spinach leaves.

Spinach naturally leads me to *spanakopita* (spinach pie) and to *pites* in general—thin, phyllo-wrapped pies. To me they represent better than any other traditional dish the home cook's ingenuity: Small scraps of almost anything—some leftover vegetable parts, a few garden herbs, together with nuts, grains, and cheese—are transformed into irresistible delicacies, enclosed in a crunchy phyllo crust that you can learn to roll with the dexterity of the potter's hand, from a dough of just flour, water, and olive oil.

A Vegetarian Journey

Through my recipes I intend to lead you on a culinary journey among fragrant herbs and spices and to help you rediscover and explore both old and new ways of cooking and combining vegetables, pulses, grains, and nuts. Marginalized, age-old ingredients of the Mediterranean, like the versatile sesame paste tahini—useful for much more than the ubiquitous hummus—will enliven both sweet and savory dishes with its rich nutty taste. Grape molasses is another ancient staple that adds a multilayered sweetness to breads and biscuits as well as to dressings and sauces; like tahini, it has been proven to be among nature's healthiest and most nourishing foods. Spices, herbs, dried fruits, and nuts impart zest, flavor, texture, and aroma to the savory and sweet dishes I include. Dried figs, dates, sultanas, black

ABOVE: *Cooked spinach roots.*

currants, almonds, walnuts, hazelnuts, and pistachios; fruity olive oil, fragrant fresh or dried herbs, musky and mildly hot Mediterranean pepper flakes; eastern Mediterranean spices such as cumin, coriander seeds, cinnamon, allspice, cloves, turmeric, and saffron—with so much to choose from, your vegetarian dishes will take on new dimensions. Experience has shown me that people can't get enough of traditional, mostly vegetarian dishes; they satisfy even the most demanding palates, and furthermore, the people who feast on them leave the table feeling well-nourished, light, and content.

Greens and herbs from Crete: (top row) sow thistle (Sonchus, a popular foraged green since antiquity), wild sage, caper bush sprigs, prickly artichokes; (second row) wild lavender, stamnagathi (a local variety of chicory, Cichorium spinosum), grape leaves, wild arugula; (bottom row) pickled kritamo (rock samphire), chard leaves, and wild fennel.

ESSENTIAL INGREDIENTS

Shop with your head up, not buried in a list; look, touch, taste, and smell what the market has to offer. Go to your local farmers' market without a recipe or shopping list in hand; choose the seasonal produce that inspires you, and only then search the pages that follow for recipes that will showcase your fresh ingredients.

Are you concerned about having the necessary ingredients to complete a dish? This book will teach you to approach your cooking and vegetable shopping differently so you never encounter that problem again. By putting together a well-stocked pantry, refrigerator, and freezer, you will cook better, eat better, and save precious time and money. Even the busiest and most overworked cooks can make fresh, healthy, and enticing meals in half an hour or less, cooking from scratch in well-planned stages (see Basic Preparations & Techniques, page 23).

Here is a brief description of the most important items to keep stocked in your pantry, refrigerator, and freezer.

I grew up eating **OLIVE OIL**—a lot of olive oil. Like most of my family, friends, and neighbors around the Mediterranean, oil *is* olive oil. A single person in Greece consumes roughly 40 pints of olive oil per year. Scientific studies have repeatedly linked the consumption of olive oil to the prevention of many common diseases, keeping our bodies and minds strong and healthy.

Some newly converted purists may find my suggestions shocking, but I don't see the point in using expensive, fruity olive oil for cooking. When heated, any olive oil inevitably loses its aroma and fruitiness. My suggestion is to have two kinds of olive oil in your pantry. Buy one ordinary and cheaper oil, which you can purchase in bulk from a reliable source, to use for cooking and baking. Then carefully choose your favorite good, fruity, and peppery olive oil for drizzling over foods just before serving; this is the oil you will use in salad dressings, spreads, and relishes

and add to raw sauces and pastes you make with spice mixtures. In the recipes that follow, I always make the distinction between the two types of oil.

Which fruity olive oil you choose is entirely a matter of taste. I suggest you get a few small bottles of different high-quality olive oils and simply taste them to decide which you prefer. You may choose one for tomato salads and another to drizzle over chickpeas. There is no right or wrong choice. Keep in mind that the fresh and assertive taste of young, newly pressed olive oil mellows as the months pass, so use last year's leftover oil for cooking, and get fresh oil each winter that will be the finishing touch to your favorite dishes.

LEMONS are omnipresent in Mediterranean recipes; you need to have two or three lemons in your fruit basket or refrigerator at all times. You probably already keep a steady supply of **GARLIC** and **ONIONS**; you should also have a bunch of **FLAT-LEAF PARSLEY** and maybe some **DILL**, **MINT**, or **BASIL**. You can grow these herbs in little pots in your garden or on the windowsill. If you buy nice fresh bunches, keep them for up to seven days or more, arranged in a jar like flowers (see page 27). **SEA SALT** is the only salt used in Mediterranean cooking, but ordinary salt is fine. Fleur de sel or any good finishing salt can add an exciting element to dishes.

In your pantry, besides a good supply of **SPICES** (see page 50), you should have **TAHINI** (see page 52), **CAPERS** (preferably the dry-salted ones; see page 83), your favorite **OLIVES**, and of course **PASTA**.

BULGUR is cracked wheat that has been steamed and dried, and it cooks quickly. It was a Mediterranean staple

OPPOSITE: *A variety of ingredients (clockwise from top left): olive oil, dry-salted olives, fresh capers, barley rusks, honey, fig leaf, salt and maraş pepper, tomatoes, green, unripe almonds, lemon, kumquat, pomegranate flower,* Apostagma *or* Raki *(local moonshine), green pistachio preserves and rose petal jam, grape molasses, grape leaf, mountain tea, Greek thyme, wild sage, and* za'atar *(Lebanese thyme).*

before rice became widely available. It comes in three grinds: Coarse and medium are best for pilafs and stuffings, and fine is preferable for salads, where it is eaten raw, just soaked in water.

FARRO and **WHEAT BERRIES** make delicious pilafs but need long cooking, so I suggest you precook them (page 35) and keep them in the freezer, along with **CHICKPEAS** and **OTHER BEANS**. That will enable you to cook a hearty meal in minutes, using fresh vegetables, greens, and fruits.

Greeks consume more cheese per person than any European—slightly more than the French, if you can believe it. **FETA** is omnipresent at the table, complementing all kinds of foods, much like the Middle Eastern *labne*—a delicious thick, creamy, spreadable cheese made by straining full-fat yogurt. Fermented *labne* acquires a pungent taste (see *Shanklish*, page 82); dried in the sun it becomes an important Middle Eastern flavoring. Greeks couldn't imagine eating string beans cooked with olive oil and tomato (page 146), or any *ladera* (olive oil–braised vegetables), for that matter, without feta and fresh country bread. Greek summers always mean a simple tomato salad, dressed with plenty of good fruity olive oil and sprinkled with oregano; the simple salad is transformed to a hearty meal with feta and good bread or *paximadia* (page 214) that absorbs the delicious juices.

Along with feta, **HALLOUMI** from Cyprus is another very popular eastern Mediterranean cheese. This semi-hard, firm white cheese has a somewhat elastic texture, similar to mozzarella. It is firmer than feta and does not crumble when sliced, making it excellent for grilling and frying, and it can also be coarsely grated. Traditionally, halloumi was made from sheep's milk, but the commercial cheese available today is made mainly from cow's milk, with some sheep's milk added for flavor. Halloumi is usually sold sprinkled with dried mint and vacuum-packed in its brine. The longer the

cheese remains in the brine, the saltier it becomes. If it is too salty, simply soak it overnight in fresh water or rinse it briefly under lukewarm running water. Unlike most cheeses, halloumi can be frozen without losing its texture or taste.

RICOTTA and **MOZZARELLA** are the most popular Italian fresh cheeses, while **PARMESAN**, probably the most exquisite aged cheese in the world, has such concentrated and complex flavor that even a few shavings can take any dish to a different level. Grana, pecorino, and aged *graviera* or *kefalotyri*—the Greek equivalents—are often used to flavor pasta, grains, and salads.

It is not an exaggeration to say that every village in Greece and certain parts of Turkey—and to a certain extent in other parts of the Mediterranean, especially on the islands—has its own variety of artisanal cheese. The majority of those delicious regional cheeses seldom travel beyond the boundaries of the communities that produce them. They are usually made with a combination of goat's and sheep's milk, from animals that wander in semi-wild conditions on hilly landscapes. These cheeses are seasonal and peak in the spring around Easter, as the production of milk depends on the fresh grass on which the animals feed. All over the world people enjoy some of the wonderful goat's- and sheep's-milk cheeses produced in the south of France. Unfortunately, very few have had the chance to taste the superb *yilomeni manoura* from Sifnos island, a semi-hard cheese that ages in wine sediment, or *divle obruk*, the exquisite cave cheese of south-central Turkey, left in sheep or goatskin sacks after draining, and then aged for four months in an ancient cave. Although production is small, I hope that some of these wonderful artisanal cheeses will eventually manage to cross the Atlantic.

An eastern Mediterranean staple since antiquity, **YOGURT** is not just the thick and creamy stuff everybody seems to adore, but comes traditionally in various forms. In Greece and throughout the Balkans, many people, my husband included, turn their noses up at the popular thick, homogenized yogurt and prefer the old traditional kind, which is not too thick and has a skin of delicious fat on the

OPPOSITE: *A selection of artisanal cheeses (clockwise from top left):* graviera *from Crete, fresh* myzithra, gilomeni manoura *aged in wine sediments (lees),* graviera *from Naxos, black-pepper cheese, San Michali cow's milk cheese from Tinos, dried* myzithra, ladotyri *from Lesbos,* krasotyri *(aged in wine), cheese aged in honey, aged* anthotyro *from Crete; in the center,* xyno *(crumbled fresh cheese).*

ABOVE: *Goat shepherd in the mountains of Peloponnese.*

surface. We used to fight over who could capture more of it on a spoon while eating from the large family-size pots.

In my family we followed my maternal grandmother's dictum: a pot of yogurt every evening, along with fruit and bread or *paximadia* (page 214). As children we had to eat at least a few tablespoons of yogurt every evening, on top of anything else we were fed. Yogurt was supposed to be no more than a light dinner, but often it was served as dessert for those who devoured copious amounts of leftover lunch

in the evening. The night "snack" turned into a family joke—"I wonder why you still have high blood pressure, since you never forget to eat your yogurt at night," my father would tease my grandmother, who claimed that yogurt was *the* panacea. It served her well—my grandmother died at ninety-eight, with almost all of her teeth, and she was still quite with it. Perhaps because she remembered to eat her yogurt every night?

SEASONAL MENU SUGGESTIONS

Festive Lunch or Dinner

Bitter Orange Drink (*Vin Apéritif à l'Orange Amère*) (page 240)

MEZE

Orange, Olive, and Baby Leek Salad
with *Verjus*-Tarragon Dressing (page 94)

Flat Bread with Dried Figs, Roquefort Cheese,
and Rosemary (*Lagana*) (page 202)

FIRST COURSE

Warm Yogurt Soup with Grains and Greens (page 124)

or

Nettle Soup with Mushrooms and Yogurt (page 112)

MAIN COURSE

Quince Stuffed with Wheat Berries, Nuts,
and Raisins (page 156)

DESSERT

Orange and Crumbled Phyllo Cake
(*Portokalopita*) (page 230)

One-Pot Family Meals

ACCOMPANY WITH SALAD AND HOMEMADE BREAD

Chickpeas and Toasted Bread with
Yogurt-Tahini Sauce (*Fattet Hummus*) (page 180)

or

Eggplant and Walnut Pastitsio with
Olive Oil and Yogurt Béchamel (page 188)

or

Youvarlakia with Mushrooms, Eggplant,
and Walnuts in Egg-and-Lemon Sauce (page 126)

or

Cauliflower Gratin with Garlic and Feta (page 131)

or

Potato Pie (*Patatopita*) (page 137)

or

Tunisian Chickpea Soup (*Leblebi*) (page 120)

Buffet Lunch or Dinner

Olive Oil Bread and Savory Biscotti
with Herbs (page 200)

Smoked Olives and Garlic Cloves
in Olive Oil (page 47)

Roasted Cauliflower with Musa's
Zahter Relish (page 102)

or

Semsa's Roasted Squash and
Bread Salad (page 103)

Spicy Levantine Cheese Balls
(*Shanklish*) (page 82)

or

Beet, Arugula, and *Shanklish* Salad with
Kumquat and Orange Dressing (page 99)

Steamed Greens (*Horta*) (page 109)

or

Oak-leaf Lettuce, Fresh Fava, and Cherry
Tomatoes with Dill-Yogurt Dressing (page 104)

Rolled Pie with Fermented Cabbage,
Peppers, Walnuts, and Raisins (page 176)

Potatoes and Olives in Onion-Tomato
Sauce (*Patates Yahni*) (page 134)

or

Chard Leaves Stuffed with Rice, Vegetables,
and Herbs (page 162)

or

Chickpea Pancakes (*Farinata* or *Socca*)
(page 78)

DESSERT

Cypriot Tahini, Cinnamon, and Walnut Cookies
in Lemon Syrup (*Tahinopites*) (page 210)

and

Rustic Chocolates with Dried Figs, Pistachios,
and Toasted Nuts (page 232)

Buffet Lunch or Dinner

"Tomato Salad" Flat Bread Topped with
Cheese and Tomatoes (page 220)

Red Pepper Spread with Hazelnuts and
Pomegranate Molasses (page 80)

Syrian Eggplant Dip with Tahini and
Yogurt (*Moutabal*) (page 89)

Baked Feta, Tomato, and Pepper with Olive Oil
and Oregano (*Bouyourdi*) (page 73)

Toasted Red Lentil and Bulgur Patties
(*Mercimek Köftesi*) (page 76)

or

Grape Leaves Stuffed with Rice, Tomatoes,
and Pomegranate Molasses (page 164)

Vegetable *Fritto Misto* in Tipsy Batter (page 68)

with

Garlic Spread (*Skordalia*) (page 70)

DESSERT

Sweet Wheat Berry and Nut Pilaf
(*Kollyva*) (page 229)

with

Greek Yogurt or Vanilla Ice Cream

or

Flourless Almond Cookies (*Amygdalota*)
from Kea (page 226)

with

Thyme Liqueur (page 241)

or

Lemon Liqueur (page 242)

One-Pot Family Meals
ACCOMPANY WITH SALAD AND HOMEMADE BREAD

Stuffed Summer Vegetables with Rice, Farro,
and Pine Nuts (page 167)

or

Zucchini Rolls Stuffed with Halloumi (page 161)

or

Eggplants *Imam Bayeldi*, Stuffed with Onions,
Peppers, Cheese, and Nuts (page 159)

Festive Lunch or Dinner

MEZE

Santorini *Fava* with Braised Capers
and Onions (page 86)

Lebanese Flat Breads with Za'atar and
Other Toppings (*Man'oushé*) (page 206)

FIRST COURSE

Cold Yogurt Soup with Cucumber, Herbs,
and Rose Petals (page 125)

or

Summer Tomato and Bread Soup
(*Pappa al Pomodoro*) (page 114)

MAIN COURSE

Pseudo-Moussaka with Spicy Tomato Sauce,
Walnuts, and Feta (page 136)

with

Roman Sautéed Greens (page 109)

or

Okra and Zucchini in Harissa-Tomato Sauce
(page 144)

with

Toasted Bulgur Pilaf (page 183)

DESSERT

Cherry Cake from Bosnia
(*Colaç od Trešanja*) (page 225)

or

Quince Preserves (*Kydoni Glyko*)
(page 236)

or

Rose Petal and Yogurt Mousse
(page 235)

BASIC PREPARATIONS & TECHNIQUES

Cooking from Scratch in Well-Planned Stages

The cuisines of the countries around the Mediterranean are ingredient-based; they rely upon and make the best of each season's produce, creatively combining the harvest to create a panoply of enticing dishes. Seasonal vegetables and greens take time to prepare, but for those who feel that cooking from scratch is the only way, take heart: With a bit of advance planning and organization, you will find that cooking from scratch is actually a misnomer—you are already close to done when you start.

When we lived in Athens, I used to shop at my neighborhood farmers' market, at the bottom of the Acropolis, early on Saturday mornings. I went with an open mind and no preconceived ideas. Strolling around, I would spot the best vegetables, fruits, herbs, and greens. Only then would I decide what to get for my salads, main courses, and occasional special meals. The season's produce guided and inspired me then as now, though the farmers' market is now a garden outside my window.

Fortunately, I learned from my mother, and by trial and error, how to treat each vegetable in order to preserve its flavor well past the harvest. The knowledge passed on to me by generations of frugal cooks who lacked our range of modern options can still be our guide. Thanks to the farmers' markets and our modern kitchen appliances, I am convinced that everybody can enjoy farm-to-table meals today, even in the world's most urban cities.

Returning home from the farmers' market, with my cart overflowing, I immediately set to work sorting and preparing the produce. Greens that I wilted would be briefly sautéed with garlic and hot pepper to become a topping for polenta (page 193) or cooked in a bulgur pilaf. Roasted peppers would complement salads, pulsed with nuts or feta to become meze spreads; or maybe they would be added to the stuffing of sumptuous Eggplants *Imam Bayeldi* (page 159), easily assembled with pre-roasted, frozen eggplants left over from previous weeks.

Chickpeas and beans need soaking and long cooking, as do wheat berries and other grains. I prepare large quantities of legumes, and always have parcooked chickpeas—my favorite legume—in the freezer, as well as cannellini or other beans; this allows me to make a hearty soup or my favorite *Fattet Hummus* (page 180) in a matter of minutes.

Leafy Greens

In *Mediterranean Grains and Greens* (1998), Paula Wolfert wrote: "I foresee a time when purslane, nettles, mallow, lamb's-quarters, and wild fennel will be on the produce counter, along with mesclun, radicchio, frisée, arugula . . ." And of course that time has come. In farmers' markets all around the country, as well as in many specialty markets, a variety of greens appears each season. In the Mediterranean tradition, many Americans and northern Europeans have started to forage for wild greens and herbs that grow in their regions. Different varieties of wild and cultivated greens can be used interchangeably for salads, pies, and other main courses. As with any produce, greens need to be utterly fresh. Get the most attractive leafy greens you find. Don't be afraid to experiment with new varieties. Ask the producers for guidance, and try new things. Taste different kinds of greens to choose the blend you prefer; the recipes are just to give you some basic techniques to forage on your own.

STORING THE GREENS

Cook the greens as soon as possible, while they are still fresh and crisp. Do not refrigerate them in a bag for longer than 48 hours. Bunches of thick leafy greens, like Swiss chard or kale, can be stored in a jar, much like a bouquet of flowers:

a time under running water to get rid of sand and dirt, discarding the tough roots and any yellow, limp stems and leaves. Drain briefly in a colander. Spread one or two tea towels—depending on the amount of greens you have—somewhat overlapping, to create a longish piece of cloth. Then spread a double layer of paper towels on the tea towels. Lay the wet greens tidily on the paper, roll the towels tightly, like a jelly roll, and refrigerate this roll for up to 3 days. The greens remain quite fresh and moist—you can chop and serve them raw or cook them briefly.

WILTING AND FREEZING

After washing tender greens like spinach, frisée, mesclun, or arugula, place handfuls—with the water that clings on the leaves—in a thick-bottomed sauté pan over medium-high heat; cover the pan for 1 to 2 minutes, then use tongs to turn the greens over, adding 2 to 3 tablespoons of water if needed to prevent burning. Transfer to a colander and continue with the rest, until all the greens are wilted. They will shrink in volume considerably. Note that the greens don't need to be fully cooked and tender at this point, as you can braise or sauté them later. Let cool and freeze in zip-top bags. You can then add the greens to soups, use them in stuffing for pies and tarts, or sauté them in olive oil for a salad or side dish (see variations on *horta*, page 109).

COOKING AND FREEZING NETTLES

Wear gloves and wash the nettles, discarding the tough stems, keeping only the tender tops. Blanch in 1½ to 2 quarts (1.5 to 2 L) boiling water—in batches, if you have a lot of nettles—for about 3 minutes, or until well wilted. Remove with tongs or with a slotted spoon and let drain in a colander. Reserve the cooking water. Pulse the wilted nettles in a blender, adding a little of the reserved water to facilitate, then freeze measured cups of the sweet, vividly green pulp to use in soups (page 112), to mix into dough for green biscotti (page 219), or to add to *horta* salad (page 108).

BOILING ROBUST AND BITTER GREENS

Tough and bitter greens, like chicory, need blanching or sometimes longer boiling in water. In a medium pot, bring

Cut a small (¼-inch/0.6-cm) piece from the bottom of each stem and arrange them in a jar or container that holds them snugly, adding enough water to come about 1½ inches (4 cm) up the stems—don't submerge the leaves in water. Keep the greens in the refrigerator for up to 5 days, adding a little water if it evaporates.

Soak tender greens and salad leaves in a large bowl of cold water for about 20 minutes. Meticulously wash a few at

3 to 4 quarts (3 to 4 L) water to a boil, adding about 1½ teaspoons salt. Depending on the quantity of greens you have to boil, you might need to work in batches. They cook better when the pot is not overfilled and you can take them out as soon as they soften, before the whole batch gets mushy. Cook successive batches in the same water. Separate the tough stems, if any, from the more delicate leaves and drop the stems into the boiling water before the leaves, as the stems take longer. Always remove the cooked greens from the pot with tongs or a large fork so that any leftover sand remains at the bottom of the pot. Never pour the greens and their cooking water through a colander. And if you like, reserve the tasty cooking water—full of vitamins and trace elements—to drink as tea with lemon, as I do. Use a ladle to transfer the water to a bottle or jar, but do so carefully. Make sure not to stir up the grit on the bottom of the pot and "muddy the waters."

Eggplants and Peppers

The freshest eggplants are firm and shiny with green, not brownish, stems. You have to cook them as soon as possible because they don't hold up well in the fridge. I keep my freshly harvested eggplants in a basket in a cool place in my kitchen for a day or two. If I don't want to cook them right away, I cut the larger eggplants in slices or halve them lengthwise, rub with olive oil, sprinkle with salt, then spread on a parchment paper–lined baking pan. I roast them in a 375°F (190°C) oven until just tender, about 25 minutes. When they are cool, I refrigerate the ones I will plan to finish cooking in the next 2 to 3 days, and freeze the rest in zip-top bags for up to 6 months.

The fleshy end-of-summer or fall peppers—green, yellow, orange, and fiery red—are firm and shiny with robust green stems. Buy large quantities when you find them in the farmers' market and roast the ones you plan to consume in the next 3 to 5 days. Halve and seed the rest, cut in ½-inch (1.3-cm) pieces, and sauté in olive oil, cooking each color separately. Refrigerate for up to 4 days or freeze in zip-top bags, separating the colors, to use for meze spreads or to

OPPOSITE: *Blanched wild greens.* ABOVE: *Sweet peppers fried in olive oil.*

brighten the flavor of salads, soups, pilafs, or pasta sauces. Sautéed peppers are ideal toppings for *man'oushé* (page 206) and other flat breads, together with cheese and herbs. Hot and sweet peppers can be added to mixed pickled vegetables (page 45) or pickled on their own.

In southern Turkey and in other parts of the Mediterranean, the plentiful summer peppers and eggplants are hollowed, threaded, and hung in the sun to dry. The multicolored dried vegetable "chains" adorn village kitchens. Cooks pick and stuff their beloved summer vegetables year-round.

Zucchini and Squash

Light-green baby zucchini—the most common variety in the Mediterranean—and the dark green ones you probably have at your market don't keep well in the refrigerator. You have to steam or boil them in water before they become limp, soft, and tasteless. Blanch the baby zucchini in salted boiling water, without trimming the ends, to keep the flesh flavorful and not watery. Cut and discard the ends after cooking. Boiled zucchini keeps for 2 to 3 days in the fridge; allow it to come to room temperature before serving.

Medium zucchini are great roasted; cut them horizontally and slice into about 1-inch (2.5-cm) pieces. Spread in a single layer on a parchment paper–lined baking sheet. Drizzle with olive oil, sprinkle with salt, Greek oregano, and pepper, toss to coat, and bake in a 400°F (205°C) oven until tender, 15 to 20 minutes; the corners should char. They are great on their own or with feta and fresh, crusty bread. They keep in the fridge for up to 5 days, but they don't freeze well. Bring to room temperature or reheat briefly in the oven before serving. Toss roasted zucchini with warm or cold bulgur and with freshly cooked pasta, drizzled with garlicky olive oil and sprinkled with feta.

With its hard skin, whole squash keeps well for days at room temperature. I like to roast diced squash much like I roast medium zucchini. Roasted squash keeps for up to 5 days in the refrigerator, but, again, it does not freeze well. To store longer, halve a large squash, remove the seeds, and roast until tender; then scoop out the flesh and puree in a blender. Cool and freeze in zip-top bags to use in bread dough (page 209) or for soups and pies.

ABOVE: *Ingredients for salad: small cucumbers, Romaine lettuce, fresh onions, tomatoes, mint, and peppers.*

Tomatoes: Raw, Half-Cooked, and Baked

When irresistible, fragrant, vine-ripened heirloom tomatoes fill the stands of your farmers' market—in late summer or early fall—preserve their tasty flesh to use in sauces, stews, and soups all year round. You won't believe how rich and complex their flavor is, even compared with the most expensive imported canned tomatoes. Baked tomatoes, or "confit," as they are often called, are very attractive and deliver a deeply concentrated tomato flavor. They are infinitely better than salty, leathery sun-dried tomatoes and make an ideal topping for flat breads and tarts. They are also a wonderful addition to pasta, bulgur, soups, and winter salads.

GRATING TOMATOES

French cooking suggests blanching, peeling, and chopping tomatoes. Mediterranean cooks have a simpler method: They grate tomatoes on an onion grater to get tomato pulp. The seeds are not discarded because they are particularly flavorful.

Halve each tomato vertically, cut off and discard the stem, then carefully grate on a large-holed grater, with the cut side facing the grater holes. Discard the skin that will remain in your hand.

FRESH TOMATO PULP

Measure 1 or 2 cups (120 or 240 g) of the grated tomato flesh and freeze it in shallow trays lined with plastic wrap for about 3 hours. Make sure that your frozen tomatoes are ½ inch (2.5 cm) thick or less. This way they melt and cook faster, and you can even cut the frozen pieces in half if you want. Take the hardened pulp out of the trays and store in zip-top bags in the freezer.

HALF-COOKED TOMATO PULP

This is a more concentrated tomato pulp, of which you will need to use less to flavor foods. In a nonreactive saucepan, bring the grated tomatoes to a boil and cook over medium heat for 15 to 20 minutes. Let cool and freeze as above.

BAKED TOMATOES (TOMATO CONFIT)

Halve the tomatoes and arrange them, cut side up, in a single layer on a shallow baking tray lined with parchment paper. Drizzle with olive oil and sprinkle with some sea salt. Bake at 375°F (190°C) for 1 to 3 hours, depending on the size of the tomatoes, until they are very soft and have shrunk to about one-third their original size. Let cool completely and freeze on a tray until hard, then transfer to zip-top bags and keep in the freezer, removing as many as you need each time.

Fresh Herbs

STORING AND DRYING

Store bunches of fresh herbs—such as parsley, dill, chervil, cilantro, mint, or tarragon—by arranging them in a jar, much like a bouquet of flowers. Trim a small (¼-inch/ 0.6-cm) piece from the stem ends and place in a jar or container that holds them upright; add enough water to come about 1½ inches (4 cm) up the stems—don't submerge the leaves in water. Keep the herb bouquet in the refrigerator for up to 5 days, adding a little water if it evaporates. Seasonal, hard-to-find herbs, like wild aromatic fennel, can be frozen. Wash the fronds, spread them on a paper towel while still wet, and slide them into a zip-top bag to store in the freezer. Preserve other herbs and herb mixtures, either in the refrigerator or in the freezer, by making aromatic pastes (page 29).

Some herbs stay fresh longer and others, like mint, deteriorate faster. Dried mint is a Middle Eastern essential. In the spring, when you get wonderfully aromatic fresh mint sprigs, buy as many as you can, tie them in small, tight bunches, and hang them upside down in a dry place. When they are completely dry, crumble the leaves and keep them in an airtight jar.

BASIL IN OLIVE OIL

My cousin from Veneto, Lorenza Berrini-Patiniotis, taught me how Italian cooks keep summer basil leaves all year round: Choosing the best, unblemished, sun-kissed leaves, she washes and thoroughly dries them on paper towels and then packs as many as she can squeeze into small jars. She fills the jars with good olive oil, runs a knife around the jar to eliminate air bubbles, and seals it. She usually makes several small jars of basil conserves, because once opened, the leaves start to lose their precious aroma. You don't need to refrigerate the jars. Just keep in a cool, dry place.

Alternatively, you can chop the leaves in a blender with olive oil and freeze in ice cube trays to have basil handy when needed. Frozen basil is slightly less aromatic than the leaves packed in olive oil.

Garlicky Cilantro Paste (*Taglieh*)   VEGAN GLUTEN-FREE

MAKES ABOUT 1 CUP (240 ML)

2 heads garlic, cloves peeled
   and halved

3 coarsely chopped bunches fresh
   cilantro, stem ends trimmed

2 teaspoons sea salt

3 tablespoons olive oil

Although you can get fresh cilantro all year round from the market, I rely on my garden's herbs. As soon as the summer days get hot, my cilantro blooms and seeds, leaving me without cilantro leaves. In Annia Ciezadlo's wonderful book *Day of Honey*, I found the recipe for this cilantro-garlic paste (*taglieh*) that has become an essential part of my repertoire. It adds flavor to all kinds of dishes, sauces, and dressings. I use a blender because I don't have the patience to mush the *taglieh* with a mortar and pestle, as Ciezadlo suggests, and the resulting paste is excellent.

In a blender, combine the garlic, cilantro, salt, and oil and pulse several times, stopping and scraping the sides with a spatula as needed, until you get a medium-chunky paste. Transfer to a container that holds the paste at a thickness of about ¼ inch (0.6 cm) and freeze. When solid, take out of the container and freeze in a zip-top bag. You can easily cut pieces each time you need to boost the flavor of beans, braised vegetables, grains, and salads.

Mixed-Herb Paste   VEGAN GLUTEN-FREE

MAKES ABOUT 2 CUPS (480 ML)

2 ounces (55 g) fresh flat-leaf parsley leaves,
   stem ends trimmed, washed and towel-dried

3 ounces (85 g) celery leaves, stem ends
   trimmed

3 ounces (85 g) dill, fennel tops, chervil, and/or
   any other fresh aromatic herb you like
   (except cilantro), washed and towel-dried

4 ounces (115 g) leeks, white part only, sliced

½ to 1 ounce (15 to 30 g) seeded jalapeño or
   other chile, to taste

2½ ounces (70 g) sea salt

Olive oil, for topping the jar

Based on an old French recipe, this salty-aromatic paste flavors soups, sauces, pilafs, and salads. Although now you can get decent fresh herbs all year round, that wasn't always the case. In the winter, when the gardens froze, women kept jars of this herb paste close at hand. I now make it regularly each spring to preserve the abundance of fresh herbs my garden produces. I add chiles, which were not part of the original recipe. This paste is extremely handy; if you try it, I am sure you will get hooked. Note that the mixture is very salty, so it is unlikely that you will need additional salt in any dish that you flavor with it.

You will need a good kitchen scale to weigh the ingredients. If the salt is not in precise proportion to the other ingredients, the mixture may spoil.

Place the herbs, leeks, and chile in the bowl of a food processor or blender. Pulse, stopping and scraping down the sides with a spatula as needed, until you get a medium-chunky paste. Transfer the mixture to a nonreactive bowl, add the salt, and stir well to mix. Pack in a 1-pint (480-ml) glass jar and top with 1 to 2 teaspoons olive oil. This will keep for up to 1 year in the refrigerator.

OPPOSITE: *In my pantry: preserved lemons, home-cured olives, pickled vegetables, dried orange slices and herbs, marmalades, fruit preserves, jams, and home-made syrups and liqueurs.*

KISHK, TRAHANA, AND TARHANA: FERMENTED EASTERN MEDITERRANEAN "PASTA"

This is an ancient staple made in the summer with coarsely ground grains—wheat or barley—and milk or yogurt. The two essential ingredients are transformed into a flavorful and nourishing "pasta" for the winter months.

The word *kishk*, used for this staple throughout the Middle East, comes from the Persian *kashk*; today, *kashk* in Iran contains no grain and is a kind of fermented whey, available in liquid and dried forms with which modern chefs in Europe and the United States have started to experiment.

Trahana is the equivalent Greek staple, called *tarhana* in Turkish. Today it usually refers to pellets of fermented and dried dough made with wheat flour and milk, occasionally including aromatics, chiles, mashed vegetables, or fruit. There is an ongoing dispute over its origins, with some scholars claiming that it can be traced back to Persia (Iran) or to the Steppes of China; the Ottomans spread it to the West, they say. Other scholars, though, insist that *trahana* was a Greek "pasta" that spread eastward. In Crete and some other Greek islands, the crumblike pasta from coarsely cracked wheat mixed with milk and yogurt is called *ksinohondros*—*ksino* means "sour," and *hondros* is the ancient word for coarsely ground grain.

Whatever the name, origin, or shape, this delicious staple is the basis for a common eastern Mediterranean porridge, a hearty, wholesome soup that nourished countless generations throughout the region. Today powdered Lebanese *kishk* is also used as a flavoring. Its musky, pungent, cheesy flavor may be an acquired taste for some.

Lebanese *Kishk* and *Ksinohondros* from Crete

I wouldn't suggest that you make your own *kishk* and *ksinohondros* if there were reliable good-quality commercial alternatives. If you are aware of one, please let me know! The process may seem long, but the actual work—the mixing, stirring, and brief cooking of the grain—takes little time. The most important step is the drying process, which traditionally took days, as the crumbled mixture was spread on clean sheets to dry in the sun. Today a dehydrator or a low oven will dry the "pasta" in a few hours. Following the old tradition, I use whole barley flour together with the bulgur.

I give you the basic recipe for the *ksinohondro* of Crete, made by briefly boiling coarse bulgur and barley flour with milk and yogurt. To make the Lebanese *kishk*, a combination of fine bulgur, barley flour, and yogurt is left to ferment. The only work needed is to stir the mixture daily until it reaches the desired sourness.

Ksinohondros

MAKES ABOUT 1 POUND (500 G) PASTA

1 quart (1 L) whole milk, preferably organic sheep's or goat's milk

3 cups (720 ml) plain sheep's- or goat's-milk yogurt (not thick)

3 tablespoons fresh lemon juice

1 teaspoon salt

1 tablespoon Maraş pepper or crushed red pepper flakes, or more to taste (optional)

2½ cups (350 g) medium or coarse bulgur or semolina

1 cup (150 g) whole barley flour

In a heavy-bottomed pot, stir together the milk, yogurt, lemon juice, salt, and Maraş pepper flakes (if using). Heat over medium heat until very warm. Whisking steadily, add the bulgur and barley flour and continue to whisk. When the mixture starts to boil, lower the heat and simmer, still stirring constantly, until very thick, at least 10 minutes. Remove from the heat and continue stirring for a few minutes more to prevent sticking.

Line two baking sheets with parchment paper and ladle about ½-cup (120-ml) pieces of the mixture onto the sheets. Flatten them with a spatula and leave about ½ inch (1.3 cm) between them. You may need more than two pans.

Let cool completely overnight. With a spatula, invert the pieces and, depending on how sour (fermented) you like your *ksinohondros*, let stand at room temperature one more day—it will start to smell very yeasty and sour. Rub the pieces to break into crumbs, and spread on the trays.

Place the trays in an oven heated to the lowest temperature (about 150°F/65°C).

Let the crumbs dry, changing the position of the trays and tossing the pieces every now and then with spatulas, for about 4 hours. Turn off the heat and crack open the oven door—use a wooden spoon to keep the door ajar. Leave the trays in the oven to cool slowly, preferably overnight.

The next day, close the door and warm the oven to 150°F (65°C). Continue drying the "pasta," changing the position of the trays and tossing the crumbs every now and then for another 3 hours or more, until bone-dry and very hard. Alternatively, you can dry *ksinohondros* in a dehydrator at 100°F to 115°F (38°C to 46°C) for about 3 days.

Let cool completely and store in airtight jars. Properly dried, *ksinohondros* keeps for years, like dried pasta.

Kishk

MAKES ABOUT 12 OUNCES (340 G)

1 cup (140 g) fine bulgur

1 cup (140 g) whole-wheat barley bulgur

2 cups (480 ml) natural goat's- or
  sheep's-milk yogurt (not thick)

1 cup (240 ml) whole milk, preferably
  sheep's or goat's milk

3 tablespoons fresh lemon juice

Depending on your kitchen's temperature, and on how sour and pungent you like your *kishk*, it will need 8 to 10 days to ferment. Stirring once or twice a day is all the work that's needed.

In a large nonreactive glass or metal bowl, mix the bulgurs with the yogurt, milk, and lemon juice, stirring well. Cover with a clean towel and let rest, at room temperature, for 24 hours.

On the next and the following 7 to 9 days, stir well every morning, and in the evening as well, if possible. It is important to stir to prevent surface molding. On the fifth or sixth day, it may start to smell quite sour. Taste and decide when you want to dry the *kishk*. Traditionally it is fermented for 9 to 10 days, but it is a matter of taste.

To dry, line two baking sheets with parchment paper and spread the mixture on the sheets, separating it into large crumbs with a fork.

Place the trays in an oven heated to the lowest temperature (about 150°F/65°C).

Let the crumbs dry, changing the position of the trays and tossing the pieces with spatulas every now and then, for about 3 hours. Turn off the heat and crack open the oven door—use a wooden spoon to keep the door ajar. Leave the trays in the oven to cool slowly, preferably overnight.

The next day, toss the crumbs, close the door, and warm the oven to 150°F (65°C). Continue drying the *kishk*, changing the position of the trays and tossing the crumbs every now and then, for another 2 hours or more, until bone-dry and very hard. Alternatively, you can dry *kishk* in a dehydrator at 100°F to 115°F (38°C to 46°C) for about 2 days.

Let cool completely. To follow the Lebanese tradition, in a blender, grind the crumbs to a powder in batches. You can also store the crumbs in airtight jars. Properly dried, *kishk* keeps for years, like dried pasta.

Ksinohondros or *Kishk* Porridge (or Soup)

SERVES 4

6 cups (1.4 L) broth or water

½ to ⅔ cup (60 to 75 g) *ksinohondros* or crumbled *kishk*

Salt, to taste

Good fruity olive oil, for drizzling (optional)

Maraş pepper or crushed red pepper flakes, for sprinkling (optional)

1 cup (120 g) crumbled feta cheese (optional)

In a thick-bottomed pan, bring the broth to a boil. Add the *ksinohondros*, stir well, and reduce the heat. Simmer, stirring every now and then, until the porridge is smooth and thick; this will take 6 to 15 minutes, or possibly longer, depending on the crumb size. Taste and add salt, if needed.

Drizzle with olive oil and sprinkle with Maraş pepper and the feta, if you like.

PRECOOKING LEGUMES, FARRO, WHEAT BERRIES, AND BARLEY

Although you can easily find canned chickpeas and beans—and friends assure me that there are some very good ones available—for me there is no comparison to the taste of the dry, organic legumes you soak and cook on your own stove. If you love legumes, you obviously feel frustrated every time you want to make a dish with beans or chickpeas and realize that you needed to have planned a day in advance. But that problem can be easily solved if you precook and freeze considerable quantities of beans, chickpeas, and grains. This way you can take out as much as you need for each dish and finish cooking them with the other ingredients. Your favorite dish can be ready in less than 30 minutes.

Precooking Beans   VEGAN   GLUTEN-FREE

FOR 6 TO 8 PEOPLE: 2 CUPS (1 POUND/ 500 G) DRIED BEANS WILL MAKE ABOUT 6 CUPS (1 KG) COOKED BEANS

1 pound (500 g) dried beans, preferably organic (such as giant, cannellini, pinto, cocos, or navy beans)

3 to 4 sprigs fresh or dried oregano or thyme, or 3 to 4 bay leaves (optional)

Soak the beans in a large bowl, adding enough cold water to cover the beans by about 4 inches (10 cm). Let stand for 10 to 12 hours. Cannellini, pinto, and navy beans need less soaking (6 to 8 hours), but you can safely soak all beans overnight.

The next morning, rinse the beans under cold water, place them in a large pot, and add water to cover by about 4 inches (10 cm). Bring to a boil over medium-high heat, cook for 5 minutes, drain in a colander, and rinse well under warm running water. Rinse the pot, put the beans back in, and cover with fresh cold or lukewarm water. Add the herbs, if you like.

Bring to a boil, reduce the heat, and simmer the beans for 15 to 20 minutes. Taste—the beans should be almost cooked. Turn off the heat and let the beans cool completely in their broth. Drain, discard the herbs if you used them, transfer to a zip-top bag, and freeze flat. The beans will keep for up to 6 months.

To cook, take out the bag, beat it on the counter to loosen the beans, and use as many as you need. Return any unused beans to the freezer.

Precooking Chickpeas (Garbanzo Beans) VEGAN GLUTEN-FREE

FOR 6 TO 8 PEOPLE: 2 CUPS (1 POUND/ 500 G) DRIED CHICKPEAS WILL MAKE ABOUT 6 CUPS (1 KG) COOKED

1 pound (500 g) dried chickpeas, preferably organic

½ teaspoon baking soda

3 to 4 sprigs fresh or dried rosemary, oregano, or thyme (optional)

Soak the chickpeas in a large bowl, adding enough cold water to cover them by about 4 inches (10 cm). Let soak for 10 to 12 hours or overnight.

The next morning, rinse the chickpeas under cold water, place them in a large pot, and add water to cover by about 4 inches (10 cm). Bring to a boil over medium-high heat, cook for 10 minutes, drain in a colander, and rinse well under warm running water. Rinse the pot, put the chickpeas back in, and cover with cold or lukewarm water, adding the baking soda and the herb sprigs, if you like. Bring to a boil, reduce the heat, and simmer for 20 minutes, or until the beans start to soften. Taste after 20 minutes—if they are still hard, cook for 15 minutes more. Taste—they should be almost soft, but not entirely cooked. Turn off the heat and let the chickpeas cool completely in their broth. Drain, discard the herbs if you used them, transfer to a zip-top bag, and freeze flat. The chickpeas will keep for up to 6 months.

To cook, take out the bag, beat it on the counter to loosen the chickpeas, and use as many as you need. Return any unused chickpeas to the freezer.

Precooking Pearl Barley, Wheat Berries, and Farro VEGAN

MAKES 2½ TO 3 CUPS (400 TO 480 G) COOKED GRAINS

1 cup (200 g) pearl barley, wheat berries, or farro

Pearl barley, wheat berries, and farro need longer cooking than rice or bulgur, but their incomparable earthy, nutty flavor is ample compensation for the extra work. In order to be able to add the grains to stuffing and pilafs whenever you feel like it, precook 1 to 2 pounds (500 g to 1 kg) of your favorite grains and keep them in the freezer.

Place the grains in a pot and add cold water to cover by 2 inches (5 cm). Bring to a boil, reduce the heat, and simmer half the time recommended on the package. Cooking times vary greatly between brands, so carefully check the cooking times suggested on the package.

Taste, and if the grains are still quite hard, continue cooking. Taste again after 5 minutes. You want the grains al dente, not mushy. Drain and let cool completely, then transfer to a zip-top bag and freeze flat. The grains will keep for up to 6 months.

To cook, take out the bag, beat it on the counter to loosen the grains, and use as much as you need. Return any unused grains to the freezer.

Homemade Phyllo Pastry VEGAN

MAKES 6 SHEETS (EACH ABOUT
16 INCHES/40 CM ROUND,
OR EQUIVALENT OVAL OR SQUARE)

2 cups (280 g) bread flour

2 cups (250 g) all-purpose flour, plus
  more for rolling

1½ teaspoons salt

¼ teaspoon instant active dry yeast
  (optional; see Note)

2 tablespoons white wine vinegar or
  cider vinegar

⅓ cup (80 ml) olive oil

Cornstarch, for rolling

Börek and *pites* (pies)—a diverse group of large and small pastries, convenient everyday dishes that can be filled with all kinds of vegetables, greens, and cheeses—are all wrapped in sheets of phyllo. These pastries are the eastern Mediterranean equivalent of sandwiches, where the tasty, crumbly phyllo plays the role of fresh bread, of equal importance to the filling. Using frozen phyllo is a poor alternative, so it is worth it to try and roll your own sheets. Use a long, thin rolling pin or dowel and follow the traditional Turkish and Greek method. I perfected this dough recipe after years of attempts and countless variations. The result is a wonderful, resilient dough that yields silky sheets. If you are not sure that you will manage to roll adequately thin phyllo, add a dash of yeast to the dough (see Note); it will lighten the thick sheets that might otherwise be too firm.

Place the flours, salt, and yeast (if using) in a food processor. Pulse a few times to mix.

With the motor running, add the vinegar and olive oil, then add ⅔ cup (160 ml) water, or just enough to make a soft dough. Let the dough rest in the processor for 15 minutes. Process the dough for 3 to 5 minutes longer, until it is smooth and elastic. Remove and let rest, covered, for 10 to 20 minutes.

On a lightly floured surface, knead the dough briefly until it is smooth and very elastic, adding a little more flour if it is sticky. Divide the dough into 6 pieces. Cover 5 of them with plastic wrap.

Begin with one piece of dough, flattening it with the palm of your hand and the rolling pin. Roll the dough as thinly as possible with restraint, just a few rolls of the pin back and forth. Dust with cornstarch and turn the dough 90 degrees clockwise. Continue to roll the pin over the dough. Use the heels of your palms on the pin to press and pull the dough as you roll forward and back.

Rotate the dough clockwise slightly, about 30 degrees.

Dust again with cornstarch and, using your fingertips, roll the edge of the dough closest to you over the rolling pin. This will allow you to "pick up" the dough with the pin. Roll the pin away from you so that the dough forms a log, wrapped around the pin. Roll the pin gently back and forth, with a continuous rocking motion, extending the heels of your palm out along the dough. You are stretching out the dough on the rolling pin.

You should roll the pin back and forth roughly four times. With the dough on the pin, pick up the pin with your hands on either side of the dough. Extend your arms and turn the pin 45 degrees clockwise. Put the pin down on the surface and unroll the dough,

pulling slightly on the pin to help extend the dough. This small 45-degree turn helps you rotate the dough to open it evenly.

Pick up the dough with the pin again and repeat the same process, dusting with cornstarch, rolling back and forth, extending the pin away, and pulling the dough back toward you. The dough will start to open as an imperfect circle. Make sure you rotate the dough as you roll so you are always picking it up in a different spot. This helps the dough open as easily and evenly as possible.

You need to make a 16-inch (40-cm) round, thin sheet. It doesn't need to be a perfect circle. By gently stretching the sheet you can form an oval; for a square or rectangular pan, the soft and resilient dough can be carefully stretched to fit. Repeat with the remaining pieces of dough.

NOTE: *If you added yeast, divide the dough into quarters and roll each piece into a 16-inch (40-cm) round sheet. Use two sheets at the bottom of your pie and another two on top.*

LEMONS: A GREEK AND EASTERN MEDITERRANEAN OBSESSION!

I was sitting with my friend, food and music writer Fred Plotkin, at a trattoria in Otranto, Italy. It was a blazing-hot summer afternoon and I was very excited because I was finally going to taste *fava e cicorie* (mashed fava beans and steamed bitter greens), a traditional country dish of the area. The *fava e cicorie* arrived warm, drizzled with fragrant green olive oil, and sprinkled with coarsely ground black pepper.

"Go on, taste it," said Fred.

"I'm waiting for the lemon," I replied, expecting the waiter to return with a plate of halved or quartered lemons.

"*Fava e cicorie* has no lemon," Fred said. "Lemon is a Greek perversion!"

He was right, of course, and only then did I become conscious of the true obsession Greeks have with lemons. It is safe to say that this obsession with lemons is shared by almost all inhabitants of the eastern Mediterranean.

Though the origin of the lemon is unknown— some think it came from Southeast Asia, others believe it originated in northern India—it is thought that lemons were introduced to the Mediterranean by the Arabs, who brought them from Persia around the eleventh century. They were immediately adopted into the culinary tradition throughout the region. Lemons soon replaced vinegar and the juices of unripe grapes, pomegranates, and all kinds of tart fruits that had been used to provide acidity to both sweet and savory dishes since ancient times.

My mother used to keep already-juiced lemon halves by the sink, and she would rub her hands often with the lemons "to keep [her hands] soft and white." Even at the age of ninety-three, after a lifetime of cooking and cleaning, her hands were still silky and beautiful.

Mediterranean cooks take lemons for granted. Every Greek kitchen has a steady supply of lemons, which, along with salt, pepper, and olive oil, are considered an essential and basic ingredient. And while northern Europeans use the juice and occasionally the zest, Moroccans preserve whole lemons in brine, creating the most pungent of lemon flavorings.

Preserved Lemons VEGAN GLUTEN-FREE

MAKES 1½ QUARTS (1.5 L)

5 to 6 organic lemons, washed and dried

½ to ⅔ cup (80 to 100 g) coarse salt, as needed

1 tablespoon whole red peppercorns

2 cinnamon sticks

2 bay leaves or leaves from a lemon tree

⅔ cup (160 ml) fresh lemon juice, or as needed

Olive oil, for topping the jar

When you make your own *citrons confits* (preserved lemons), an indispensable ingredient in French-speaking North Africa and throughout the eastern Mediterranean, you come to better understand one of the most powerful flavorings in our cuisine. Like all preserves, lemons need time to develop their flavor, which is very different from the lemon zest that I have often seen as a substitute in recipes. If you are in an absolute hurry to have a sneak preview of your preserved lemons' flavor while they slowly ferment in the salty juices, make Salt- and Olive Oil-Marinated Lemon Slices (see Variation, page 40).

To use preserved lemons, cut strips of the rind and rinse them under cold running water. Most of the flesh will wash off. Add ½ teaspoon of the brine to dressings, sauces, stews, and marinades in place of salt.

Roll and press each lemon on a work surface to soften and break the inner membranes. Working over a bowl, quarter each lemon, not fully detaching the pieces and stopping before you cut all the way to the center rind. Salt the inside of the lemon generously and place in a 1½-quart (1.5-L) Mason jar. Continue with the rest of the lemons—as you work, add the peppercorns, cinnamon sticks, and bay leaves between the lemons and sprinkle with salt after each layer of lemons. Press hard on the lemons as you stuff and squeeze them into the jar. Depending on the size of the lemons, you may not be able to fit all of them in the jar.

Add the lemon juice and any juices that have accumulated in the bowl. Press the lemons again. They will be almost covered by liquid, but even if they are not, don't add more juice yet. Press the lemons down, close the jar, and set aside at room temperature. In a day or two the liquid should cover the lemons completely. If it does not, then add a little more lemon juice, after pressing down hard on the lemons once more.

Top with some olive oil and let the lemons ferment for about 4 weeks, until their skins soften and become almost translucent. As you take lemons out to chop and use, add new ones to the brine, slashing them as you did with the first ones, but salting lightly.

SALT- AND OLIVE OIL–MARINATED LEMON SLICES (FAST "PRESERVED" LEMONS)

MAKES A 12-OUNCE (375-ML) JAR

2 lemons, cut lengthwise into eighths

¼ cup (40 g) salt

¼ cup (60 ml) olive oil, or more as needed

These are by no means the equivalent of the authentic preserve, but they will give you a preview of the taste and possibilities of preserved lemons.

Place the lemon pieces in a zip-top bag and freeze for 12 to 24 hours.

Take out of the bag, transfer to a glass or stainless-steel container, and let come to room temperature. Sprinkle with the salt, toss thoroughly, and let macerate for 24 hours. Drizzle with the olive oil, toss, and set aside for another 24 hours.

You can now taste and use the softened lemon skins. Transfer to a 12-ounce (375-ml) jar, adding more olive oil, as needed, to cover them, and keep in the refrigerator. Use these within 10 days, until your real preserved lemons are ready, because they will eventually spoil.

Pink Fermented Cabbage   VEGAN   GLUTEN-FREE

MAKES ABOUT 4½ QUARTS (4.5 L)

1 medium-small green cabbage and 1 small red cabbage (5½ to 6 pounds/2.5 to 3 kg total)

3 tablespoons sea salt

½ cup (50 g) finely chopped seaweed (*dulce, wakame, porphyra,* or any other kind), soaked in 2 cups (480 ml) lukewarm water for 30 to 45 minutes

2 to 3 stalks celery (optional)

1 tablespoon caraway or coriander seeds (optional)

Water or brine from a previous batch, as needed (see Note)

I ferment shredded, not whole, cabbage (see page 43), an easier and faster process that never fails. I mix green and red cabbage together. After about five days I have vividly pink, crunchy strands of cabbage that I can't stop eating. Following the basic instructions from Sandor Ellix Katz's first book, *Wild Fermentation,* I use salt sparingly together with seaweed. The container you use for the fermentation is quite important. A large, wide-mouthed, transparent jar is ideal. After trying different crocks, I chose a heavy, wide-mouthed five-quart glass cookie jar, perfect for the two cabbages I usually prepare. I also discovered special clay vats with the appropriate heavy tops (see Sources, page 244), but for the time being I am very happy with my cookie jar, a saucer, and a large jar of olives, preserved lemons, or my marmalade for weighing the cabbage down.

Halve the cabbages, cut off the hard stems, and shred the cabbage into ¼- to ⅓-inch (0.6- to 0.8-cm) strands.

Transfer to a large bowl and sprinkle with the salt. Add the seaweed and pour its soaking juice over the cabbage, along with any leftover brine or water (see Note). Start rubbing and tossing the strands, and continue for at least 10 minutes, until they reduce in volume and start to soften. Add the celery and spice (if using), toss, and transfer to a 5-quart (5-L) cylindrical jar, pressing down hard with your palms. The liquid will almost reach the top of the cabbage; if not, add a little more water. Cover the entire surface of the shredded cabbage with plastic wrap and place a plate, almost as large as the jar, on top. On top of the plate, put a large, heavy can or jar—at least 4 pounds (2 kg). Leave on the kitchen counter overnight. The next day you will see tiny bubbles rising from the bottom of the jar as the cabbage ferments. This happens faster if you have used brine from a previous fermentation. Depending on the room temperature, it could take a couple of days before you see the first results of the fermentation process. Be sure to check every day, pressing the shredded cabbage down. Gradually the green and red strands will change to a uniform pink color. Make sure that the cabbage is submerged in the brine at all times.

Taste the cabbage after 4 or 5 days to see if you like it. At this point I usually transfer it to smaller jars, pour enough brine over to cover the cabbage completely, then add a bag filled with clean stones as a weight to keep the cabbage covered in brine. I close the lids and store the fermented cabbage in the refrigerator. The cabbage will continue to ferment slowly in the refrigerator, and after 4 to 5 months it may eventually become too sour and pungent. Mine seldom lasts for more than a few weeks (see Note).

NOTE: *As Sandor Ellix Katz suggests, start a new batch before you finish the old one. I remove the last pieces with a slotted spoon and then pack the jar with freshly shredded cabbage, which I mix with the leftover brine, adding some salted water made by stirring 1½ to 2 teaspoons salt for each 1 cup (240 ml) water. This cabbage will ferment faster—try it on the third day—and it usually develops a more complex flavor.*

VARIATION

FERMENTED CABBAGE WITH RADISHES AND TURNIPS

I first tried this more pungent variation as a solution for the abundance of radishes and turnips from my garden. It is by no means a substitute for plain fermented cabbage, which I find more satisfying and useful for all kinds of dishes. This mixture ferments faster, so make sure you start tasting around the end of the third day.

Omit the red cabbage. Choose a larger green cabbage (about 3½ pounds/1.6 kg); core and shred it as described on page 40. Add 1 pound (500 g) radishes and 1 pound (500 g) turnips, coarsely shredded or julienned on a mandoline. Mix the cabbage, radishes, and turnips in a bowl, add the salt and the soaked seaweed, rub, and proceed as described above.

FERMENTED CABBAGE (NOT SAUERKRAUT)

Fermented cabbage is part of a traditional meze spread and an indispensable part of Mediterranean cuisine. In Lebanon, cabbage and other pickled vegetables are a customary part of breakfast; in the Balkan countries, they are served at the beginning of every meal "to help digestion," as my Albanian neighbor's father told me. The important health benefits of fermented cabbage and other vegetables have now been scientifically proven, and there is increasing interest in all kinds of fermented foods.

As fall progresses and the nights get longer and cooler, cooks in the north of Greece and all through the Balkans and the Middle East start to ferment the year's cabbage. People usually ferment whole, large heads, making a deep conical cut to remove the core and filling the cavity with coarse salt. They have special large vats or buckets that hold two or three cabbages snugly—they top them with special well-cleaned stones to weigh down the cabbages and keep them submerged in *armià*, the salted juices released as the heads slowly ferment.

Coming from an urban, southern Greek home, I first tasted home-fermented cabbage in the late 1980s, when I visited Maria Papadinas's home in Kastoria. While researching my first book, *The Foods of Greece*, I spent days cooking with some wonderful women all over the country; Maria was one of the best. Her pork-stuffed cabbage leaves—the traditional New Year's fare in Greek Macedonia—were unlike anything I had ever tasted before. I took notes as Maria described the recipe. When she said, "We take as many leaves as we need from the *armià* cabbage," I asked about the cabbage, since I had never encountered the word—a local term—before. Maria was totally puzzled. Didn't we ferment cabbage in my home? How could we prepare winter dishes without it?

Eating not just the stuffed leaves, but also Maria's braised chicken with fermented cabbage, the pies throughout Thrace, the rice and legume dishes as well as the salads whose flavor is boosted with fermented cabbage, I got hooked. This home-fermented cabbage is nothing like commercial sauerkraut. Its crunchiness and tangy-floral flavor can be addictive. As you will discover while easily making your own, you can fine-tune its taste, deciding how sour or pungent you like it, before you move it from the countertop to the refrigerator.

Pickled Eggplants Stuffed with Garlic, Pepper, and Parsley VEGAN GLUTEN-FREE

MAKES 12 EGGPLANTS

12 small eggplants (each 4 to 5 inches/
10 to 12 cm long)

1 large bunch fresh flat-leaf parsley, chopped
(about 1½ cups/90 g)

8 to 10 large cloves garlic, finely diced

½ red bell pepper, seeded and finely diced

2 fresh red chiles, seeded and finely diced, or
1 to 2 tablespoons Maraş pepper or crushed
red pepper flakes

12 sprigs leaf (wild) celery (see page 51), or
4 to 5 stalks celery, cut lengthwise into long
flexible strands, to tie the stuffed eggplants

3 cups (720 ml) white wine vinegar, or more
as needed

3 cups (720 ml) salt brine (see Note), or more
as needed

Good, fruity olive oil, for serving (optional)

Eggplants, the vegetable of choice throughout the eastern Mediterranean, are not just fried and baked as appetizers and main dishes. They are also cooked into a syrup for one of Greece's most exotic preserves. Pickled stuffed eggplants are a ubiquitous feature in the meze spread and come in many variations. I learned this southern Albanian version from Drita Aliay, my friend Ela's mother. We prepared it together in the fall using the garden's last eggplants. I suggested we steam, instead of boil, the eggplants, and Drita loved my recommendation. We were able to skip the long draining-and-drying process needed to get rid of the water the eggplants absorb before stuffing and marinating them in the sour-salty brine.

Fill a large saucepan with water to a depth of 1 inch (2.5 cm) and bring to a boil. Peel the eggplants in strips so the eggplants have lines of skin and flesh. Make a long, deep slash along the length of each eggplant, stopping about ¼ inch (0.6 cm) from the stem and the tip. Place the eggplants in a steamer basket or on a sieve that will fit over the pan of boiling water. The eggplants must not touch the water. Cover and steam until the eggplants are fork-tender, at least 10 minutes. Do not let them get too soft. Transfer to paper towels and let cool.

In a bowl, mix the parsley, garlic, bell pepper, and chiles. Stuff a teaspoon or more of this mixture inside the slash of each eggplant, packing in as much as you can. Tie the eggplant with the celery, being careful to keep the filling inside the eggplant. Place the eggplants in three 1-quart (1-L) jars, pressing to fit snugly. Divide any remaining stuffing among the jars and add a few celery sprigs and leaves to each. Add enough vinegar to come halfway up the jar, then top with brine, making sure the eggplants are completely submerged. Seal the jars and turn them upside down a couple of times to blend the brine. Let stand at room temperature for 2 to 3 weeks. Take out 1 or 2 eggplants, cut into pieces, and serve drizzled with fruity olive oil, if desired.

NOTE: *To make basic salted brine, stir 3½ to 4 tablespoons (70 to 75 g) sea salt into 1 quart (1 L) water until completely dissolved. It is easier if you use lukewarm water, but let it come to room temperature before proceeding. I make 2 to 3 quarts (2 to 3 L) at a time and keep the brine in a glass bottle to have ready whenever I need it for pickles, olives, or other uses.*

OPPOSITE: *Pickled stuffed eggplants, Green Chickpea Hummus (page 93), Raw Pepper Spread (page 81), sliced Spicy Levantine Cheese Balls (*Shanklish, *page 82).*

Pickled Celeriac with Carrots VEGAN GLUTEN-FREE

MAKES ONE (1½-QUART/(1.5-L) JAR

1 pound (500 g) trimmed and peeled celeriac
(celery root), halved

2 large carrots

3 to 4 fresh or dried chiles, slashed lengthwise
and seeded

5 leaf (wild) celery sprigs (see page 51) or
3 stalks celery

2 tablespoons coriander seeds

4 bay leaves

About 1½ cups (360 ml) white (pickling) vinegar

2 cups (480 ml) salt brine (see Note, page 45),
or more as needed

Good, fruity olive oil, for serving (optional)

MAKES ABOUT 2 QUARTS (2 L)

1 pound (500 g) unripe green tomatoes,
halved or quartered, depending on size

1 pound (500 g) cauliflower florets

2 medium onions, quartered

2 small beets, trimmed and diced

2 to 3 dried chiles

2 to 3 bay leaves

2 tablespoons coriander seeds

2 cups (480 ml) white (pickling) vinegar,
or more as needed

2 cups (480 ml) salt brine (see Note,
page 45), or more as needed

Pickled vegetables are an eastern Mediterranean staple. The traditional brine is salty-sour, usually without sugar, and efforts are made to preserve the crunchiness of the produce.

Choose the best, freshest seasonal produce, picking vegetables that are underripe and firm. Pickle them as soon as you reach home, and your pickles will be crisp and wonderful. The most common combination, usually prepared in the fall, includes green tomatoes that have no chance of ripening, cauliflower florets, turnips, the last green peppers, plus a few sliced beets that add a vivid pink color to the pale pickled morsels (see Variation). I often pickle long sticks of fresh green garlic to add to my salads and spreads all year round. I also pickle okra with plenty of hot chiles.

Using a mandoline, carefully cut the celeriac into thin slices. Slice the carrots diagonally and place all the slices into a 1½-quart (1.5-L) jar, adding the chiles, celery, coriander seeds, and bay leaves between the slices. Pour in enough vinegar to come about halfway up the jar, then top with the brine. Make sure all the vegetables are submerged in the liquid. Seal the jar and turn it upside down a couple of times to blend the brine. Let stand at room temperature, shaking the jar every now and then, for 2 to 3 weeks. Take out slices as needed and serve, drizzled with fruity olive oil, if you like.

VARIATION

PINK, MIXED FALL PICKLES

Fill one or two smaller jars snugly, equally dividing the various ingredients. Fill halfway with vinegar and top with salted brine, then proceed as described above.

Smoked Olives and Garlic Cloves in Olive Oil VEGAN GLUTEN-FREE

MAKES TWO (1¼-PINT/600-ML) JARS

1½ cups (360 ml) white wine

1 cup (240 ml) white wine vinegar or cider vinegar

Salt, to taste

15 to 20 large cloves garlic

2 cups (360 g) firm, good-quality Kalamata olives

About 3 cups (720 ml) olive oil

½ cup (75 g) wood chips mixed with dried herb sprigs (if using a homemade smoker)

Any kind of olive can be smoked, and you can experiment to see which ones you prefer. I like to smoke Kalamata olives and store them in olive oil. Along with the olives, I smoke garlic cloves; it took me some time to find a good way to safely store the garlic cloves in olive oil. Finally I decided to first blanch them in a mixture of vinegar and wine, as I do with artichokes (see page 48). You can keep smoked olives and garlic together or in separate jars. Serve on their own, as meze, or add to legumes, salads of boiled or roasted vegetables, or stuffing for breads, vegetables, and pies.

In a saucepan, bring the wine, vinegar, salt, and 1 cup (240 ml) water to a boil. Add the garlic, return to a boil, then reduce the heat and cook for 5 minutes. Remove the garlic with a slotted spoon and spread it on paper towels to dry completely.

Drain the olives on paper towels. In a bowl, toss the garlic cloves with 2 teaspoons of the olive oil and rub to coat, then spread the cloves on paper towels to get rid of any excess oil.

If you have a stovetop smoker, follow the manufacturer's instructions and smoke the olives and garlic for 30 minutes. If you do not already have one, you can easily create a stovetop smoker using a large pot with a tight-fitting cover: Line the bottom of the pot with aluminum foil and layer it with about ½ cup (75 g) wood chips mixed with some dried sprigs of herbs (such as thyme, oregano, and bay leaves). Place a steamer basket so that it sits just above the chips, and in it arrange the olives and garlic. Cover the pot with a piece of aluminum foil, then the lid. Cover the seal around the pot with more foil to make sure no smoke escapes. Turn the heat to high for 5 to 7 minutes, or until you start to smell the smoke. Turn off the heat and let the pot smoke on the stove for 30 minutes.

Remove the lid from the smoker, then the foil, then the olives and cloves. Taste to see if they are smoky enough. If not, repeat the process with new wood chips.

Let the olives and garlic cool, then pack them into two jars, either separately or mixed. Fill the jars with the remaining olive oil and seal them. You can use them immediately, if you like, or they will keep at room temperature for at least 6 months.

Artichokes in Olive Oil (*Carciofi Sott'Olio*) VEGAN GLUTEN-FREE

MAKES ONE (1-QUART 1-L) JAR

3 to 4 medium artichokes, or 8 baby artichokes, peeled (see Note)

¼ cup fresh lemon juice (for peeling; see Note)

1 lemon, quartered (for peeling; see Note)

1½ cups (360 ml) white wine

1 cup (240 ml) white wine vinegar or cider vinegar

1 tablespoon salt

1 small fennel bulb, cut into eighths

1 tablespoon fennel seeds, coarsely crushed with a mortar and pestle

1 tablespoon coriander seeds

1 tablespoon whole pink peppercorns

1½ cups (360 ml) good, fruity olive oil, or more as needed

2 to 3 bay leaves

2 small chiles, slashed lengthwise with scissors from the tip, almost to the stem (not detached)

I always have jars of artichokes in the refrigerator, using my garden's crop of small, thorny, purple Kea artichokes. In the spring, when you find the best artichokes at the farmers' market, dedicate a day to peeling and preparing them, filling jars with delicious artichokes that can become the base for all kinds of dishes. Add them to salads, appetizers, grains, or pasta. I stuff small breads with the leftovers from the bottom of the jar and use the olive oil in sauces and dressings or keep it for next year's artichoke preserves.

The recipe is based on the traditional Italian way of preserving in olive oil and can be used to preserve not just artichokes, but also pearl onions, green garlic, peppers, fresh fava, peperoncini, and more.

Quarter the medium artichokes or halve the baby ones, removing any fuzzy choke with a spoon. Rub the cut sides with the lemon quarters reserved from peeling the artichokes (see Note).

In a saucepan, combine the wine and vinegar, add the salt, bring the mixture to a boil, and add the artichokes. Cook for 4 minutes, or until barely fork-tender. Be careful not to let the artichokes get soft. Remove them with a slotted spoon and spread them on paper towels to drain.

Blanch the fennel bulb in the wine-vinegar mixture for 3 minutes, then drain on the paper towels along with the artichokes.

When the artichokes and fennel are dry, transfer to a bowl and sprinkle with the fennel seeds, coriander seeds, and peppercorns. Add 3 to 4 tablespoons of the olive oil and toss well to mix.

Transfer the artichokes to a 1-quart (1-L) jar, inserting the bay leaves and chilies between the artichokes. Pour in enough olive oil to cover the pieces, pressing them down and making sure the oil comes about ⅔ inch (1.5 cm) above the vegetables.

Let stand at room temperature for 2 days, then refrigerate for up to 6 months. Bring the pieces you want to serve to room temperature, as the olive oil solidifies in the refrigerator. If you want to keep them longer on the shelf, you can properly seal the jar by boiling it, lid on, for 15 minutes in a large pot of water that covers the jar by 2 inches (5 cm).

NOTE: *To peel the artichokes, follow the method on page 97.*

Spice It Up!

Wisely combined spice mixtures are at the center of the Mediterranean flavor arsenal. It is incredible what a difference one or two teaspoons of mixed spices can make to the most common foods: cooked rice, boiled lentils, or roasted potatoes. Try these with and without seven-spice (*baharat*, page 54); add a teaspoon of Aegean Herb and Hot Pepper Mix (page 55) to steamed cauliflower or boiled pasta drizzled with olive oil. I am sure that you will quickly understand why even the smallest amounts of indigenous and imported seeds, barks, roots, leaves, and buds have played such a crucial role in the kitchen since antiquity.

Not just food, but the flavorings in food were the major means of keeping people healthy or restoring strength to the ill. Locally grown herbs and imported spices were believed to be therapeutic and a form of preventive medicine; many were considered aphrodisiacs. But in choosing the ingredients and spices in the recipes that follow, my main concern was to create dishes with profound and layered flavors. The health benefits are a welcome bonus, as far as I am concerned.

What follows is a list of some of the less familiar, at times exotic, flavorings used in the recipes. I include some substitutes, although most items are widely available in ethnic markets, in specialty stores, or online (see Sources, page 244).

MARAŞ, CHILES, AND PEPERONCINI The sunny, predominantly dry climate of the Mediterranean produces very tasty hot and sweet peppers. In most recipes I use Maraş pepper, the seeded and dried Turkish *pul biber* (pepper flakes), similar to Aleppo pepper, from the neighboring eponymous Syrian town—a famous stop along the old Silk Road. Maraş pepper is medium-hot, with wonderful fruity and aromatic undertones; some people find it similar to ancho chili. It is cultivated, dried, and exported from the Kahraman Maraş province, near the Syrian border. Bear in mind that the flavor and heat of Middle Eastern peppers

vary from one year to the next. Their production is still artisanal and, according to my Turkish friends, potency depends on the weather conditions. Maraş pepper is widely available in the United States (see Sources, page 244).

In Europe, chiles are classified only by their level of heat. Italians call the hot chiles used in the cooking of Sicily and Calabria *peperoncini* (small peppers). Peperoncini are closely related to cayenne, but they are not tongue-burning; besides heat, they have a deep, fruity flavor and aroma. *Piment d'Espelette*, ground sun-dried chiles grown in particular regions of the French Basque country, are probably the most expensive European hot peppers, with DOC status.

WILD FENNEL (*FINOCCHIO SELVATICO*) Intensely aromatic fennel grows wild all over Greece, in the south of Italy, and in many parts of California. Its thick fronds are added to spinach, green pies, stuffing for vegetables and grape leaves, and fish dishes. You occasionally find *finocchio selvatico* in American markets in May, and if you live in California you can forage with great success along the coast. If wild fennel is not available, substitute crushed fennel seeds combined with chopped fennel bulb and fronds.

GRAPE MOLASSES This is a classic ingredient of Greek, Turkish, and southern Italian pantries, but chefs from all over the world now experiment with this precious, old-fashioned, and very healthy sweetener. The molasses is produced by reducing grape must for hours, until it becomes dark and syrupy. The lengthy process makes it expensive and often hard to find, as the small quantities produced in the fall disappear fast. Grape molasses was one of the ancient sweeteners, together with honey, before the production of sugar. It is not just sweet; it has a complex flavor with slightly bitter undertones. In the old days, fruits such as apples, pears, and quince were cooked in grape molasses to make preserves. Teaspoons of grape molasses enhance salad dressings; I use it in the dough of traditional barley *paximadia* (page 214).

Herbs: Fresh versus Dry

There is a big difference in flavor and aroma between fresh and dry oregano, cilantro (fresh coriander) and coriander seeds, and fresh and dried mint. In Mediterranean cooking dried herbs are used in stews and all kinds of cooked or baked dishes, while fresh herbs are added to salads, spreads, and occasionally to marinades. A small pinch of dry, wild Greek oregano goes a long way. Its potent aroma permeates meat and vegetable dishes, but it particularly shines when sprinkled over feta cheese. It miraculously transforms a simple olive-oil-and-lemon dressing into the perfect sauce for grilled fish and seafood. Dried mint is a Middle Eastern essential, added to many spice blends and to vegetable and yogurt spreads. It is steeped in boiling water to become the quintessential tea of Morocco and other North African countries. Fresh mint is added to salads, pies, sauces, and dressings. Because dried mint is not readily available, you can easily dry a bunch (see page 27).

MAHLEP Consisting of the small seeds of a kind of wild cherry and about the size of apple seeds, *mahlep* gives a sweet and smoky aroma to breads and other baked goods. Its grains should be the color of café au lait; a dark-brown color indicates that the spice is old and probably stale. *Mahlep* is sold in most Middle Eastern stores (see Sources, page 244). Buy whole grains, not the powder. Keep them in sealed jars in the freezer and grind small quantities as needed to make the spice blend for breads (page 54).

MASTIC Mastic is the crystallized sap of the mastic shrub (*Pistacia lentiscus*), a kind of wild pistachio that grows only on southern parts of Chios island. Very popular in Arab countries and throughout the Middle East, mastic is used as a flavoring mainly in sweets, ice cream, breads, and drinks. Mastic was the chewing gum of the ancients—hence the word "masticate." Mastic is sold in Middle Eastern and ethnic grocery stores (see Sources, page 244). Store in a cool, dry place or in the freezer. When grinding mastic in a spice grinder, always mix the crystals with sugar and other spices you need for the recipe to prevent the heat of the motor from melting the mastic, which could otherwise stick to the blades of the grinder.

NIGELLA These tiny black seeds have a licorice-like flavor and aroma, similar to aniseed. They are used as a bread topping or mixed into the dough itself for breads and crunchy savory or sweet biscuits. Sometimes called "black cumin" or "black sesame seeds," nigella seeds come from *Nigella sativa*, a plant with delicate blue flowers, native to the Mediterranean. Nigella seeds are sold at Middle Eastern and Indian groceries and spice shops (see Sources, page 244). Aniseeds, caraway seeds, or a combination can be used as a substitute.

FLAT-LEAF PARSLEY AND "WILD" CELERY Flat-leaf parsley is the most prevalent herb in the Mediterranean. Its flavor is more prominent and aromatic than the decorative curly variety, which is rarely used in this part of the world.

Mediterranean, or French, celery is a thin-stalked, dark-green leafy plant that Americans call "wild" celery. Although it does grow wild in the mountains, it is also cultivated for consumption. This leafy celery has a strong taste with a slight bitter undertone, and it is rarely consumed raw. You can find it in Asian markets under the name *kun choi* or *kin tsai*. You can also grow your own (for seeds, see Sources, page 246). If you find it in your farmers' market, buy a lot: Wash it, chop it coarsely, and store in zip-top bags in the freezer; it will keep for about six months. Thick-stalked American celery with some flat-leaf parsley can be substituted, but the taste is much milder.

POMEGRANATE MOLASSES The cooked-down juice of mostly unripe pomegranates becomes a dark, syrupy, tart, fruity condiment, truly unlike any other. It is a basic ingredient in many Middle Eastern and North African salads and vegetable dishes. There are now many brands, both domestic and imported, available in markets. They range in flavor and some are quite sweet. For these recipes I suggest the more sour kinds, like Lebanese pomegranate molasses (see Sources, page 244), which give the most authentic taste to the dishes I propose. If you have a sweet molasses, add some lemon.

DRIED ROSE PETALS AND ROSEBUDS Small, dried, fragrant rosebuds are popular eastern Mediterranean

flavorings, and not just for sweet dishes. They are added to spice mixtures that flavor stews or soups in Iran, the broader Middle East, and the Maghreb (the Arab areas of North Africa). "Olive Oil Scented with Roses" was found inscribed on clay tablets dating from about the thirteenth century BC, unearthed in the palaces of Knossos, Crete. Although it is not clear if the ancient Greeks used that oil in foods or for cosmetic purposes, we know that the Byzantines liked to add rose water with *garum*, a fermented fish sauce, to their meat and game dishes.

SUMAC The tangy, deep-red fruits of sumac (*Rhus corioria*) are ground and sprinkled over yogurt sauces, spreads, onions, and a range of salads. In the old days, cooks used to steep whole dried sumac fruits in water and use the liquid for flavoring. Sumac is part of the large wild pistachio family. One very close relation is the Italian *lentiscus* (*skinos* in Greek), a shrub with small, hard, fragrant leaves that grows in clusters on the driest and rockiest Mediterranean shores. Ancient Greeks used to flavor olive oil with branches of *skinos*, and today you will find green olives scented with *lentiscus* leaves. Mastic, the popular flavoring from Chios (see page 51) that flavors breads and sweets, comes from the resin of another plant (*Pistacia lentiscus*) that belongs to the same family.

ABOVE LEFT: *Turmeric powder deepens the flavor of legumes and vegetable stews.* ABOVE RIGHT: *The stunning blossoms that will become pomegranates.*

TAHINI An oily paste used since ancient times, tahini is made from pounded sesame seeds and is used in both sweet and savory dishes. You probably know tahini as a basic ingredient in hummus. But it also flavors the Syrian Eggplant Dip on page 89 and, mixed with yogurt and garlic, becomes a delicious topping for *fattet hummus* (page 180). In traditional Cypriot *tahinopites* (page 210), tahini is mixed with sugar, cinnamon, and walnuts to make the stuffing for a unique vegan bun. Chose good-quality, organic tahini made from whole sesame seeds, and store it in the fridge after opening. Stir well before using, because the oil tends to separate and float to the top.

TURMERIC This deep yellow powder—a key ingredient in almost all Indian curry blends—has a musky, earthy aroma that deepens the flavor of legumes and vegetable stews. Turmeric is a rhizome related to and very much resembling ginger, but it has bright orange flesh when peeled. It is native to Southeast Asia, and although it is commonly used in dried and powdered form in North Africa and the Middle East, recently the fresh root has become available in specialty markets. Some scientists have found that it has important antioxidant and antimicrobial properties that may help prevent salmonella poisoning. Others claim that curcurmin, the basic substance in turmeric, prevents and heals arthritis and other inflammatory diseases.

Mediterranean Bouquet Garni VEGAN GLUTEN-FREE

MAKES 1 BOUQUET

ONE SPRIG OF EACH, OR AS MANY AS
YOU CAN GET, OF THE FOLLOWING:

Fresh thyme, if possible both wild and
cultivated

Fresh rosemary

Dried bay leaf

Basil (fresh or dried)

Fresh fennel or fresh dill (or both)

Fresh mint

Fresh Greek sage

Celery leaf

Fresh flat-leaf parsley

Oregano (fresh or dried)

Savory (fresh or dried)

Fresh chervil

1 cinnamon stick

1 piece dried orange peel (page 56)

1 green part of a scallion or leek, to tie the
bundle (optional)

My version of the classic bouquet garni includes whatever herbs grow in the garden at any given time, plus cinnamon and dried orange peel. Tie the bouquet together with scallion or leek leaves or with kitchen string if you use it in a broth that you will pass through a sieve; if you add the bouquet to a sauce or stew, enclose it in cheesecloth to make removal easy. When the food is cooked and the bouquet has released its flavors you can discard it, after pressing firmly with a spoon to extract every single aromatic drop from it.

Lebanese Seven-Spice Mixture VEGAN GLUTEN-FREE

MAKES ABOUT ⅓ CUP (35 G)

1 tablespoon finely ground black pepper

1 tablespoon ground allspice

1 tablespoon ground cinnamon

1 teaspoon freshly grated nutmeg

1 teaspoon ground coriander

1 teaspoon ground cloves

1 teaspoon ground ginger

This aromatic spice mixture is the Lebanese version of *baharat*—the word means "spice" in Arabic. A good pinch added to lentils with onions (page 186) or to quince stuffing (page 156) transforms the flavors into something exceptional. As with all spice blends, it comes in various combinations, and every cook has his or her own version. My good friend Anissa Helou, Lebanese food authority, gave me her recipe.

Mix all the spices and store in an airtight container in a cool, dark place.

North African *Baharat* VEGAN GLUTEN-FREE

MAKES ABOUT ½ CUP (50 G)

3 to 4 tablespoons crumbled dried organic rose petals or rosebuds, stems discarded (see Sources, page 244)

2 tablespoons whole black peppercorns

2 cinnamon sticks, each about 2 inches (5 cm) long

2 tablespoons cumin seeds

2 tablespoons coriander seeds

5 to 6 whole cloves

1 teaspoon freshly grated nutmeg

2 to 3 cardamom pods

1 tablespoon dried mint (optional)

Good pinch of saffron threads (optional)

1 teaspoon grated lemon zest (optional)

This is a basic recipe with optional components. Add or subtract, increase or decrease the amounts of each spice to create your own mix.

Grind the spices in a spice grinder or a clean coffee grinder. Transfer to a sealed jar and keep in a cool, dark place.

Spices for Bread VEGAN GLUTEN-FREE

MAKES ABOUT 1 CUP (100 G)

⅔ cup (70 g) coriander seeds

3 tablespoons *mahlep* (see page 51)

1 teaspoon mastic (see page 51)

3 tablespoons aniseeds, or 1½ pieces star anise

Inspired by festive Greek breads, this blend enhances the flavor of savory and sweet breads as well as biscotti. I usually add two to three teaspoons for each pound of flour in a bread recipe.

Grind the spices in a spice grinder or a clean coffee grinder. Transfer to a sealed jar and keep in a cool, dark place.

Aegean Herb and Hot Pepper Mix **VEGAN GLUTEN-FREE**

MAKES ABOUT 1 CUP (100 G)

7 tablespoons (65 g) Maraş pepper, or
  ¼ cup (25 g) crushed red pepper flakes
  plus 3 tablespoons paprika

¼ cup (25 g) dried Greek oregano, crumbled

2 tablespoons fennel seeds, freshly ground
  or crushed with a mortar and pestle

1 tablespoon ground cumin

3 tablespoons ground dried orange zest,
  preferably homemade (page 56)

2 tablespoons dried basil, crumbled

1 tablespoon dried mint, crumbled

Along Turkey's Aegean coast and on the neighboring Greek island of Chios, cooks use a wonderfully aromatic spice-and-herb blend to flavor all kinds of dishes. I was amazed by the pairing of dried mint and basil with orange peel and cumin. These cooks turn up the heat with the addition of locally grown, mildly hot peppers to create a unique combination of fascinating flavors. Here is my version of the fragrant, mouth-warming, alluring mix: an all-purpose seasoning that enhances the flavor of grilled vegetables, beans, sauces, and dressings.

In a small bowl, mix together all the ingredients. Transfer to a jar and keep in a cool, dark place for up to 6 months.

Dried Orange Peel VEGAN GLUTEN-FREE

Non-treated oranges, preferably organic

Much more interesting and deep-flavored than orange zest alone, dried orange peel is very easy to make and incredibly flavor-enhancing. Use the dried orange strips for savory and sweet dishes alike, to flavor sauces, pulses, and stews. They will add an extra dimension to tomato sauces in particular. Grind the dried peel to add to spice mixtures, vinaigrettes, breads, cakes, and syrups.

VARIATION

Dry tangerine peels in the same way, either to use as a substitute for or together with orange peels. Freshly picked tangerines can have a very intense, overpowering aroma, so use them sparingly.

Whenever you find fresh organic oranges in the market, before cutting them to eat or juice, remove thin strips of their skin with a vegetable peeler. Arrange the strips on a tray lined with a kitchen towel. Leave the orange peels on the counter for about 3 days, until they curl up and dry completely.

Alternatively, you can dry them on a baking sheet lined with parchment paper in a 180°F (82°C) oven for 30 to 40 minutes. Make sure they are absolutely dry and cooled before you store them in an airtight jar. They will keep their taste and aroma for 6 months or more.

Za'atar VEGAN GLUTEN-FREE

MAKES ABOUT 2 CUPS (200 G)

1 cup (100 g) sesame seeds

½ cup (50 g) dried thyme, preferably Mediterranean

⅓ cup (35 g) dried savory

¼ cup (25 g) dried marjoram

½ cup (20 g) sumac (see page 52)

1 teaspoon sea salt

½ to 1 teaspoon ground cumin (optional)

½ to 1 teaspoon ground caraway seeds (optional)

Za'atar is not just a flavoring but a nourishing paste, mixed with olive oil and spread on *man'oushé* flat breads (page 206) or pita. It is traditionally eaten for breakfast in Lebanon, and people believe that it gives strength and clears the mind. The za'atar spice blend derives its aroma from a particular kind of thyme indigenous to Syria and Lebanon, the variety of which is known simply as *za'atar* in Arabic and *zahter* in Turkish (see the photo on page 11). That herb is very different from wild Greek or European thyme. The herb za'atar itself is not readily available, so I propose a combination of dried marjoram, thyme, and savory, which together create a very similar aroma. Za'atar has become popular in recent years, and you will find ready-made blends in your local markets. Nevertheless, since it is easy to make your own, I give you my recipe with some optional ingredients.

Warm a skillet over medium-high heat and toast the sesame seeds, tossing with a spatula until just golden, 3 to 4 minutes. Let cool completely.

In a small bowl, mix together the thyme, savory, marjoram, sumac, salt, cumin, and caraway and add the toasted sesame seeds. Keep in a sealed jar in a cool, dark, dry place. Za'atar will gradually start to lose its flavor and aroma after 2 months.

Dukkah VEGAN GLUTEN-FREE

MAKES ABOUT 3½ CUPS (350 G)

1½ cups (about 200 g) hazelnuts, almonds, or a combination of both

⅔ cup (70 g) sesame seeds

1 cup (105 g) coriander seeds

⅓ cup (35 g) cumin seeds

1 teaspoon sea salt (preferably fleur de sel or finishing salt)

1 to 1½ teaspoons freshly ground black pepper, to taste

Egyptian dukkah is a crunchy, nourishing spice, nut, and seed blend that can be used as topping for all kinds of salads; it makes a delicious and unexpected pasta sauce when tossed with garlicky olive oil. It is common for people to dip flat bread in olive oil and then sprinkle it generously with dukkah—a nourishing meal on the go. You can also sprinkle it on yogurt, ricotta, or goat cheese. It is very easy to make: Sesame seeds, almonds, cheese, and pistachios or hazelnuts are spiced up with cumin, coriander seeds, and pepper. The proportion of spices can vary greatly per cup of nuts, from 2 to 3 tablespoons to ½ cup (50 g) of the spice mixture. Here is my version; use it as a base to make one that suits your taste.

Preheat the oven to 375°F (190°C). Spread the nuts on a tray and roast, tossing once, until just golden and fragrant. Be careful not to burn them. Set aside to cool.

Warm a skillet over medium-high heat and toast the sesame seeds, tossing them with a spatula until just golden, 3 to 4 minutes. Transfer to a bowl. Add the coriander seeds to the skillet and toss until they start to puff up. Transfer to the bowl with the sesame seeds. Toast the cumin seeds in the same manner. Let cool completely.

Place all the seeds in a clean coffee or spice grinder along with the salt and pulse to a coarse grind. You don't want to make a fine powder.

In a blender or food processor, pulse the nuts to a medium-fine consistency. Add the seeds and pepper and pulse once more to mix thoroughly. You want to make a dry, mealy dukkah, not an oily paste.

Store in a sealed jar in a cool, dark, dry place. Dukkah will keep its flavor for at least 3 months. You can also freeze it for at least 1 year. Bring to room temperature before using.

ABOVE: *Breads and pastries in a Beirut bakery.*

CRUNCHY BITS

Toasted or olive oil–fried bread crumbs are the "Parmesan of the poor," often more flavorful than cheese, according to Marcella Hazan. And they are simple to make. The unforgettable cook and teacher of authentic Italian cuisine proved her point in one of her inspiring workshops at the Worlds of Flavor conference in Napa, where she prepared a variety of toasted bread crumbs. The multicolored medley was flavored with herbs and anchovies, spices, garlic, and different nuts, and colored with carrots and beets. Tasting those deliciously crunchy bits alongside "ordinary" grated Parmesan, the king of cheeses, was a real revelation for me.

Ever since then, I have been experimenting, building on Marcella's ideas. I used my leftover homemade bread, mixing the crumbs with chopped olives (plain or smoked) or with good capers. Both make great toppings for steamed or roasted vegetables, especially cauliflower, broccoli, zucchini, or squash. Recently I ground dried porcini mushrooms with bread crumbs before sautéing them with rosemary-scented olive oil. The resulting bouquet of flavors astonished me; sprinkled over steaming pasta, they imparted an incredibly rich flavor. Sun-dried tomatoes and good-quality tomato paste are other avenues that you can explore. The possibilities are truly endless, and the effort required is minimal.

Sicilian *Conza* Bread Crumbs   VEGAN

MAKES ABOUT 2 CUPS (220 G)

2 tablespoons olive oil

1½ cups (150 g) bread crumbs, from bread
at least 1 to 2 days old (see Notes)

1 cup (100 g) coarsely ground or chopped
almonds, preferably unskinned

2 tablespoons chopped fresh flat-leaf
parsley, thyme, fennel, rosemary, or
any herb you like

½ to 1 teaspoon Maraş pepper, or a pinch
of crushed red pepper flakes, to taste

Salt

1 to 2 tablespoons grated Parmesan or
pecorino cheese (optional; see Notes)

Sicily is renowned for its bountiful and delicious almonds. Though famous for
their almond sweets, Sicilians use them to make *conza* as well, a mixture of
bread crumbs, almonds, and parsley that is fried in olive oil and used as topping
for grilled prawns and sardines or for pasta and vegetable dishes. Use any kind
of leftover bread, but preferably whole-wheat or multigrain. One- or two-day-
old bread is good, but even older is better, giving extra texture and crunch to the
conza.

Heat the olive oil in a heavy skillet over medium heat and add the bread crumbs and
almonds. Sauté, stirring, until the mixture turns golden brown. Add the parsley, season
to taste with the Maraş pepper and salt, and toss for 30 seconds. Remove from the
heat, transfer to a bowl, and taste to correct the seasoning. Toss, adding the cheese (if
using), and sprinkle on seafood, salad, or pasta while still warm. You can also let the
conza cool completely and store it in a sealed jar for up to 1 week, refrigerating it if
you have added cheese. *Conza* usually remains crisp, but if it feels soggy, reheat it
briefly under the broiler before using.

NOTES: *To make gluten-free* conza*, substitute rolled oats for the bread crumbs.*

*Substituting 3 to 4 drained anchovy fillets for the cheese, and adding 1 to 2 minced
garlic cloves, will turn this into a more substantial topping for pasta or any kind of
steamed vegetables and greens.*

VARIATION

BREAD CRUMBS WITH OLIVES OR CAPERS

MAKES ABOUT 2 CUPS (220 G)

2 cups (200 g) bread crumbs, from bread
at least 1 to 2 days old (see Notes, above)

1 cup (180 g) pitted, coarsely chopped olives,
preferably Kalamata, or smoked olives
(page 47), or ⅔ cup (90 g) salt-packed
capers, washed under running water and
dried on paper towels.

2 tablespoons olive oil

½ to 1 teaspoon Maraş pepper, or a pinch
of crushed red pepper flakes, to taste

In a blender, pulse the bread crumbs with the olives to get a coarse mixture. Heat the
olive oil in a heavy skillet over medium heat and sauté the bread crumb mixture,
tossing constantly, until dry and crisp, about 8 minutes. Add the Maraş pepper and
toss, then transfer to a plate lined with paper towels and let cool. Transfer to a jar,
cover, and store in a cool, dark place for 4 weeks or more.

Concentrated Vegetable Broth VEGAN GLUTEN-FREE

2 large onions, halved, peeled, and thickly
  sliced

3 leeks, white and light-green parts halved
  lengthwise and quartered crosswise, green
  tops reserved

2 fennel bulbs, quartered

2 green bell peppers, cored, seeded, and
  halved

1 head garlic, halved crosswise

3 carrots, halved lengthwise

10 button mushrooms

3 tablespoons olive oil

1 to 2 tablespoons coarse sea salt or kosher
  salt

2 tablespoons whole black peppercorns,
  coarsely crushed with a mortar and pestle

1 tablespoon whole allspice berries, coarsely
  crushed with a mortar and pestle

2 cups (about 200 g) chopped Swiss chard or
  spinach stalks, plus a few leaves (optional)

Asparagus trimmings, or stalks from parsley or
  other herbs (optional)

2 ripe tomatoes, halved

1 cup (100 g) coarsely chopped green beans

5 to 6 sprigs fresh flat-leaf parsley

2 celery sprigs

2 Mediterranean Bouquet Garni (page 53)

1 cup (240 ml) dry white wine

Baking some of the vegetables before boiling makes a strong broth that goes
a long way. I suggest you use it sparingly in recipes, probably half or two-thirds
of the amount specified. Taste and decide if you need to add more broth or
just water.

The trimmings of parsley and other herbs will add flavor to your stock. If you
have freezer space, keep them in zip-top bags to use for your next stock. Adding
seaweed makes the broth even more intense (see Variation).

Preheat the oven to 400°F (205°C) and line a baking sheet with parchment paper.

In a large bowl, place half the onions, half the leeks (not the green tops), half the
fennel bulbs, and half the bell peppers. Add the garlic, carrots, and mushrooms and
toss with the olive oil.

Spread on the baking sheet and sprinkle with the salt, peppercorns, and allspice.
Bake until the edges of the vegetables start to brown and caramelize, 20 minutes
or more.

In a large pot, combine the baked vegetables, the spices, and all their juices, the
remaining raw vegetables, greens, herbs, and the bouquet garni. Pour in enough
water to cover by 4 inches (10 cm), bring to a boil, then reduce the heat to low and
simmer, partially covered, for about 1½ hours, until all the vegetables are very soft and
mushy. Add the wine, cook for 5 minutes more, then strain, pressing down on the
vegetables to extract all their juices. Discard the solids.

Let the broth cool and refrigerate; the broth keeps for up to 5 days in the refrigerator.
But I suggest you freeze a few small containers. Remove the frozen blocks of broth
from the containers and keep them in a heavy-duty zip-top bag. This way small
quantities are available to use as you need them. Frozen, the broth will keep for up to
6 months.

VARIATION

CONCENTRATED VEGETABLE AND SEAWEED BROTH

When you add the raw vegetables to the pot include: ½ to 1 cup (50 to 100 g) *wakame,*
sea lettuce, or any combination of dried seaweed—preferably Spanish or French (see
Sources, page 244). Pour in the water and cook as described above.

Basic Tomato Sauce VEGAN GLUTEN-FREE

MAKES 2½ TO 3 CUPS (600 TO 720 ML),
ENOUGH FOR 1 POUND (500 G) OF PASTA

⅓ cup (80 ml) olive oil

1 cup (160 g) finely chopped red onions

1 tablespoon tomato paste

1 cup (240 ml) sweet wine, such as Mavrodaphne or Marsala

1 teaspoon Aleppo pepper, or ¼ to ½ teaspoon crushed red pepper flakes

2½ cups (300 g) grated vine-ripened tomatoes (about 1½ pounds/680 g), or 1 (16-ounce/ 455-g) can diced tomatoes (with their juice)

1 cinnamon stick

1 (4-inch/10-cm) piece fresh or dried orange peel

1 teaspoon sea salt, plus more to taste

1 teaspoon sugar (optional)

½ cup (70 g) raisins, pureed in a blender with 1 to 2 tablespoons of wine or water (optional)

In recent years most Greek restaurants have added celery to their all-purpose tomato sauce, inspired by the Italian marinara. But the older versions of all-purpose tomato sauce were scented with bay leaves and cinnamon, Eastern-inspired aromatics. I love to include orange peel, too, as they do in the Peloponnese. The wine sweetens the tomatoes, so I seldom add sugar. But if you like your sauce sweeter, I suggest you pulse a handful of raisins in the blender, which adds one more layer of flavor along with sweetness to the sauce.

Heat the olive oil in a medium, heavy-bottomed saucepan over medium heat. Add the onions and sauté, tossing often, until soft, about 5 minutes. Add the tomato paste and cook, stirring, for 1 minute, or until glossy. Add the wine and pepper and simmer for 1 minute. Add the tomatoes, cinnamon stick, orange peel, salt, and the sugar or raisins, if you like. Bring to a boil, then reduce the heat to low, cover, and simmer for 15 to 20 minutes, until the sauce thickens. Taste and adjust the seasoning.

Remove from the heat and discard the cinnamon stick and the orange peel.

Use immediately or let cool, cover, and refrigerate. The sauce will keep for up to 5 days.

VARIATIONS

For an earthy, spicy tomato sauce: add 1 teaspoon turmeric and 1 to 2 tablespoons *h'rous* (page 62) or harissa, to taste.

For a fragrant, spicy tomato sauce: add 1 to 2 teaspoons Lebanese seven-spice blend (*baharat*, page 54).

For an Italian-inspired tomato sauce: add 2 minced garlic cloves with the tomato paste. Omit the cinnamon and orange and add 2 chopped celery sprigs with the tomatoes.

Pepper, Onion, and Turmeric Paste (*H'rous*)

VEGAN GLUTEN-FREE

MAKES ABOUT 2 CUPS (480 ML)

2 pounds (1 kg) purple onions, halved and cut into half-moons

⅓ cup (about 100 g) coarse sea salt

2 tablespoons ground turmeric

6 ounces (170 g) dried chipotle peppers or dried New Mexican chile peppers

⅓ cup (about 35 g) coriander seeds

5 tablespoons caraway seeds

2 to 3 tablespoons dried rosebuds (see Sources, page 244)

1 teaspoon ground cinnamon

⅓ cup (75 ml) olive oil, plus more to top the jar

Less popular than harissa—Moroccan pepper paste—*h'rous*, the spicy condiment of southern Tunisia, is for me a more complex and interesting flavoring. It is made with fermented onions, turmeric, rosebuds, and other spices. This recipe is based on Paula Wolfert's *h'rous* from her classic book *The Cooking of the Eastern Mediterranean*. I like the mild, smoky flavor of chipotle peppers, but you can make the paste hotter by combining different kinds of dried chiles, since the Tunisian varieties are not readily available. I use *h'rous* to deepen the flavor of any vegetable stew or meze spread. I add it to my basic tomato sauce (page 61) or mix some with olive oil to serve as a dipping sauce for toasted pita or savory biscotti.

In a large bowl, toss the onions with the salt and turmeric. Let ferment at room temperature, tossing every now and then, for about 3 days, until the onions become very soft and translucent. Transfer the onions to a sieve lined with cheesecloth and let them drain. Gather the ends of the cloth and squeeze the onions to extract their liquid. It is easier to squeeze the onions in two batches.

Wearing gloves, cut off the stems and discard the seeds of the dried peppers; with scissors, cut them into pieces. In a blender or food processor, grind the chiles in batches with the coriander seeds, caraway seeds, and rosebuds. Be careful to avoid irritating your nose and eyes with the peppery dust. Add the onions, cinnamon, and olive oil and pulse to mix.

Pack into 2 to 3 small jars and top with more olive oil. *H'rous* will keep for about 4 months in the refrigerator.

RECIPES

MEZE & SALADS

It is always time to taste meze. A combination of small, shared plates, served in the middle of the table, meze can mean appetizer, dessert, or the meal itself in different eastern Mediterranean countries. To serve an interesting meze spread, you should plan ahead, as most dishes can be cooked more than one day in advance and served at room temperature— and many of the flavors improve over the course of a couple of days. A main course may or may not follow. If you plan an all-meze meal, follow the Mediterranean tradition and start with spreads, pickles, and cold vegetable dishes, then continue with cold fish or seafood and finish with the warm plates— the fried vegetables, grilled octopus or fish, a pie or a casserole.

On the other hand, if meze is a mere prelude to a lunch or dinner, choose one or two pickled vegetables and one or two spreads. You can also prepare a light vegetable or fish dish, set on a side table, for when your guests arrive. They can help themselves as they enjoy their aperitifs. Note, though, that some eastern Mediterranean meze tend to have strong flavors that can overpower delicate wines. Ouzo or *raki*—the strong anise-scented drink with a sweet aftertaste—is the most common eastern Mediterranean aperitif, served diluted with two parts water and an ice cube. Whites or rosés, demi-sec wines both flat and sparkling, are my suggestion. We serve them to our guests before dinner or lunch, while they taste a variety of olives, spicy Green Pepper, Feta, and Pistachio Spread (page 71), Pickled Eggplants Stuffed with Garlic, Pepper, and Parsley (page 45), or any of the meze I place on the sideboard.

PREVIOUS SREAD: *Ela Allamani, my neighbor and invaluable assistant, holding a plate of Braised Artichokes and Fava with Lemon and Fennel (see Variation on page 139).*

RIGHT: *A selection of meze: Pink Fermented Cabbage (page 40), home-cured olives, Raw Pepper and Nut Spread (page 81), pickled peppers, Green Chickpea Hummus (page 93), Artichokes in Olive Oil (page 48), sliced Spicy Levantine Cheese Balls (Shanklish, page 82), and Pickled Eggplants Stuffed with Garlic, Pepper, and Parsley (page 45).*

Vegetable *Fritto Misto* in Tipsy Batter with Garlic Sauce VEGAN (EXCEPT FOR THE STUFFED ZUCCHINI BLOSSOMS)

SERVES 6 TO 8

FOR THE TIPSY BATTER:

Olive oil, or a combination of olive and sunflower oil, for frying

1 cup (130 g), plus 2 tablespoons cornstarch

1½ cups (185 g) all-purpose flour

1½ teaspoons baking powder

1 cup (240 ml) ouzo, Pernod, *raki*, or vodka

⅔ cup (160 ml) club soda, or more as needed

6 or more zucchini or squash blossoms stuffed with feta or other cheese (see Note)

Choose at least 2 or 3 vegetables from the list below, the season's best. You should have about 2½ pounds (1.2 kg) total. Keep each sliced vegetable in a separate bowl:

Medium eggplants, sliced vertically or horizontally, cut into ½-inch (1.3-cm) rounds or slices, salted liberally and left for 30 minutes, then rinsed well and dried on paper towels

Medium or small zucchini or squash, sliced horizontally into ¼-inch (0.6-cm) slices

Small tender carrots, halved lengthwise

Red or green peppers, quartered and seeded

Baby artichokes, trimmed and thinly sliced (for preparation, see Note page 97)

Tender green beans or green fava pods, trimmed

Handful of sage leaves (optional)

1 small organic lemon, ends cut off, sliced into paper-thin rounds (optional)

1 medium shallot or 3 to 4 scallions, thinly sliced (optional)

Sea salt

Garlic Spread (*Skordalia*), for serving (page 70; optional)

Zucchini and squash blossoms—especially stuffed with feta or spicy cheese and fresh mint—are the undisputed stars of this parade of crunchy fried vegetables. Good luck bringing them to the table—my guests crowd the kitchen and grab the golden, crispy vegetables, dripping with hot olive oil, as they come out of the frying pan.

Traditionally we shallow fry in Greece using all-purpose olive oil, although recently people mix olive oil with less expensive sunflower oil. But olive oil is still king, imparting its royal and luxurious flavor to vegetables, potatoes, and even fish. Myriad vegetables—zucchini, squash, bell peppers, green beans, baby artichokes, sliced shallots, scallions, thin slices of lemon, and leaves with body like chard and kale—are all fried. We like to add fragrant sprigs of marjoram from our garden, while Italians adore fried sage leaves, which beautifully complement this *fritto misto* (mixed fry). My favorite vegetables are sweet, tender carrots, which I slice lengthwise, and whole tender fava pods in spring. Eggplant is the only vegetable that needs extra preparation in advance—salted, left to wilt, rinsed, patted dry and dipped in batter, they are soon ready for the sizzling oil. Simple fried eggplants with some sage leaves are a real treat! The tipsy batter, which I also use for fish, creates a wonderfully crisp exterior that keeps the vegetables inside juicy and tender.

We tend to fry vegetables most often in summer, using our outside burner to manage the unavoidable mess that frying creates. But I have devised a system to help you fry in any kitchen. If you have an electric range, like me, fully cover the space around the frying pan with newspaper; if you have gas burners, spread aluminum foil to keep the surface free of oil spatters. Once you see how easy cleanup can be, you will start to enjoy this irresistible meze in any season.

We traditionally accompany the fried vegetables with garlic spread or any zesty spread, like Green Pepper, Feta, and Pistachio Spread (page 71) or Caper, Scallion, and Parsley Spread (page 85). Musa's *Zahter* Relish (page 102), mixed with a few tablespoons of thick yogurt, is a more unusual but equally delightful addition.

Line a baking sheet with a double layer of paper towels. Add olive oil to a large pan, preferably with high sides, to a depth of 1½ to 2 inches (4 to 5 cm).

Heat the oil to 375°F (190°C), and just before it reaches temperature, mix the batter: In a bowl whisk together the cornstarch, flour, and baking powder. Add the ouzo and

NOTE: *Stuffing for each zucchini blossom: About 1 teaspoon crumbled feta sprinkled with some Maraş pepper or crumbled Shanklish (page 82). Green Pepper, Feta, and Pistachio Spread (page 71) also goes well. Regardless of the stuffing you choose, add 1 mint leaf or a sprig of dill for a bit of extra freshness. Place the stuffing deep inside the blossom, fold to close, and then dip in the batter and fry as described.*

club soda, whisking to incorporate. It should be runny, with the consistency of light cream. If too thick, add a little more club soda.

When the oil is hot, pick up stuffed zucchini blossoms, alternating with slices of vegetables, with tongs. Dip the vegetables, sage leaves, lemons slices, and shallots, if using, briefly in the batter, lift to drain for a few seconds, then drop carefully in the hot oil. Fry, turning once, until golden brown, 1 to 3 minutes, depending on the vegetable and the thickness of the slice. Transfer to the paper towel–lined baking sheet and then to a serving platter. Sprinkle with salt and serve hot with the garlic spread, if using.

Garlic Spread (*Skordalia*)

MAKES ABOUT 1 QUART (1 L)

5 to 10 cloves garlic, peeled and quartered, to taste

1½ teaspoons sea salt

1 cup (125 g) blanched almonds, soaked in water for 3 hours and drained

2 to 3 tablespoons fresh lemon juice, or more to taste

About 3½ ounces (100 g) country bread, crusts removed, soaked in water and squeezed dry

1 cup (210 g) mashed cooked potato, cold

About ⅔ cup (160 ml) good, fruity olive oil, plus extra for drizzling

½ to 1 teaspoon ground white pepper, to taste

1 cup (250 g) Greek-style yogurt (preferably full-fat), or more to taste

1 teaspoon fine lemon zest

1 teaspoon sumac (optional)

This is a basic recipe I play around with, depending on my whims and the season—the two of which are inseparable. I love to make it with ramps or green garlic whenever my garden is so generous. Besides fried vegetables, *skordalia* can be served with fried mussels or any batter-fried fish. It is also delicious with stuffed chard leaves (page 162). Diluted with some white wine or water, it becomes a dressing for steamed broccoli, cauliflower, *horta* (see page 109), beets, or green beans.

In the bowl of a food processor or blender, combine the garlic (start with 5 medium cloves), salt, almonds, and 2 tablespoons lemon juice. Process to get a fine but grainy mixture. Add the bread and potato and process briefly. With the motor running, slowly pour in the olive oil to get a thick and creamy paste. Add the white pepper and taste, adjusting the seasoning with more lemon juice or olive oil. Add more garlic if you like and process a few more seconds. Keep in mind that the flavor will mellow somewhat with the addition of the yogurt.

Transfer to a bowl, cover with plastic wrap, and refrigerate for a few hours or up to 3 days. Just before serving, fold in the yogurt and the lemon zest. Taste and adjust the seasoning.

Drizzle with good olive oil and a sprinkling of sumac, if you like, and serve.

Green Pepper, Feta, and Pistachio Spread GLUTEN-FREE

SERVES 8 TO 10

6 tablespoons (90 ml) olive oil

2 large green bell peppers, seeded and coarsely chopped

2 jalapeños, seeded and chopped

⅔ pound (300 g) feta cheese, crumbled

2 to 4 tablespoons Greek-style yogurt (preferably full-fat), as needed

1 cup (120 g) coarsely ground pistachios

This is one of my staple spreads—very simple to make, but with a beguiling flavor. The combination of sweet and spicy fried peppers, complemented by sour-salty feta and crunchy pistachios, will have your guests enthralled and asking for the recipe. The spread keeps for days in the refrigerator, and you can serve it in a bowl with raw vegetables to dip or spread it on toasted bread or pita. It can also be used as topping for *friselle*, drizzled with tomato juice and fruity olive oil (page 75).

In a skillet, warm the olive oil over medium heat. Add the bell pepper and jalapeño and sauté, stirring often, until soft, about 8 minutes.

In a blender or the bowl of a food processor, combine the cheese, 2 tablespoons of the yogurt, and the sautéed peppers with their cooking oil. Pulse until smooth. Transfer to a serving dish and fold in most of the pistachios, reserving some to sprinkle on top. Cover and refrigerate. The spread will keep well for at least 1 week.

Take out of the refrigerator 30 minutes before serving. If the spread is too hard or thick, stir in some additional yogurt to soften. Sprinkle with the reserved pistachios and serve with toasted pita or crudités.

Baked Feta, Tomato, and Pepper with Olive Oil and Oregano (*Bouyourdi*) GLUTEN-FREE

SERVES 4

1 large vine-ripened tomato

About ½ cup (120 ml) good, fruity olive oil

1 jalapeño, seeded and finely sliced, or a few pinches of Maraş pepper or crushed red pepper flakes, to taste

1 medium green bell pepper, seeded and sliced into thin rings

4 slices feta cheese (about ⅔ pound/ 300 g total)

1 tablespoon dried Greek oregano, or more to taste

Thick slices of fresh, crusty bread (optional)

Bouyourdi hardly needs a recipe. One or two slices of good tomato, a lavish slice of feta cheese, and pieces of bell and hot pepper are doused with olive oil, generously sprinkled with oregano, and grilled in a very hot oven. *Bouyourdi* is brought to the table directly from the oven, often in individual clay pots, and enjoyed with plenty of fresh crusty bread to sop up the scrumptious oil. Although served as a meze in Greece, it can also be a wonderful breakfast or brunch dish for the whole family.

Preheat the oven to 430°F (220°C) with a rack in the middle.

Spread a double layer of paper towels on a large dish. Core the tomato carefully, slice it horizontally into 5 or 6 pieces, and spread them on the paper towels to drain.

Oil a shallow 8- or 9-inch (20- or 23-cm) baking dish, or four individual ramekins, and spread the tomato slices over the bottom, reserving 4 nice slices for the top. Sprinkle with some jalapeño and bell pepper slices. Arrange the feta pieces on top, place one tomato slice on each piece of cheese, and finally place 2 or 3 bell pepper rings on the tomato. Drizzle liberally with olive oil, sprinkle with oregano and the remaining jalapeño, and transfer to the oven. Bake for 15 minutes, or until the feta turns a light golden color and the oil is sizzling. Serve immediately with warm bread, if you like.

BREAD SALAD TURNED ON ITS HEAD

Originally from Puglia, *friselle* (see page 217) have now spread all over Italy. The eponymous summer appetizer consists of dried bread rings topped with diced fresh tomatoes. The variations are endless— garlic and fruity olive oil, anchovies, capers, peperoncini—to name but a few options. The end result is akin to a large bruschetta, but with a much more interesting texture because of the dense, crisp *friselle*.

Cretan *dakos* or *paximadia* are the Greek equivalent of *friselle*. They are traditionally shaped like a doughnut and sliced horizontally. They can also be formed into baguettes and cut into thick slices before drying, as in the photo

above. Today the ancient island staples are baked with a combination of barley and wheat flour (see page 214), and they are crunchy, but no longer rock-hard. The juices from the chopped tomatoes and the olive oil are sufficient to soften the rusks while they still retain their shape and bite, which is vital to this simple appetizer.

If these dried breads were crushed in a bowl, and the tomatoes cut into larger pieces, you would end up with a traditional bread salad, which is always a delicious option. But isn't this a much more imaginative and enjoyable way of dressing up an ingredient with the season's best produce?

Friselle or *Paximadia* with Chopped Tomato, Herbs, and Feta

SERVES 4 TO 6

2 pieces *friselle* (page 217) or 4 to 6 pieces *paximadia* (page 214), depending on the size

4 medium vine-ripened tomatoes

1 cup (60 g) coarsely chopped fresh parsley, purslane, or arugula, or a mixture

½ cup (50 g) thinly sliced scallions

2 cloves thinly sliced smoked garlic (see page 47; optional)

3 tablespoons chopped fresh mint leaves

2 tablespoons chopped fresh thyme

2 to 3 jalapeños, seeded and finely chopped

4 tablespoons (35 g) capers, rinsed and drained

FOR THE SAUCE:

⅓ cup (80 ml) good, fruity olive oil, or more as needed

2 tablespoons fresh lemon juice

1 tablespoon balsamic vinegar

1 to 2 cloves garlic, minced (optional)

2 teaspoons lemon zest

Salt

1 teaspoon sumac (optional)

1½ cups (180 g) chopped feta cheese, or a few home-marinated sardines (optional; see Note)

1 teaspoon dried Greek oregano

1 to 2 teaspoons Bread Crumbs with Olives or Capers (optional; page 59)

You can simply top the dry rusks (the crunchy dried bread) with tomatoes and olive oil, or you can make this more elaborate topping that will transform the *friselle* or *paximadia* into a more substantial meze. The dish can even become a light lunch, especially if you choose to complement it with feta, home-marinated sardines, salted anchovies, or *boquerones*.

Place the *friselle* or *paximadia* in a shallow dish that holds them snugly. Halve the tomatoes over a medium bowl and squeeze lightly with your hand to remove some loose seeds. Using a sharp serrated knife, dice the tomatoes. Transfer to a sieve set over a small bowl to collect the juices. Transfer the diced tomatoes to the medium bowl and add the parsley, scallions, smoked garlic (if using), mint, thyme, jalapeños, and capers.

Pour the tomato juice from the small bowl over and around the rusks.

Make the sauce: In a bowl, whisk together the olive oil, lemon juice, vinegar, garlic (if using), lemon zest, salt, and sumac, if using. Pour the sauce over the chopped tomatoes and herbs and toss. Taste and adjust the seasoning.

Spread tablespoons of this mixture over the *friselle* and drizzle the sauce that remains in the bowl over and around the rusks.

Refrigerate for 15 to 20 minutes before serving to give the flavors time to meld. Just before serving, scatter the feta over the top. Sprinkle with oregano, drizzle with more olive oil, sprinkle with the bread crumbs (if using), and serve.

NOTE: *You can also use 3 to 4 good-quality anchovies in olive oil, drained and chopped or* boquerones *(see Sources, page 244; optional) in place of the feta.*

Toasted Red Lentil and Bulgur Patties (*Mercimek Köftesi*) VEGAN

MAKES ABOUT 25 PATTIES;
SERVES 6 TO 8

1 cup (290 g) red lentils

⅔ cup (95 g) fine bulgur

1½ teaspoons salt, or more to taste

¼ cup (60 ml) olive oil, plus more as needed

1 cup (160 g) chopped onion

1 teaspoon ground turmeric

2 tablespoons tomato paste

2 to 3 teaspoons Maraş pepper, or crushed red pepper flakes, to taste

1 cup (40 g) finely chopped fresh flat-leaf parsley

2 scallions, white and most of the green part, very finely chopped

1 tablespoon fresh lemon juice, or more to taste

1 teaspoon ground cumin

3 to 4 sprigs fresh tarragon, finely chopped, or 1 teaspoon dried tarragon (optional)

Lettuce leaves, for serving (optional)

Garlic Spread (*Skordalia*, page 70) or Caper, Scallion, and Parsley Spread (page 85), for serving

Traditionally these lentil-and-bulgur patties, a very common meze in southern Turkey, are served raw. They are shaped with wet hands to prevent sticking. Although they can be delicious raw if the spicing is right, the texture is on the mushy side. José Andrés adds his own brilliant touch, briefly toasting the *mercimek köftesi* he serves at Zaytinya, his eastern Mediterranean restaurant in Washington, D.C. The toasting makes all the difference.

In a medium saucepan, combine the lentils and 2½ cups (600 ml) water and bring to a boil. Reduce the heat and simmer, stirring often and adding more water, if needed, until the lentils are soft and mushy. About 1 cup (240 ml) of the water must be left in the pan. If need be, add more, and when it returns to a boil add the bulgur and salt. Stir, remove from the heat, cover, and let stand for about 15 minutes, until the bulgur softens.

In a skillet, heat the olive oil over medium heat. Add the onion and sauté until it softens and starts to color. Add the turmeric, tomato paste, and Maraş pepper and sauté, stirring, for 1 minute. Add the onion-tomato mixture to the lentils and bulgur, stir well to mix, and transfer to a bowl. Let cool, cover, and refrigerate for at least 2 hours, but preferably overnight.

You can complete preparation to this point up to 3 days in advance.

Add the parsley, scallions, lemon juice, cumin, and tarragon (if using), and stir well to mix. The mixture should be soft, a bit moist, and easy to shape. If it feels too dry, add 1 to 2 tablespoons water and some olive oil. Taste and adjust the seasoning with more salt, pepper, and lemon, if you like.

Take heaping tablespoons of the mixture and form them into flat, oval patties.

Heat a ridged stovetop grill or a nonstick skillet. When it is very hot, brush a few patties at a time lightly with olive oil and toast for about 2 minutes per side, until well-browned. Flip carefully with two spatulas and brown on the other side. They don't need to cook through, just get a nice crust. Sear the rest of the patties, brushing them with oil just before placing them on the hot pan.

Serve, placing each patty on a lettuce leaf, if you like, and accompany with Garlic Spread or Caper, Scallion, and Parsley Spread.

Zucchini, Herb, and Feta Fritters (*Kolokythokeftedes*)

MAKES ABOUT 20 PATTIES;
SERVES 6 TO 8

2 pounds (1 kg) zucchini, coarsely grated

1 teaspoon salt

1 bunch scallions, white and most of the green parts, finely chopped

1 bunch fresh dill, finely chopped

1 tablespoon dried oregano, crumbled

½ pound (225 g) feta cheese, crumbled

Freshly ground black pepper

2 eggs, lightly beaten

1 cup (100 g) dried bread crumbs, or more as needed

½ cup (60 g) all-purpose flour, or more as needed

Olive oil and safflower oil, for frying

There are as many different preparations of *kolokythokeftedes* as there are cooks in Greece—and I am not exaggerating. Throughout the summer this very popular meze is served in taverns all over the country. With cold wine or beer, Greeks nibble on *kolokythokeftedes* until the main courses arrive. The fried patties have to be very crunchy, with a soft, fresh center. This recipe is adapted from the patties served at Magazes, my friend Stephanos Alexandrou's fish tavern on Kea.

In a colander, combine the zucchini with the salt. Mash and squeeze handfuls to extract most of its moisture. Transfer the zucchini to a bowl and add the scallions, dill, oregano, feta, and a few grindings of pepper. Add the eggs and toss to mix.

In a bowl, combine the bread crumbs and the flour. Add ½ cup (about 50 g) of the bread crumb mixture to the zucchini mixture, stirring together to get a soft dough—you might need to add more bread crumbs and flour. Spread the rest of the bread crumb mixture on a plate.

In a large, deep skillet, heat 1½ inches (4 cm) of combined olive oil and safflower oil over medium-high heat to 350°F (175°C).

Make a test patty: Stir the zucchini mixture and, using a spoon, scoop up an amount about the size of a large walnut. With the help of a second spoon, dredge it in the bread crumb mixture, shaping it into a small patty as you roll it. Place the test patty carefully in the hot oil. Fry, turning once, until browned, about 3 minutes. Taste the patty and adjust the seasonings in the remaining zucchini mixture, if necessary.

Shape and fry the remaining patties in batches. Prepare more bread crumb–flour mixture, if needed, maintaining a ratio of approximately 2 to 1.

Transfer the fried patties to paper towels to drain briefly, then serve hot, warm, or at room temperature.

Chickpea Pancakes (*Farinata* or *Socca*) VEGAN GLUTEN-FREE

MAKES 6 TO 8 PANCAKES, OR
ONE 13-INCH (33-CM) *FARINATA*

1 cup (140 g) chickpea flour

1 teaspoon sea salt

1½ teaspoons freshly ground black pepper

2 tablespoons olive oil, plus more for the pan

2 tablespoons fresh oregano or thyme, finely chopped (optional)

2 tablespoons Maraş pepper, or a pinch of crushed red pepper flakes (optional)

2 tablespoons *h'rous* (page 62) or harissa, diluted in 1 to 2 tablespoons olive oil

In the maze of Genoa's narrow streets, deep within what is believed to be Europe's largest medieval quarter, bakeries display huge pans of *farinata*, described as "chickpea pizza" to entice the puzzled tourist. The locals don't need an explanation, of course, and come to get a piece of this addictive delicacy, delivered simply on parchment paper and devoured quickly on the spot. Farther west along the coast, in neighboring Nice on the French Riviera, the chickpea pancake is called *socca* and is equally popular.

I suggest you mix the batter the night before you plan to serve this wonderful meze; it needs to rest for several hours before cooking, so plan ahead.

Whisk the chickpea flour in a bowl, adding the salt and black pepper. Slowly pour in 2 cups (480 ml) water, whisking vigorously to mix into a smooth batter. Be careful that you have no lumps in your batter. Stir in the olive oil. Cover and refrigerate overnight, or up to 3 days. Bring to room temperature before proceeding.

To make the *farinata* pancakes: Preheat the broiler and place a rack close to the heat source.

Heat two 8-inch (20-cm) nonstick, ovenproof sauté pans over medium-high heat. Add 1 teaspoon olive oil to each pan. Whisk the batter—it will be watery and thin—and pour ¼ cup (60 ml) of the batter into each pan. Tilt the pans so that the batter forms a thin layer all around the base. If you like, sprinkle with some herbs and Maraş pepper. Cook for 3 minutes, or until the edges brown and start to curl. Place the pans under the broiler for 1 minute to brown the tops. Transfer the broiled pancakes to a plate and continue cooking the rest of the batter in the same manner. Serve with some *h'rous* while still warm.

To bake a large, pizzalike *farinata*: Preheat the oven to 450°F (230°C).

VARIATION

FARINATA DEL BOSCO: FARINATA WITH DRIED MUSHROOMS AND ROSEMARY

In a blender or food processor, combine ½ cup (35 g) dried porcini mushrooms and 2 tablespoons rosemary leaves. Whisk with the chickpea flour, salt, pepper, and 2 cups (480 ml) water to make the batter. Allow the batter to rest and cook as described at right, preferably making one large *farinata*.

Place a 13-inch (33-cm) nonstick pizza pan on a rack in the lower part of the oven. Once the pan is very hot, remove it carefully and add 3 tablespoons olive oil. Whisk the batter and pour it into the pan. Sprinkle with herbs, if you like. Carefully place the pan into the very hot oven and bake for 10 minutes, or until the edges brown and start to curl. If the top has not colored sufficiently, heat the broiler and move the pan close to the heat source for a minute, until golden.

Using a spatula, cut into squares or wedges and serve with *h'rous* while still warm.

Red Pepper Spread with Hazelnuts and Pomegranate Molasses VEGAN

MAKES ABOUT 2 CUPS (480 ML);
SERVES 8 TO 10

3 large red bell peppers, halved and seeded

2 to 3 dried mildly hot dried peppers

2 to 3 tablespoons *h'rous* (page 62) or good-quality imported Turkish hot pepper paste (see Sources, page 244), or 2 to 3 teaspoons Maraş pepper or crushed red pepper flakes, or more to taste

1½ cups (200 g) hazelnuts, toasted

3 tablespoons pomegranate molasses

1 teaspoon ground cumin

1 teaspoon ground coriander seeds

Salt

1 to 3 tablespoons finely ground whole-wheat crackers or toasted whole-wheat bread crumbs (optional)

Fresh lemon juice (optional)

Grilled pita triangles or thin slices whole-wheat bread, toasted, for serving

This dish is inspired by *muhammara*, a Syrian pepper-and-walnut spread, flavored with the distinct taste of pomegranate molasses. Most recipes call for grilled peppers, but I find that sautéing the peppers in olive oil deepens their flavor, plus it is simpler and spares you the time of removing the skins. I choose to make it with roasted hazelnuts, but walnuts work just as well. My guests find this brick-colored spread irresistible, especially when I make it with my homegrown peppers and *h'rous* pepper paste. Note also that this is a rare spread in that it contains no garlic.

Cut the bell peppers into 1-inch (2.5-cm) strips. In a skillet, heat the olive oil over medium heat and sauté the bell peppers, tossing often with a spatula, until they soften and start to color, 10 to 15 minutes.

In a blender or a food processor, combine the sautéed bell peppers and their oil with the dried hot peppers, *h'rous*, toasted hazelnuts, pomegranate molasses, cumin, coriander seeds, and salt to taste. Process into a chunky paste.

Transfer to a bowl. If the spread is too thin for your liking, stir in 1 tablespoon bread crumbs (or more to taste). Taste and correct seasoning, adding more *h'rous*, pomegranate molasses, or some lemon juice, if you like.

Cover and refrigerate for at least 3 hours or overnight.

Serve with toasted pita or bread.

Raw Pepper and Nut Spread (*Muhammara*) VEGAN

¼ cup (35 g) almonds

½ cup (50 g) walnuts

⅓ cup (35 g) pine nuts

½ cup (75 g) roasted peanuts, preferably unsalted

1 medium white onion, coarsely chopped

3 medium red or yellow bell peppers (about 1 pound/500 g total), halved, seeded, and cut into 1-inch (2.5-cm) pieces

½ cup (50 g) finely ground whole-wheat crackers or toasted whole-wheat bread crumbs

1 to 2 teaspoons Maraş pepper, or crushed red pepper flakes, to taste

2 tablespoons pomegranate molasses

½ cup (120 ml) good, fruity olive oil

Salt

¼ cup (30 g) shelled unsalted pistachios, coarsely chopped or ground

Warm pita, for serving

Syrian-born chef Mohammed Antabli offers a very different *muhammara* in Al Waha, his renowned London restaurant. Apparently the original Aleppo *muhammara* was made with raw, not roasted, peppers. Although I usually have an aversion to uncooked peppers, I love this nutty spread that is totally different from the previous recipe, not just in taste and texture, but also in color. When I serve the two dishes together, to emphasize their differences and to add even more color, I often make this raw spread with yellow bell peppers, which have a sweet flavor similar to that of red bell peppers.

Preheat the oven to 375°F (190°C) with a rack in the middle.

Spread the almonds and walnuts on a baking sheet and toast in the oven for 8 minutes. Toss, add the pine nuts, and toast for 6 to 8 minutes more, until golden and fragrant. Let cool.

Transfer the almonds, walnuts, roasted peanuts, and pine nuts (reserving 1 tablespoon pine nuts for serving) to a food processor. Pulse to chop the nuts finely. Transfer to a medium bowl.

Place the onion and bell peppers in the food processor and pulse until finely chopped. Pour the mixture through a fine-mesh sieve into a bowl and press with a spatula to drain excess liquid. Add the pepper-onion mixture to the chopped nuts and stir in the ground crackers.

Add the Maraş pepper, pomegranate molasses, olive oil, and salt to taste. Stir well and taste to adjust the seasoning. Sprinkle with the pistachios and reserved pine nuts. Serve with warm pita.

Spicy Levantine Cheese Balls (*Shanklish*) GLUTEN-FREE

MAKES ABOUT 32 GOLF-BALL-SIZE PIECES

FOR THE CHEESE BALLS:

¾ pound (340 g) feta cheese, crumbled

2 cups (500 g) full-fat Greek-style yogurt

4 cloves garlic, minced

3 teaspoons Maraş pepper, or crushed red pepper flakes, to taste

1 tablespoon dried Greek oregano

FOR THE SPICE MIXTURE:

⅓ cup (about 15 g) fresh thyme leaves

⅓ cup (about 35 g) coarsely ground coriander seeds

3 tablespoons coarsely ground pink peppercorns

¼ cup (25 g) dried thyme

2 to 3 teaspoons Maraş pepper, or crushed red pepper flakes, to taste

Olive oil, for preserving

Sun-drying *laban*—a fresh cheese made by straining yogurt—was one means, before the invention of cold storage, to preserve perishable dairy products. The cheese was shaped into balls and then rolled in an aromatic mix of seasonings—za'atar, red pepper flakes, or a mixture of local herbs and spices—and then dried completely until rock-hard, finally ready for extended storage in clay jars.

These fermented, extremely pungent *shanklish* balls are a multipurpose spice in their own right. Ground with a mortar and pestle, they can be used to provide different dimensions of flavor to salads and vegetable dishes. Syrian-born chef Mohammed Antabli makes a modern version of this age-old cheese with a mixture of yogurt and feta, rolled in spices, which he serves at Al Waha, considered one of London's top Middle Eastern restaurants. I varied the spices slightly, but I followed his brilliant way of making these wonderful cheese balls. Crumble them over salads, like the one with beets and arugula (page 99), or slice the log-shaped cheese and serve it on its own as an appetizer, drizzled with good, fruity olive oil (pictured on page 44). You can preserve *shanklish* in jars, submerged in olive oil, in the refrigerator. They will keep for up to 4 months.

Make the cheese balls: In a bowl, whisk together the feta, yogurt, garlic, Maraş pepper, and oregano.

Line a tray with parchment paper. Scoop out about ⅓ cup (80 ml) of the cheese mixture at a time (use a small ice cream scoop, if you have one) and place dollops on the tray, next to one another but not touching.

Place the tray in the refrigerator, uncovered, and leave for at least 2 days, until the mixture is dry enough to shape into balls.

Make the spice mixture: In a bowl, blend all the spice mixture ingredients well. Then spread the mixture on a plate. Roll the cheese balls in the spices to coat on all sides. Alternatively, you can knead 2 to 3 balls together and shape the mixture into small logs, then roll them in the spice mixture and dry. They can then be sliced and served on bread or drizzled with olive oil.

Place the formed *shanklish* (either the balls or logs) on a clean parchment paper–lined tray. Let dry in the refrigerator for 2 to 3 days more.

Fill a jar with the dried cheese balls and add just enough olive oil to cover. Keep in the refrigerator, but take out an hour before serving and let come to room temperature, as the oil solidifies in the fridge.

THE GREAT CAPER AND THE TINY IMPOSTER

Across Greek islands and throughout the Mediterranean, caper bushes grow wild, hanging majestically off rocky cliffs overlooking the sea, scoffing at the idea of being restricted to a garden. Though they have surged in popularity recently, capers have been a Mediterranean staple for centuries. There is a widespread belief that tiny capers are the best, but I disagree strongly. They are more widely available than their superior cousins, which perhaps explains their ubiquity in books and blogs, but small capers lack the flavor and aroma unique to the larger variety. Try them yourself and you will be hooked for life.

When harvested, the caper buds, shoots, leaves, and fruits of the shrub are bitter; they must be cured and pickled in a salt-vinegar brine. For those far from fresh Mediterranean buds and shoots, capers in vinegar are widely available in supermarkets. But I suggest you opt for the ones preserved in salt, like the capers from Pantelleria (see Sources, page 244). They retain flavors that are lost in commercial vinegar brining. Salted capers need to be rinsed well under lukewarm running water before use. Dry thoroughly on paper towels.

Caper berries, which look like small, elongated almonds, are the fruits of the caper bush. Cured in vinegar, they are meatier and have a milder taste than capers. On Chios and other islands, the berries are stuffed with garlic cloves and served as an appetizer. Pickled caper shoots and leaves are also served as meze, and are of course added to salads, pasta sauces, grilled fish, and all kinds of vegetable dishes.

Caper, Scallion, and Parsley Spread VEGAN

MAKES ABOUT 2½ CUPS (600 ML);
SERVES 8 TO 10

1 cup (140 g) capers, preferably
 salt-packed

4 to 5 scallions, white and most of the
 green parts, coarsely chopped

1½ cups (60 g) fresh flat-leaf parsley leaves

3 to 4 tablespoons fresh lemon juice,
 or more to taste

½ cup (105 g) mashed cooked potato,
 cold

¼ cup (60 ml) good, fruity olive oil

4 sprigs wild fennel or dill

Salt and freshly ground black pepper

Pita triangles or thin slices of toasted
 whole-wheat bread, for serving

Handful of cherry tomatoes, halved, for
 serving (optional)

This recipe, from the Greek island of Tinos, is based on a traditional Lenten meze. Serve as an appetizer with fresh and crusty bread or toast, or use as a dressing for steamed potatoes or cauliflower. It can also work as a refreshing sauce for summer pasta dishes, best served at room temperature. The quality of the capers is crucial. I suggest you avoid the small, commercial capers commonly found in supermarkets. Large salt-packed capers (see Sources, page 244) are the best choice.

Rinse the capers thoroughly under running lukewarm water. Dry them well on paper towels. In a food processor, combine the capers, scallions, parsley, and 3 tablespoons lemon juice and process into a smooth paste. Add the potato, olive oil, fennel, and salt and pepper to taste and process until incorporated. Taste and adjust the seasonings, adding more lemon juice, salt, and pepper, if needed.

Transfer to a serving bowl, cover, and refrigerate for at least 2 hours or overnight.

Serve with pita or bread, with the cherry tomatoes on the side, if you like.

Santorini *Fava* with Braised Capers and Onions VEGAN GLUTEN-FREE

SERVES 8

FOR THE *FAVA*:

3 tablespoons olive oil

1 medium onion, finely chopped

2 teaspoons salt

2 cups (250 g) yellow split peas, picked over and rinsed

2 bay leaves

1 tablespoon ground turmeric

FOR THE BRAISED CAPERS AND ONIONS:

1 cup (140 g) good-quality medium or large capers, preferably salt-packed

½ cup (120 ml) olive oil

3 cups (480 g) halved and thinly sliced purple onions

1 cup (240 ml) sweet red wine, such as Mavrodaphne or sweet Marsala

2 to 3 tablespoons good red wine vinegar (optional if using brine-packed capers)

Maraş pepper or freshly ground black pepper, for serving

Good, fruity olive oil, for drizzling

Long before Santorini became one of the world's most popular tourist destinations, it was one of Greece's most destitute islands. In a place poor in natural resources and badly exposed to the harsh winds of the Aegean, Santorini's impoverished but ingenious inhabitants survived on whatever they could forage or cultivate in small terraced gardens on steep, rocky hills. Capers were plentiful, so they were often treated like any other foraged green, elevated from a flavoring to the principal ingredient of a dish; large, meaty capers were braised with plenty of onions and olive oil to make a frugal but hearty meal, consumed with bread or *paximadia*. Braised capers are also served as a topping for the local *fava*, the trademark dish of Santorini. *Fava* is usually prepared with mashed yellow split peas (*dal*) but in the old days it was made from an indigenous legume, a variant of *Lathyrus sativus*— chickling vetch or grass pea, *cicerchia* in Italian. Traces of this ancient legume have been found in the island's Bronze Age settlement, Akrotiri.

Make the *fava*: Heat the olive oil in a skillet over medium heat, add the onion, sprinkle with salt, and sauté for about 5 minutes, until just soft. Place the split peas in a large pot, add the sautéed onions with their oil, cover with water by 4 inches (10 cm), and bring to a boil. Reduce the heat to low and simmer for 5 minutes.

Add the bay leaves and turmeric and simmer for about 30 minutes, stirring occasionally. Add a little warm water, if needed, to keep the peas covered as they cook. The peas are done when they are very soft and almost dry. Remove the bay leaves. Puree with an immersion blender or transfer to a food processor and process. Let the puree cool completely; it will thicken considerably. (The split peas can be prepared to this point up to 3 days in advance. Store them, covered, in the refrigerator and bring to room temperature before serving.)

Make the braised capers and onions: If using salt-packed capers, place them in a colander and rinse under running lukewarm water for 2 to 3 minutes, or until they lose their excessive saltiness. If using brine-packed capers, rinse them well to remove most of their tartness. Dry the capers on paper towels.

In a deep skillet, heat ¼ cup (60 ml) of the oil over medium heat and sauté the onions, tossing often until soft, about 8 minutes. Add the capers and the remaining oil and cook for 2 to 3 minutes, or until the capers start to sizzle. Pour in the wine and cook for 1 minute. Add ½ cup (120 ml) water, reduce the heat to low, and cook for 8 minutes.

Turn the heat to high and cook, stirring, until the water has evaporated and the onions start to caramelize. Remove from the heat and add vinegar (if using) and Maraş pepper to taste; you may not need to add vinegar if using capers that were packed in brine. Let cool before serving.

The capers and onions can be made up to 3 days in advance, covered and refrigerated; bring to room temperature before serving.

To serve: Transfer the cooled split pea puree to a shallow bowl and spread it out with a spoon, leaving about 1 inch (2.5 cm) of space between the edge of the bowl and the puree. Use the spoon to create a well in the center of the puree. Spread the onion-caper topping in and around the well. Drizzle with good, fruity olive oil and sprinkle with Maraş pepper, if you like.

THE VERSATILITY OF SMOKY EGGPLANT

Charcoal-grilled and roasted eggplants with . . . sweet and hot peppers? Sliced zucchini or squash? Lemon or vinegar? Olive oil and chopped garlic? The options are endless, giving flavor to rustic salads and summer spreads all around the Mediterranean. My Albanian neighbors serve a wonderful, minimalist dish that begins by halving and grilling the eggplant. They take it right off the fire, its charred skin contrasting with the snow-white flesh that glistens with drops of olive oil and lemon. A final touch of coarsely chopped garlic gives some bite.

Over the years, I have tried several variations on grilled and roasted eggplant. Recently, though, I have decided to go back to the core of this irresistible appetizer. The two eggplant spreads I propose on the following pages both start from the exact same roasted, smoky eggplants, mashed with a fork and flavored with garlic and lemon. In a Provençal variation, olive oil, chopped olives, parsley, and basil give a fresh spring flavor to the appetizer; tahini and yogurt, on the other hand, make *moutabal* a totally different yet equally irresistible spread with an earthy, nutty flavor.

Eggplant and Olive Spread Provençal (*Aubergines à la Matrasso*) VEGAN GLUTEN-FREE

3 to 4 large eggplants (about 2 pounds/
1 kg total)

¼ cup (60 ml) good, fruity olive oil,
plus more for drizzling

1 cup (40 g) packed fresh flat-leaf
parsley leaves

3 cloves garlic, quartered

2 to 3 tablespoons fresh lemon juice,
or more to taste

1 cup (200 g) Kalamata or other juicy black
olives, pitted and chopped

Leaves from 4 sprigs fresh basil, coarsely
chopped

Freshly ground black pepper

Salt (optional)

1 to 2 sprigs fresh parsley or basil, for garnish
(optional)

Slices of toasted multigrain or whole-wheat
bread, for serving (optional)

Melintzanosalata (eggplant spread) became a standard item on Greek restaurant menus during the mid-1960s, as the number of tavernas all over Greece grew rapidly, competing to attract tourists and an expanding Athenian middle class. People loved the creamy concoction of roasted eggplant, garlic, and mayonnaise that most places served. In English the appetizer was referred to as "eggplant caviar," a direct translation from the French *caviar d'aubergine*. In *La Table d'un Provençal*, renowned French chef Guy Gedda writes that in the beginning of the twentieth century the appetizer was called *aubergines à la Matrasso*, but then the more pretentious *caviar d'aubergine* caught on. If you squint at the dish long enough—after enough ouzo—this eggplant salad might start to look like caviar!

Pierce each eggplant in several places around the stem with a skewer, toothpick, or fork. Place on a rack about 1 inch (2.5 cm) from the coals on a gas or charcoal grill, or under a very hot broiler. Turn the eggplant methodically, exposing all sides to the heat. The skin will char evenly and the flesh will soften in about 10 minutes (see Note for Syrian Eggplant Dip, opposite). The slower and longer you roast the eggplant, the smokier the taste. If you're using an electric stove, roast the eggplants over moderate to low heat on a ridged stovetop grill (which allows their liquid to drain), turning as above, for 20 to 30 minutes.

Transfer the eggplants to a colander. Using a sharp knife, halve them lengthwise and let them drain for 10 minutes. Scoop out the flesh, discarding the skin and hard seeds. Mash the flesh with a fork and transfer to a medium bowl.

In a blender or a food processor, combine the olive oil, parsley leaves, garlic, and 2 tablespoons lemon juice and process into a smooth paste.

Stir the parsley-garlic puree into the mashed eggplant, then add the chopped olives and basil leaves. Stir, add pepper to taste, and taste, adding more lemon juice and maybe salt, but beware that olives are usually quite salty. Cover and refrigerate for at least 1 hour or overnight.

Transfer to a serving bowl, drizzle with good, fruity olive oil, garnish with parsley and/or basil sprigs, and serve with toasted bread if you like.

Syrian Eggplant Dip with Tahini and Yogurt (*Moutabal*)

MAKES ABOUT 2 CUPS (480 ML);
SERVES 8 TO 10

3 to 4 medium eggplants (about 1½ pounds/ 680 g total; see Note)

⅓ cup (80 ml) tahini, preferably whole-grain, imported from Greece or from the Middle East (see Sources, page 244), well stirred

4 cloves garlic, crushed with ½ teaspoon salt

3 to 4 tablespoons fresh lemon juice, or more to taste

1 cup (250 g) Greek-style yogurt

Salt

1 tablespoon good, fruity olive oil

¼ cup (40 g) pomegranate seeds, fresh or frozen (if frozen, thaw)

Toasted pita or thin slices of toasted multigrain or whole-wheat bread, for serving (optional)

This is the traditional Syrian eggplant spread. The final dish requires no pretentious name, no exotic spices or other fancy ingredients—it doesn't even have pepper! You can omit the pomegranate seeds—though the red jewels make the grayish spread more attractive, they don't really add any extra flavor to the nutty, earthy dip. I am following the recipe given to me by Paula Wolfert, the doyenne of Mediterranean foods, which she found going through old notes from a 1989 trip to Syria. I am grateful to her for preparing, fine-tuning, and sharing the recipe with me.

Pierce each eggplant in several places around the stem with a skewer, toothpick, or fork. Place on a rack about 1 inch (2.5 cm) from the coals on a gas or charcoal grill, or under a very hot broiler. Turn the eggplant methodically, exposing all sides to the heat. The skin will char evenly and the flesh will soften in about 10 minutes. The slower and longer you roast the eggplant, the smokier the taste. If you're using an electric stove, roast the eggplants over moderate to low heat on a ridged stovetop grill (which allows their liquid to drain), turning as above, for 20 to 30 minutes.

Transfer the eggplants to a colander. Using a sharp knife, halve them lengthwise and let them drain for 10 minutes. Scoop out the flesh, discarding the skin and hard seeds. Mash the flesh with a fork and transfer to a medium bowl.

In a blender or a food processor, combine and pulse the tahini, garlic, 3 tablespoons lemon juice, and yogurt. Add this puree to the eggplant and stir. Taste and adjust the seasoning with salt and/or more lemon juice. Refrigerate for at least 1 hour or overnight before serving. The *moutabal* keeps for up to 5 days in the refrigerator.

About 30 minutes before serving, spread the mixture in a shallow dish, drizzle with olive oil, and sprinkle with pomegranate seeds. If you like, serve with toasted pita or with thin slices of toasted whole-wheat or multigrain bread.

NOTE: *Syrian cook and blogger Ghinwa Alameen (www.syriancooking.com)—who has an almost identical* moutabal *recipe—writes that every time she or her husband fire the grill they roast a couple of extra eggplants on the side. They then cool them, scoop out the pulp, and store it in bags in the freezer. When she needs to create* moutabal, *or any other smoky-flavored eggplant dish, she simply places the frozen pulp in a colander to thaw and drain. It is a wonderfully efficient method of saving time and effort when preparing almost any eggplant spread.*

Sautéed Olives and Carrots with Preserved Lemon and Thyme   VEGAN GLUTEN-FREE

SERVES 6 TO 8

3 tablespoons olive oil

1 clove garlic, smashed

⅔ pound (about 300 g) full-flavored, brine-cured black olives (like Pelion or Niçoise), rinsed and dried on paper towels

2 cups (480 ml) Orange and Olive Oil Carrots (recipe follows)

¼ preserved lemon peel, rinsed, dried, and cut into thin strips

2 teaspoons dried thyme, or Aegean Herb and Hot Pepper Mix (page 55)

1 teaspoon Maraş pepper or a pinch of crushed red pepper flakes, or more to taste

1 tablespoon finely chopped fresh thyme

1 lemon, cut into eighths (optional)

"This preparation is a recipe from my father," writes French chef Guy Gedda, describing a combination of sautéed carrots and olives, cooked either with milk or rich, thick crème fraîche. Sweet carrots and salty-bitter olives complement one another beautifully, probably better than the braised onions and olives that have been in my repertoire of quick bites for years. Inspired by Gedda's dish, I decided to rework my mother's recipe for carrots with orange juice and olive oil, as I remember them from my childhood (recipe follows). She called them "caramelized" to appeal to our sweet tooth, I guess, but she never used sugar, just freshly squeezed orange juice and olive oil. I prefer to keep the olives unpitted to preserve as much flavor as possible. Slivers of preserved lemon and a combination of dried and fresh thyme, or my Aegean Herb and Hot Pepper Mix, add the final touches to this very simple dish.

Heat the olive oil in a skillet over medium-low heat. Add the garlic and toss for a few seconds until fragrant, then discard. Add the olives, carrots, and preserved lemon to the skillet and sauté, stirring carefully, for 2 to 3 minutes, until just heated through.

Remove from the heat and add the dried thyme and Maraş pepper, and toss. Transfer the mixture to a shallow dish, sprinkle with the fresh thyme, and serve warm or at room temperature, with lemon wedges for squeezing, if you like.

Orange and Olive Oil Carrots   VEGAN GLUTEN-FREE

MAKES ABOUT 4 CUPS (ABOUT 600 G)

½ cup (120 ml) olive oil

1½ pounds (680 g) medium carrots, preferably organic, sliced into ⅛-inch (0.3-cm) rounds (use a mandoline or a food processor fitted with a slicing disc)

1 teaspoon salt, plus more to taste

1 cup (240 ml) fresh orange juice

Maraş pepper, red pepper flakes, or freshly ground black pepper, to taste

You can halve the recipe. I like to keep a bowl in my refrigerator ready to add to salads, grain pilafs, and soups, or just to eat with grilled cheese or fish. My dogs love them, too, so I use them as treats!

Heat the olive oil in a large, deep, heavy-bottomed sauté pan and add the carrots. Sprinkle with the salt and sauté, tossing often, for 2 to 3 minutes, until the carrot slices are coated with olive oil.

Add the orange juice and cook, uncovered, tossing often, for about 10 minutes, until the carrots are tender and the orange juice has evaporated. Add Maraş pepper, taste, and correct the seasoning. Let cool, cover, and refrigerate for up to 4 days.

Red Cabbage with Yogurt and Walnuts GLUTEN-FREE

SERVES 6 TO 8

⅔ cup (160 ml) olive oil

1 medium red cabbage, halved, cored, and thinly sliced

1 teaspoon salt, or more to taste

4 cloves garlic, finely chopped

1 to 2 teaspoons Maraş pepper, or a good pinch of crushed red pepper flakes, to taste (plenty of freshly ground black pepper will also suffice)

2 cups (500 g) Greek-style yogurt

1 cup (240 ml) full- or low-fat natural yogurt

1 cup (150 g) Pink Fermented Cabbage, drained (page 40; optional)

⅔ cup (90 g) raisins

⅔ cup (55 g) walnuts, roasted and coarsely ground (see Note)

2 tablespoons chopped cilantro (optional)

A kind of Turkish coleslaw, this salad is inspired by the recipe for *Yoğurtlu Kırmızı Lahana*, described by Sende Pişir, a Turkish food blogger from Izmir. Dressing cabbage or greens with garlic and yogurt is common in Turkey and throughout the Balkans. In Greece we eat cabbage in the winter only, but our neighbors enjoy cabbage throughout the year, and therefore have spring and summer recipes that are cool and refreshing. Sende wilts the red cabbage in plenty of olive oil, then mixes garlic cloves with thick yogurt to create a healthy, creamy dressing. I briefly sauté the garlic with the cabbage and add some of my fermented cabbage as well as a few raisins, which add a hint of sweetness to this attractive, colorful salad.

Heat the olive oil in a heavy-bottomed pan over medium heat, add the raw cabbage, sprinkle with the salt, and sauté, tossing often, for 10 minutes or more, until the cabbage is just wilted. Add the garlic and Maraş pepper and toss for a few seconds, then remove from the heat and transfer to a colander placed over a bowl to drain. Transfer the drained cabbage to a large serving bowl. Return the juices released by the cabbage to the pan and boil vigorously until reduced to about 2 tablespoons. Pour over the cabbage and let cool completely.

In a medium bowl, whisk the yogurts together. If using, add the fermented cabbage to the wilted cabbage. Add the raisins and most of the walnuts to the cabbage, reserving 1 tablespoon of the walnuts for serving. Toss to mix. Add the yogurt mixture, toss again, and taste to correct the seasoning.

Transfer the salad to a bowl, cover, and refrigerate for at least 2 hours or overnight. The salad keeps for at least 3 days.

Just before serving, sprinkle with the reserved walnuts and the cilantro (if using).

NOTE: *To roast the walnuts, preheat the oven to 400°F (205°C), spread the walnuts on a baking sheet, and roast for about 15 minutes, until they are fragrant and begin to color. You can substitute hazelnuts for the walnuts, if you like.*

Green Chickpea Hummus   VEGAN

SERVES 6 TO 8

2 cups (400 g) shelled fresh chickpeas
(see Note)

2 cloves garlic, halved

1 teaspoon salt, or more to taste

1 cup (125 g) blanched almonds, presoaked
in water for 2 to 3 hours, and drained

2 to 3 tablespoons fresh lemon juice, to taste

1 cup (40 g) fresh flat-leaf parsley leaves

½ cup (20 g) fresh cilantro leaves

¼ cup (60 ml) tahini, preferably whole-grain,
imported from Greece or from the Middle
East (see Sources, page 244)

Freshly ground black pepper

¼ preserved lemon, rinsed, or zest from
½ lemon

Good, fruity olive oil, for drizzling

2 tablespoons pine nuts, toasted

Toasted pita or thin slices of toasted
multigrain or whole-wheat bread (optional)

Fresh green chickpea pods, each enclosing two green garbanzos, appear at Mediterranean markets in the spring. In Turkey and in the Middle East they are painstakingly shelled, peeled, steamed, and added to salads. They are often mixed with yogurt or a fetalike cheese and garlic and served as meze. They are also a delicious raw snack, much like fresh fava beans or snow peas.

In the bowl of a food processor, combine the chickpeas, garlic, salt, almonds, lemon juice, parsley, and cilantro and process to get a coarse mixture. Occasionally stop and scrape down the sides of the bowl with a spatula as you process.

Stir the tahini, as the oil tends to rise to the surface, and add it to the chickpea mixture, along with some pepper and the preserved lemon. Process for a few seconds to get a creamy spread.

Transfer the hummus to a bowl and taste to correct the seasoning, adding more lemon juice, salt, or pepper, as needed. Cover and refrigerate for at least 2 hours or overnight.

Drizzle with some olive oil and sprinkle with the pine nuts. Serve the hummus with toasted pita or bread, if you like.

NOTE: *If fresh chickpeas are not available, you can use fava beans or peas. You can also use frozen peas (a 10-ounce/280-g bag), steamed according to the package instructions.*

Orange, Olive, and Baby Leek Salad with *Verjus*-Tarragon Dressing VEGAN GLUTEN-FREE

SERVES 4 TO 6

4 baby leeks, white and light-green parts only, thinly sliced (keep the rest for use in broth)

Salt

3 tablespoons cider vinegar

3 Valencia oranges

2 cups (360 g) full-flavored brine-cured black olives (such as Pelion or Niçoise), rinsed and dried on paper towels

FOR THE DRESSING:

¼ cup (60 ml) good, fruity olive oil

3 tablespoons *verjus* (see Notes)

Salt

Good pinch of Maraş pepper, or crushed red pepper flakes, to taste

2 tablespoons snipped fresh tarragon (see Notes)

This pairing of olives and juicy oranges is yet another brilliant combination of ingredients, dictated by necessity. My Albanian friends explained that the oranges their gardens produced were sour and full of pips, nothing like today's sweet, lush and pip-less fruits. Paired with salty olives and sweet baby leeks or onions, and often complemented with shredded cabbage (see Variation), the oranges became a robust and delightful treat.

In the old days, this salad would have been dressed simply with olive oil, the natural tartness of the oranges adding depth to the dish. I compensate for the sweeter oranges you are likely to find with a fragrant *verjus* (see Sources, page 244) or lemon dressing. Fresh or dried mint is the most commonly used herb in Albania, but I also like to add tarragon when available. In place of oranges, thick-skinned sweet lemons, like the ones from Amalfi, are often made into a similar salad.

Place the leeks in a bowl, sprinkle generously with salt, add the vinegar and 2 tablespoons water, and toss. Cover and let marinate for 30 minutes to 1 hour.

Peel the oranges, halve them, discard any pips, and remove the hard central membrane. With a sharp knife, carefully cut each half into ½-inch (1.3-cm) slices. Arrange on a shallow platter and add the olives.

Drain the leeks and press between double layers of paper towels to dry. Sprinkle the leeks over the sliced oranges.

Make the dressing: In a bowl, whisk together the olive oil, *verjus*, a pinch of salt (keep in mind that olives are usually quite salty), the Maraş pepper, and the tarragon. Taste, correct the seasoning, pour over the salad, and serve.

NOTES: *You can substitute 2 tablespoons fresh lemon juice and 1 tablespoon white wine for the* verjus, *if you like.*

If you cannot find fresh tarragon you can substitute 3 tablespoons mint leaves.

VARIATION

ORANGE, CABBAGE, AND OLIVE SALAD

In a bowl, mix 3 cups (210 g) finely shredded green cabbage—or a combination of green and red—with 1 teaspoon fresh lemon juice and a good pinch of salt. Rub with your fingers to soften the cabbage. Toss with the drained leeks, and add to the orange and olive salad, proceeding with the dressing as described above.

Artichokes, Baby Carrots, and Fennel with Orange Vinaigrette VEGAN GLUTEN-FREE

SERVES 4 TO 6

8 baby artichokes

½ cup (120 ml) fresh lemon juice, for peeling

2 large lemons, quartered, for peeling

6 to 8 baby carrots, scrubbed under running water

1 small tender fennel bulb, hard parts and stems discarded, fronds chopped and reserved

FOR THE DRESSING:

2 scallions, thinly sliced

¼ cup (60 ml) good, fruity olive oil

3 tablespoons sherry or fruit vinegar

3 tablespoons fresh orange juice

2 teaspoons finely grated orange zest

1 teaspoon ground aniseeds

Finishing salt and freshly ground black pepper

This is a delicate, slightly crunchy salad with a complex sweet-and-salty taste. The strong lemony marinade keeps the thinly shaved artichokes from oxidizing and also tenderizes all the vegetables without altering their fresh spring flavors. The fragrant orange-aniseed vinaigrette, inspired by a recipe by José Andrés, complements this dish beautifully and works well with a variety of green salads. This unique salad can be enjoyed only during a few weeks of the year because the season for baby artichokes is so brief. But keep the recipe for the dressing in your repertoire for use throughout the year—it will give new life to a number of your standards and favorites.

Prepare the artichokes: Fill a bowl with 1½ quarts (1.5 L) cold water, add the lemon juice, and squeeze most of the juice from the lemon quarters into it—reserve the lemon quarters. Working with one artichoke at a time, trim the stem to about 1 inch (2.5 cm). Snap off the bottom three rows of leaves, rubbing the cut surfaces frequently with the lemon quarters as you work to keep the artichokes from discoloring. Cut off the tip of the artichoke and rub the cut side with lemon. Drop the peeled artichoke in the bowl of lemon-water and continue peeling the rest of the artichokes.

Using a mandoline, very carefully shave the artichokes, almost paper-thin, dropping the slices back into the lemon-water bowl. Shave the carrots and the fennel bulb vertically on the mandoline and drop the pieces into the bowl with the artichokes. Cover and refrigerate for up to 3 hours.

Make the dressing: Mix the scallions, olive oil, vinegar, orange juice and zest, and aniseeds in a jar with a tight-fitting lid. Shake the jar vigorously to combine.

Assemble the salad: Line a tray with three layers of paper towels. Using a slotted spoon, carefully lift and transfer the vegetable shavings to the tray. Dab the vegetables carefully with the paper towels to dry completely.

Arrange the vegetables on a shallow platter and pour the dressing on top, sprinkling with the reserved fennel fronds and salt and pepper, to taste. Serve immediately.

Beet, Arugula, and *Shanklish* Salad with Kumquat and Orange Dressing GLUTEN-FREE

SERVES 4 TO 6

2 pounds (1 kg) medium or small red beets (see Note)

3 tablespoons fresh lemon juice

1 cinnamon stick (optional)

3 kumquats or 1 tablespoon slivered orange zest

FOR THE DRESSING:

½ cup (120 ml) fresh orange juice

½ teaspoon honey, or 2 teaspoons pomegranate molasses

2 tablespoons fresh lemon juice, or more to taste

¼ cup (60 ml) good, fruity olive oil

1 bunch wild arugula leaves, washed and dried

2 crumbled *shanklish* balls (page 82), or ⅔ cup (80 g) crumbled spicy Gorgonzola

Salt and freshly ground pepper (optional)

Fresh lemon juice (optional)

We take our sweet, tender Mediterranean beets for granted. We boil them in water, and they are perfectly succulent with any dressing, even eaten plain, skin removed. When I first tasted roast beets in the United States, I realized that the strain of sweet beets that thrive in our garden is very different from the one cultivated here, which lacks the fruitlike flavor of Mediterranean beets. But I was determined to get my kind of tender sweetness out of common American beets, and here is my recipe.

Wash the beets and trim their tops. Place the beets in a saucepan, add water to cover, the lemon juice, and the cinnamon stick (if using). Bring to a boil, reduce the heat, and simmer for about 30 minutes, until the beets are fork-tender. You may have to remove the smaller beets and cook the larger ones a bit longer. Drain and let cool, then peel them easily by rubbing off the skin. Halve or quarter the larger beets and transfer to a bowl.

Halve the kumquats and use a spoon to remove the bitter flesh—discard or reserve to use in the orange cake syrup (see page 230)—and cut the skin into slivers.

Make the dressing: In a small saucepan, simmer the orange juice with the honey for 2 to 3 minutes, until reduced to about ¼ cup (60 ml) and fully incorporated. Pour into a bowl and let cool. Add the lemon juice and the olive oil and whisk to combine.

Pour half of the dressing over the beets and toss. Transfer the beets to a shallow bowl or a platter and add the arugula leaves. Sprinkle with crumbled *shanklish* and pour the rest of the dressing on top, sprinkling with the slivered kumquat. Taste and adjust the seasoning by adding salt, pepper, or more lemon juice, to taste.

NOTE: *You can use golden beets for this salad, or a combination of red and golden. I love golden beets, and I can't stop eating them when I'm in the United States. I have brought seeds back with me to Greece and have tried to grow them here for years, but to no avail.*

Steamed Zucchini and Roasted Peppers with Tomato-Garlic Dressing VEGAN GLUTEN-FREE

SERVES 4 TO 6

2 pounds (1 kg) small light-green zucchini or baby green zucchini

1 tablespoon salt

2 large red bell peppers

FOR THE DRESSING:

1 small juicy plum tomato, quartered (skin removed, if you like)

1 medium clove garlic, quartered

1 teaspoon Dijon mustard

¼ cup (60 ml) good, fruity olive oil

1 to 2 teaspoons cider vinegar or fresh lemon juice, to taste

1 teaspoon salt, or to taste

1 to 2 teaspoons Maraş pepper or a pinch of crushed red pepper flakes, to taste

1 to 2 tablespoons chopped fresh oregano, marjoram, or thyme, to taste

Finishing salt (optional)

June in Greece means zucchini. Some days we are overwhelmed with zucchini of all sizes. The light-green Middle Eastern zucchini cultivated in our part of the world are incredibly delicious and tender. Choose freshly harvested small zucchini for this salad, and boil them without trimming the ends. This way the zucchini keep their flavor and texture. If fresh zucchini are not available, make the salad with green beans (see Variation). The tomato-garlic dressing is my favorite—the perfect addition to zucchini, peppers, or any steamed vegetable or greens.

In a large pot, bring 5 quarts (5 L) water to a boil. Wash the zucchini but do not trim the ends. (If the ends are trimmed, the water will penetrate the flesh and the zucchini will turn to mush.) Add the zucchini to the pot with the salt and boil for 15 to 20 minutes (or more, depending on the size), checking often with a pointed knife. The zucchini are cooked when the knife pierces them very easily. Remove carefully with a slotted spoon and drain in a colander.

Roast the bell peppers over the gas flame on your stovetop, holding them with tongs and turning to get the skin black and blistery on all sides. Peel off the skin and cut the roasted peppers into strips. (Alternatively, heat the broiler. Quarter and seed the peppers. Line a baking sheet with aluminum foil and arrange the pepper quarters, skin side up, on the tray. Broil 4 to 5 inches/10 to 12 cm from the heat source until the skin is black and blistery. Peel and slice as above.)

Cut the zucchini vertically or into rounds. Transfer to a platter and add the bell pepper strips. Cover and set aside until ready to serve.

Make the dressing: In a blender, combine the tomato, garlic, mustard, olive oil, and vinegar—start with 1 teaspoon only of vinegar, since the tomato is often sour enough—salt, and Maraş pepper. Process to get a creamy sauce. Taste and adjust the seasoning, making sure your dressing is sour and spicy to balance the sweet zucchini and peppers. The dressing can be prepared up to 2 hours ahead.

Just before serving, whisk the dressing and pour over the zucchini and peppers. Sprinkle with the oregano and pass finishing salt at the table, if desired.

GREEN BEANS AND ROASTED PEPPERS WITH TOMATO-GARLIC DRESSING

Instead of zucchini, substitute 1½ pounds (680 g) tender green beans, with ends trimmed. Bring 2 inches (5 cm) water to a boil in a pot and steam the beans in a steamer basket until tender, about 10 minutes. Remove the steamer from the pot and transfer the beans to a platter; add the roasted peppers, make the dressing, and proceed as described opposite. To finish, sprinkle the salad with 3 tablespoons toasted pine nuts or slivered almonds, if you like.

Roasted Cauliflower with Musa's *Zahter* Relish VEGAN GLUTEN-FREE

SERVES 4 TO 6

Florets from a 3- to 3½-pound (1.5- to 1.6-kg) cauliflower

2 to 3 tablespoons olive oil

FOR THE ZAHTER RELISH:

1 medium onion, finely chopped

4 scallions, finely chopped

Salt

1 bunch fresh thyme

1 bunch fresh oregano

¼ cup (60 ml) good, fruity olive oil

1 jalapeño, seeded and finely chopped

3 tablespoons pomegranate molasses

1 bunch fresh flat-leaf parsley, finely chopped

1 tablespoon dried thyme or summer savory

Maraş pepper or freshly ground black pepper

1 to 2 tablespoons fresh lemon juice, to taste (optional)

Sprigs of fresh oregano or thyme, to decorate (optional)

Musa Dağdeviren is *the* most inspired and inspiring chef I know. I am dying to be able to converse with him in Turkish, the only language he speaks. Tasting his food at Ciya Kebab and Ciya Sofrasi, in Istanbul's Kadikoy district, I was bowled over by the enticing and complex flavors he creates in dishes that look simple and straightforward, like this refreshing *zahter* relish: a fragrant, tangy mixture of minced aromatic eastern Mediterranean thyme shoots (*zahter* in Turkish), parsley, onion, and scallions dressed in olive oil with lemon and pomegranate molasses. Musa serves "*zahter* salad" with his wonderful kebabs, wrapped in pita breads baked fresh by the minute in his restaurant's kitchens. I find that this pungent relish complements roasted or steamed cauliflower very well and makes a unique potato salad (see Variation). Serve it with grilled portobello or ear mushrooms, or any roasted vegetable—squash, carrots, zucchini, or eggplants, for example. Diluted with a few tablespoons of white wine, the *zahter* relish becomes an excellent dressing for grilled or poached fish.

Preheat the oven to 430°F (220°C) with a rack in the middle. Line a baking dish with parchment paper.

In a bowl, toss the cauliflower florets with 2 to 3 tablespoons olive oil, making sure the florets are well oiled all over. Spread them on the baking dish, cover loosely with a sheet of parchment paper, and place in the oven. Bake until tender, about 25 minutes— lift the paper to check for doneness. Transfer to a platter.

Make the *zahter* relish: In a bowl, combine the onion and scallions. Add a pinch of salt, rub with your fingers, and let macerate for 15 to 30 minutes. Drain.

Remove the hard stems from the fresh thyme and oregano (reserve the stems to add to broths and sauces) and finely chop the sprigs.

In a bowl, whisk together the olive oil, jalapeño, pomegranate molasses, and salt to taste. Add the parsley, onion and scallions, thyme, and savory. Toss well, cover, and let stand for at least 15 and up to 30 minutes.

Taste and adjust the seasonings with salt, pepper, or lemon juice, if you like. Pour over the cauliflower and serve, decorated with fresh oregano or thyme sprigs, if desired.

STEAMED NEW POTATOES WITH *ZAHTER* RELISH

In place of cauliflower, substitute 2½ pounds (1.2 kg) new potatoes, scrubbed and halved lengthwise (or quartered if they are large). Place the potatoes in a steamer basket over boiling water. Cover and steam for about 15 minutes, until the potatoes are tender. Transfer to a shallow bowl or platter and pour the *zahter* relish on top. Drizzle generously with good, fruity olive oil and serve the potato salad hot, warm, or at room temperature.

Semsa's Roasted Squash and Bread Salad

SERVES 4 TO 6

4 (½-inch/1.2-cm) slices day-old sourdough bread, torn to about 1-inch (2.5-cm) pieces—remove only the very hard crusts

⅔ cup (160 ml) olive oil

About 2½ pounds (1.2 kg) kabocha, buttercup, or any other squash with dense flesh, peeled, seeded, and cut into 1-inch (2.5-cm) cubes

2 teaspoons dried Greek oregano or thyme

Salt

A few pinches of Maraş pepper or crushed red pepper flakes, to taste

Yogurt-tahini sauce (see *Fattet Hummus*, page 180)

1 bunch fresh mint, coarsely chopped

Good pinch of dried mint (optional)

Good, fruity olive oil, for drizzling

Finishing salt, for sprinkling

Semsa Denizsel, the celebrated Istanbul chef and owner of Kantin Lokanta, is a passionate baker. Her sourdough bread is one of the best I have tasted. Very cleverly, she supplements many of her seasonal vegetable and fish dishes with toasted bread slices. In this simple winter salad, the creamy roasted squash is paired with crunchy olive oil croutons and complemented with yogurt-tahini sauce, creating an irresistible combination.

Preheat the oven to 400°F (200°C) and line a baking sheet with parchment paper.

In a large bowl, toss the bread with half of the oil, spread it on the baking sheet, and toast in the oven for 10 minutes or more, until golden brown and dry. Transfer to a tray. Leave the oven on.

In the same large bowl, toss the squash with the remaining olive oil, adding the oregano and salt and Maraş pepper, to taste. Spread on the parchment paper–lined baking sheet and roast in the oven for about 20 minutes or more, until tender. Let cool a little.

Spread half the yogurt-tahini sauce on a shallow serving dish. Arrange alternating pieces of squash and toasted bread on the sauce, sprinkle with the fresh mint and the dried mint (if using), drizzle with fruity olive oil, and sprinkle with finishing salt.

Serve warm or at room temperature, passing the rest of the yogurt-tahini sauce on the side at the table.

Fresh and Pickled Cabbage Salad with Herbs VEGAN GLUTEN-FREE

SERVES 4 TO 6

5 cups (350 g) finely shredded green cabbage (about ½ medium-small cabbage)

1 large carrot, peeled and coarsely grated or julienned with a mandoline

2 scallions, white and most of the green parts, thinly sliced

3 to 4 tablespoons freshly squeezed lemon juice, to taste

Salt

1 clove garlic, minced (optional)

2 cups (300 g) Pink Fermented Cabbage (page 40)

½ cup (30 g) chopped fresh mint leaves

¼ cup (15 g) finely chopped fresh flat-leaf parsley

½ cup (30 g) finely chopped fresh cilantro

¼ cup (60 ml) good, fruity olive oil

Pinch of Maraş pepper or crushed red pepper flakes

1 to 2 tablespoons toasted Bread Crumbs with Olives or Capers (page 59; optional)

This is a winter salad that I simply can't stop eating. It is inspired by Lebanese and Cypriot cabbage salads, but I substitute my attractive Pink Fermented Cabbage for pickled cucumbers or other common vegetables. Add more or less lemon depending on the sourness of your fermented cabbage—I enjoy mine before it gets too sour. The toasted bread crumbs with olives add another layer of flavor and a delicious crunch to my favorite winter salad.

In a large bowl, combine the green cabbage, carrot, and scallions with 3 tablespoons lemon juice and salt to taste. Rub and squeeze with your hands to soften. The mixture will reduce by almost half in volume. Add the garlic, if using, and toss to mix.

You can prepare the salad up to this point 3 to 4 hours in advance; cover and refrigerate until ready to serve.

In a serving bowl, combine the fresh cabbage mix with the pickled cabbage, mint, parsley, and cilantro. Drizzle with the oil, sprinkle with the Maraş pepper, and toss. Taste to adjust the seasonings, adding more lemon juice, if needed. Sprinkle with the bread crumbs, if you like, and serve.

Oak-leaf Lettuce, Fresh Fava, and Cherry Tomatoes with Dill-Yogurt Dressing GLUTEN-FREE

Any lettuce will be equally delicious in this simple salad, but the dark oak-leaf variety makes for a dramatic presentation and contrast in colors. The salad is one of my "accidental" recipes. Oak-leaf lettuces thrive in our garden and last much longer than romaine, which wilts early, when the days get longer and warmer in the spring. Oak-leaf lettuce is still tender when the fava pods ripen and the first cherry tomatoes from southern Crete appear in our supermarkets. To dress the salad, I pulse the last fronds of dill I find in the garden—somewhat tough and starting to blossom—with a little mustard and yogurt. The dill releases all of its flavor, leaving behind none of its toughness. This dressing is great with any green salad.

4 cups (200 g) coarsely chopped oak-leaf lettuce (see Notes)

2 cups (340 g) cooked and skinned fava beans, fresh or frozen (see Notes)

10 to 12 cherry tomatoes, halved

4 scallions, white and most of the green parts, thinly sliced

FOR THE DILL-YOGURT DRESSING:

1 teaspoon Dijon mustard

1 tablespoon sherry vinegar

½ cup (30 g) coarsely chopped fresh dill

1 tablespoon Greek-style yogurt

3 tablespoons good, fruity olive oil

Salt and freshly ground pepper

In a serving bowl, combine the lettuce with the fava beans and tomatoes. Sprinkle with the scallions.

Make the dill-yogurt dressing: Place the mustard, vinegar, dill, yogurt, and olive oil in a blender and pulse to get a creamy sauce. Scrape the sides with a spatula, add salt and pepper to taste, and pulse again to incorporate. Taste and adjust the seasoning, then pour over the salad and serve.

NOTES: *If oak-leaf lettuce is not available, romaine or any other tender-crunchy lettuce leaves work well.*

You can replace the fava beans with flageolet beans or fresh sweet peas.

Mung Bean and Pepper Salad with Pomegranate Molasses VEGAN GLUTEN-FREE

SERVES 4 TO 6

½ pound (225 g) dried mung beans

1½ cups (150 g) thinly sliced scallions

2 medium cloves garlic, minced

3 tablespoons fresh lemon juice

1 teaspoon salt

¼ cup (60 ml) good, fruity olive oil, plus
  more for drizzling

1 to 2 tablespoons pomegranate molasses,
  or more, to taste

½ to 1 teaspoon Maraş pepper, or a pinch
  of crushed red pepper flakes, to taste

1 cup (60 g) chopped fresh flat-leaf parsley

½ cup (30 g) chopped fresh mint leaves

3 tablespoons chopped fresh dill

2 red bell peppers, roasted, seeded, skinned,
  and cut into ¼-inch (0.6-cm) strips (see Note)

Inspired by a recipe from Gaziantep, celebrated Istanbul chef Musa Dağdeviren created this fresh, tangy salad. In my version of his recipe, I add roasted bell peppers in place of the raw peppers he suggests and marinate the scallions and garlic with salt and lemon juice before adding them to the dressing. Bursting with flavor, the mung bean salad should be accompanied by freshly baked bread, as in Musa's restaurants, or toasted pita. You can also serve it as a main course with Toasted Bulgur Pilaf (page 183), rice, or pasta.

In a pot, bring 3 quarts (3 L) water to a boil. Add the mung beans and return the water to a boil. Reduce the heat and simmer for about 30 minutes, stirring every now and then, until the beans are tender. Drain and let cool.

While the beans are boiling, in a small bowl, toss the scallions and garlic with the lemon juice and salt. Set aside.

In a large bowl, whisk the olive oil with the pomegranate molasses and Maraş pepper to taste. Add the drained mung beans, the scallion mixture, the parsley, mint, and dill and toss well. Taste and adjust the seasonings, adding more pomegranate molasses if necessary; the salad should be sour-spicy. Transfer to a shallow serving dish, cover, and let stand for 30 minutes, or refrigerate for up to 4 hours. Bring to room temperature, add the roasted bell peppers, toss, drizzle with some more olive oil, and serve.

NOTE: *Roast the bell peppers over the gas flame on your stovetop, holding them with tongs and turning to get the skin black and blistery on all sides. Peel off the skin and cut the roasted peppers into strips. Alternatively, heat the broiler. Quarter and seed the peppers. Line a baking sheet with aluminum foil and arrange the pepper quarters, skin side up, on the tray. Broil 4 to 5 inches (10 to 12 cm) from the heat source until the skin is black and blistery. Peel and slice as above.*

Cucumber Salad with Feta and Mint GLUTEN-FREE

SERVES 4 TO 6

1 large cucumber

1 cup (60 g) purslane, chopped
(if available; optional)

1 cup (120 g) crumbled feta cheese

½ cup (30 g) chopped fresh mint leaves

2 to 3 tablespoons fresh lemon juice

¼ cup (60 ml) good, fruity olive oil

Freshly ground black pepper

Sumac, for sprinkling (optional)

This salad is so simple that I wasn't going to include the recipe. But countless guests have devoured the salad and asked for the recipe, so I feel compelled—and delighted—to include it here. The crunchy, refreshing cucumber, seasoned with feta and lemon and scented with mint, complements perfectly grilled fish, octopus, poultry, lamb, or any grilled meat. In a recipe so simple, the quality of the cucumber is critical, so use the best ones you can find. Serve it with Eggplant *Pastitsio* (page 188) or any hearty pasta or bean dish.

Wash and dry the cucumber. If you like, peel the cucumber with a vegetable peeler. Halve it horizontally, then slice thinly—this is easily done with a mandoline. Arrange the slices in a shallow salad bowl, add the purslane (if using), and toss. Scatter the feta and the mint over the cucumber.

In a jar or in a small bowl, whisk together the lemon juice, olive oil, and a few grindings of pepper—no salt is needed, as feta is already quite salty.

Just before serving, pour the dressing over the salad and, if you like, sprinkle with a good pinch of sumac.

HORTA: WILD AND CULTIVATED GREENS

Though *horta* are simply boiled or steamed greens, they are not at all simple. Both wild and cultivated greens are called *horta* in Greek. Every self-respecting taverna serves some variety of *horta*, and the mixtures are seasonal and endless. The wild varietals tend to be more interesting, but some of the cultivated *horta* are equally delicious and more easily found. These greens can taste sweet, tart, or bitter, and some are wonderfully aromatic. Apart from the greens collected from the hills and mountains, there are also some, like purslane, nettles, and orache, that grow as weeds in gardens among cultivated crops.

My grandfather, like many Greeks, used to drink the broth in which the greens were boiled, adding plenty of lemon juice. I drink it too, not because I believe that it is "cleansing" and a "superfood" of some kind, but because I love the taste! Every time I boil greens I put aside bottles of the cooking liquid in my refrigerator to enjoy in the coming days. For those of you in the American South, this will come as no surprise, as you share the same tradition.

You may not have access to all the wonderful greens that grow on the hills of the Greek islands, but you have different and equally interesting options within arm's reach, no matter where you are. Here are some greens, readily available in markets near you, that can be used for a *horta* salad: mustard greens, chard, spinach, miner's lettuce, pea shoots, orache, amaranth shoots, and the outer leaves of escarole or romaine lettuce.

Chinese markets are also an excellent resource. They carry lots of hearty greens with which you can experiment. Some, like sweet, aromatic chrysanthemum shoots, are very popular in Crete and in other parts of the Mediterranean. You will also find different varieties of robust amaranth shoots in Chinese markets. Greeks call them *vlita*, and they are cultivated for summer *horta* salad, when even the most resilient wild greens wither under the blazing sun.

Blanched Greens (*Horta*) VEGAN GLUTEN-FREE

SERVES 4 TO 6

1½ to 2 pounds (680 g to 1 kg) mixed greens: baby spinach, Swiss chard leaves, mustard greens, miner's lettuce, pea shoots, orache, amaranth shoots, outer leaves of escarole or romaine lettuce, beet greens

Good, fruity olive oil

Finishing salt

1 juicy lemon, quartered

If you learn to combine different greens to create the perfect blend of sweet, bitter, spicy, and aromatic flavors, *horta* will become a staple in your diet. I can tell you my favorite combination, but we might not share the same bitter palate, and your local greens will have their own ranges of flavor. So I suggest you experiment, using the greens on my list as a base, choosing two, three, or more, depending on what is available and fresh. Find the combinations that suit you; explain to your guests how you've created your own dish. If you prefer a more complex, garlicky, or spicy salad, try the Italian and Moroccan variations below. These can be delicious even with common spinach or chard leaves.

Wash and drain the greens well (see page 24). Separate the tough leaves and stalks from the more tender ones that will cook faster.

Bring 4 quarts (4 L) water to a boil and add the tougher leaves and stalks first. Cook them for 2 to 4 minutes, or until they start to soften, then add the more delicate greens that will cook quickly. Stir the pot with a long fork and taste after 2 minutes. If the greens are done to your liking—they should be tender with a very slight bite—remove with a fork or a large slotted spoon. Don't pour the cooked greens into a colander as we do with pasta, because any leftover sand from the bottom of the pot will end up on the cooked *horta*.

(If you want, use a ladle and transfer the top portion of the broth to jars or bottles. Let cool and refrigerate, then warm a cup or two at a time to drink with plenty of lemon.)

Chop the cooked greens and transfer them to a shallow bowl. Drizzle with olive oil and sprinkle with finishing salt. Pass the lemon quarters at the table so everyone can season their greens according to taste.

VARIATIONS

ROMAN SAUTÉED GREENS

Heat ¼ to ⅓ cup (60 to 80 ml) olive oil in a heavy-bottomed pan or deep skillet, and add 2 to 3 coarsely chopped garlic cloves. Toss for a minute, and as the garlic starts to color, add the cooked and drained greens. Toss for about 2 minutes, just to heat the greens through and coat them with the garlicky oil. Transfer to a platter and serve warm or at room temperature, sprinkled with salt and pepper and drizzled with more olive oil, if you like. Italians don't usually add lemon.

MOROCCAN GREENS

Heat ¼ to ⅓ cup (60 to 80 ml) olive oil in a heavy-bottomed pan or deep skillet, and add 2 to 3 coarsely chopped garlic cloves. Toss for a minute, and as the garlic starts to color, add 2 tablespoons harissa or *h'rous* (page 62) and the finely chopped cooked and drained greens. Toss for about 3 minutes, to heat the greens through and coat them with the spicy oil. Transfer to a platter and serve warm, sprinkled with salt and Maraş pepper and drizzled with lemon juice.

SOUPS
LIGHT & HEARTY

A steaming bowl of brothy legumes, plain or combined with vegetables and greens, or a rich creamy *kishk* or *trahana* porridge, made with homemade fermented pasta (page 33) are the most common eastern Mediterranean soups. They are fundamentally nourishing meals, eaten as a breakfast or a dinner, not as a separate course in the classic French tradition, where a soup is served before the main course.

Paula Wolfert told me that Moroccan cooks usually chop up leftover food from lunch, fry some onions or garlic, add water, yogurt, or broth, and make it into a dinner soup, a trait they share with my frugal mother.

Cold, refreshing soups, like the one with yogurt, cucumber, herbs, and rose petals on page 125, are summer favorites that I often serve in small glasses, passing them around during my buffet dinners or lunches. On the other hand, the hearty Tunisian *leblebi* (page 120), with chickpeas, twice-baked bread, capers, and egg, or the mushroom and eggplant *boulette*s in *avgolemono* (page 126) are substantial and satisfying one-pot meals that the whole family will enjoy.

LEFT: *Nettle Soup with Mushrooms and Yogurt (page 112).*

Nettle Soup with Mushrooms and Yogurt GLUTEN-FREE

SERVES 4 TO 6

1 pound (500 g) tender nettle tops, washed with gloves on; thick stems discarded (see page 24 and Note)

⅓ cup (80 ml) olive oil

1½ teaspoons chopped garlic

⅔ cup (about 50 g) dried porcini mushrooms, soaked in 1 cup (240 ml) warm water for 30 minutes, water reserved

6 to 12 fresh or dried morels (if using dried morels, soak in warm water for 30 minutes) (optional)

1 cup (240 ml) dry white wine

6 large outer green leaves of romaine lettuce, coarsely chopped

3 bunches fresh flat-leaf parsley, coarsely chopped, stems discarded

Salt

1 cup (240 ml) vegetable broth

1 cup (250 g) Greek-style yogurt, plus more for serving

Freshly ground black pepper

Good, fruity olive oil, for drizzling

Bunch of chervil or cilantro leaves, for garnish

Throughout the Balkans, foraged nettles are one of the most sought-after greens. Their deep, sweet flavor differentiates them from other wild leafy greens. On Kea, our garden fills with nettles in the winter and we gather them while still tender, before they suffocate the spinach, kale, chervil, and the other herbs we plant. Wearing gloves, I wash the nettles, discard the thick stems, then blanch the tops in salted water for a few minutes, until just wilted. I drain them but keep the cooking liquid, which makes a wonderful herbal tea that I love to drink with a squeeze of fresh lemon.

I pulse the blanched nettles in the blender and then cool and freeze the dark-green pulp in zip-top bags that I weigh and label. The frozen pulp makes a convenient year-round base for a number of recipes. I add some nettle pulp to my dough when I make green savory biscotti (page 200).

Traditional nettle soup from the north of Greece is thick and creamy, fortified with toasted flour to make it a nourishing winter dish. I suggest this lighter version (pictured on the previous spread), which I serve as a first course, either hot or cold. If you keep wilted nettles in your freezer, as I do, you can enjoy them year-round.

Blanch the nettles in 1½ quarts (1.5 L) boiling water for about 3 minutes, until well wilted. Remove with tongs or a slotted spoon and let drain in a colander. Reserve the cooking broth.

In a medium pot, warm the olive oil over medium-high heat. Add the garlic and sauté for 1 minute. Add the porcini and their soaking liquid as well as the morels (if using). Sauté until tender, 3 to 4 minutes, then carefully remove the morels only and set them aside. Pour in the wine and add the romaine, parsley, and some salt. Toss several times, until the greens are wilted and soft.

In the bowl of a food processor, combine the greens-and-porcini mixture from the pot with the drained nettles. Add a few tablespoons of the reserved nettle broth and pulse several times to make a paste. You will have to scrape down all the bits that stick to the sides of the bowl as you process. At this point, classic French cuisine would have you pass the paste through a fine sieve in order to make a perfectly smooth soup. I love a chunky texture so I omit this step, but it is up to you.

Pour the green pulp back into the pot and add the vegetable broth and 1 cup (240 ml) of the reserved nettle broth. Bring the soup to a slow boil, and then reduce the heat. Simmer, half-covered, stirring every now and then, for about 15 minutes, until the soup thickens.

Remove from the heat and stir in the yogurt and plenty of pepper. Taste and adjust the seasoning.

Serve in bowls, adding 1 to 2 morels to each serving, if using. Drizzle with good, fruity olive oil and garnish with the chervil leaves. Serve extra yogurt on the side.

NOTE: *If nettles are not available, replace them with ⅔ pound (300 g) tender spinach leaves. The taste will be different but still delicious. Serve warm or cold.*

ANCESTRAL SOUPS REVISITED

I find it remarkable that even today, with a seemingly endless supply of fancy ingredients from around the world at our fingertips, we are still drawn to simple, frugal peasant food, and particularly to the bread soups of the past! They were invented by cooks all around the Mediterranean who had nothing but leftover stale bread, garlic, olive oil, and maybe some vegetable scraps and foraged herbs or greens. These soups were served for breakfast, lunch, or dinner.

I am hesitant to fiddle too much with the basic, age-old recipes; their appeal is in their simplicity. There is no need for upgrade or invention if we respect the basic ingredients and obey the rules of nature. With such recipes, every ingredient must be superior in quality. The quality of the bread is just as important as that of the seasonal ingredients, but fortunately even if you don't bake your own you can certainly get excellent whole-wheat or multigrain loaves that have bite. They do cost more than fluffy white breads, but good bread is essential. I have also provided many recipes that make sure none of your bread will go to waste. *Paximadia* (barley rusks, page 214) and *friselle* (page 217), the Italian equivalent of twice-baked hard, savory biscotti—both staples that date back at least to medieval times—can be stored in a cupboard almost indefinitely and are an ideal substitute for, if not better than, stale bread in these basic and comforting soups.

Summer Tomato and Bread Soup (*Pappa al Pomodoro*) VEGAN

¼ cup (60 ml) olive oil

1 large onion, chopped

1½ teaspoons salt, plus more as needed

4 cloves garlic, thinly sliced

2 pounds (1 kg) fresh vine-ripened tomatoes, briefly dipped in boiling water and peeled, then coarsely chopped (keep all the juices)

2½ to 3 cups (600 to 720 ml) vegetable broth, preferably homemade (page 60)

3 thick slices stale whole-wheat or country bread, diced

⅓ cup (20 g) fresh basil leaves, coarsely chopped, plus sprigs for garnish

Good, fruity olive oil, for drizzling

Freshly ground black pepper (optional)

Rich with the flavor of slow-cooked, vine-ripened tomatoes, sweetened with plenty of bread that soaks up the red broth, infused with the aroma of garlic and fresh basil . . . One could go on waxing poetic about this Tuscan soup, which is equally delicious warm or cold. Here is the basic recipe, adapted from that of my good friend Elizabeth Minchilli, who is a Rome-based food writer and blogger but scouts to the far ends of Italy to discover the most interesting restaurants and food shops. She writes that the soup "will be very, very thick. Just about thick enough to eat with a fork." Almost!

Heat the olive oil in a soup pot over medium-low heat. Add the onion, sprinkle with the salt, and sauté until soft, about 8 minutes. Don't let the onion brown. Add the garlic, stir for a few seconds, and pour in the tomatoes and any juices. Bring to a boil and cook until the tomatoes are fully cooked, about 15 minutes.

Add 2½ cups vegetable broth, stir, and bring to a boil. Add the bread, turn off the heat, cover the pot, and let the soup sit for 10 minutes. Stir in the chopped basil, cover again, and let sit for 10 minutes more. Stir with a wooden spoon to break up the bits of bread that have absorbed the tomato broth and are very soggy. If the soup is too thick, add a little more broth and stir. Taste and adjust the seasoning with more salt, if you like.

Serve warm or at room temperature, drizzle with good, fruity olive oil, and, if you like, add a few grindings of pepper. Decorate with basil sprigs.

Garlic and Bread Soup with Sage and Bay Leaf, from Provence (*Aigo Boulido*)

SERVES 2

3 cups (720 ml) water or homemade vegetable broth (page 60)

6 cloves garlic

Salt

7 fresh sage leaves

3 bay leaves

4 thin slices day-old whole-wheat or country bread

2 tablespoons grated Gruyère, *graviera*, or aged cheddar cheese

Good, fruity olive oil, for drizzling

Freshly ground black pepper (optional)

Guy Gedda, the celebrated French chef and cooking instructor, apologizes to his readers for including such a primitive soup in *La Table d'un Provençal*. "I had promised to exclude all dishes that are 'too rustic,'" he writes, but "this evening having a bad migraine […] a mysterious voice shouted in my ears that I was suffering because I had decided to drop and forget *Aigo Boulido*." Then he goes on describing the virtues of this "soup of the old folks," which was not just soothing, but a "sacred therapeutic and preventive infusion!" I, on the other hand, urge you to enjoy it because it is so delicious and will undoubtedly lift your spirits even on a dark, miserable midwinter evening. The healthy properties are just an added bonus. No apologies necessary, Guy.

Pour the water or broth in a saucepan, add the garlic and a pinch of salt, and bring to a slow boil. Cover and simmer for 15 minutes. Add the sage and bay leaves to the pot, remove from the heat, cover, and let infuse for 3 minutes.

While the broth is cooking, heat the broiler and toast the bread, then sprinkle each slice with some cheese and broil again briefly, until the cheese is bubbling.

Using a slotted spoon, remove the sage and bay leaves from the broth, mash the garlic with a fork, and stir.

Place 2 slices of cheese-topped bread in each bowl and pour the broth on top. Drizzle with olive oil and, if you like, add a few grindings of pepper. Serve immediately.

Red Lentil Soup with Spicy Aromatic Basil Oil VEGAN

SERVES 6 TO 8

¼ cup (60 ml) olive oil

1 cup (160 g) chopped onions

1 teaspoon salt

1 cup (220 g) red lentils, rinsed in a colander under running water

2 medium carrots, thinly sliced

1 cup (160 g) precooked wheat berries (page 35)

½ cup (100 g) precooked chickpeas (page 35)

1 tablespoon ground turmeric

3 tablespoons tomato paste

1 to 2 teaspoons Maraş pepper, or ½ to 1 teaspoon crushed red pepper flakes, to taste

1½ to 2 teaspoons Aegean Herb and Hot Pepper Mix (page 55) or a combination of cumin and dried basil, to taste

⅓ cup (80 ml) good, fruity olive oil

¼ cup (15 g) chopped fresh basil leaves, plus slivered leaves for garnish

1 teaspoon dried basil, or more to taste

Freshly ground black pepper

Sumac, for sprinkling (optional)

Variations on this heartwarming soup are infinite. The creamy red lentils regain their attractive color, which is lost when they are boiled alone, when they are cooked with tomato paste and plenty of Maraş pepper. My recipe is inspired by the soups of Gaziantep, which often combine bulgur and/or chickpeas with the lentils. The pulses are usually cooked with lamb or beef bones to add body, and the soup is finished with aromatic-infused butter, though olive oil is an excellent alternative.

Vegetarians can make the soup more substantial by adding diced feta or complementing it with grilled halloumi cheese.

In a heavy-bottomed pot, warm the olive oil over medium heat. Add the onions, sprinkle with the salt, and sauté for about 6 minutes, until the onions are soft.

Add the lentils and carrots, turn a couple of times in the oil, and pour in 2 quarts (2 L) water. Bring to a boil, reduce the heat, and simmer, stirring occasionally, for 20 minutes, adding more water as needed to keep the lentils covered.

Add the wheat berries, chickpeas, turmeric, tomato paste, Maraş pepper, and herb mix. Stir to incorporate and add more water to cover. Bring to a boil, then reduce the heat and simmer for at least 20 minutes, until all the ingredients are very soft. Taste and adjust the seasoning.

Puree the soup to a thick, chunky consistency with a stick blender, or transfer to a food processor and pulse several times.

In a skillet, warm the good, fruity olive oil over very low heat with the fresh and dried basil and plenty of black pepper.

Serve the soup in bowls, adding swirls of the basil-infused oil, garnished with basil leaves and sprinklings of sumac, if you like.

Lentil Soup with Home-Pickled Cabbage VEGAN GLUTEN-FREE

SERVES 6 TO 8

2 cups (440 g) brown or green lentils, picked over and rinsed

⅓ cup (80 ml) olive oil

4 large cloves garlic, thinly sliced

1 tablespoon tomato paste

1 cup (120 g) diced ripe tomatoes or canned tomatoes, with their juices

½ cup (120 ml) dry red wine

2 bay leaves

1 to 3 teaspoons Maraş pepper, or a pinch of crushed red pepper flakes, to taste

1 tablespoon ground turmeric

Salt

3 cups (720 ml) vegetable stock or water, or more as needed

1 teaspoon dried thyme, crumbled

1 tablespoon Dijon mustard

1 to 3 teaspoons red wine vinegar, or more to taste

Freshly ground black pepper

2 cups (300 g) Pink Fermented Cabbage (page 40), plus more for serving

Good, fruity olive oil, for drizzling

Along with chickpeas, lentils are the most popular of the old-world legumes, but lentils require far less time and effort to cook. My mother has made this simple lentil soup all my life, but the idea of adding pickled cabbage came to me recently when I read an ancient and unexpected description of lentils. Described as a food for heroes and warriors, lentils were paired with pickled *volvoi*, bitter grape hyacinth bulbs—what southern Italians call *lampascioni* (see Variation). The fruity sourness of home-pickled cabbage, with its crunchy texture, complements beautifully the earthy sweetness of the lentils and potatoes.

Place the lentils in a large saucepan and add cold water to cover. Bring to a boil, remove from the heat, and let stand for 15 minutes, then drain.

In a large pot, heat the olive oil over medium heat. Add the garlic and sauté for 1 minute, but do not let it color; add the tomato paste and sauté for 1 minute more. Add the lentils, tomatoes (with juice), wine, bay leaves, Maraş pepper, turmeric, and salt to taste. Bring to a boil, add the stock and thyme, and return to a boil. Reduce the heat to low, cover, and simmer for 20 minutes, or until the lentils are very tender.

Add the mustard, 1 teaspoon vinegar, and a few grindings of black pepper and simmer for 3 minutes more. Remove from the heat, add the cabbage, toss, and taste. If your cabbage is not particularly sour, the soup will need more vinegar.

Serve hot or warm, drizzled with good, fruity olive oil. Pass a bowl of pickled cabbage at the table to serve either in the soup or on the side.

VARIATION

LENTIL SOUP WITH PICKLED *VOLVOI* (GRAPE HYACINTH BULBS)
Crunchy, bitter *volvoi* are usually gathered from the wild and were in high demand in ancient Greece as an alleged aphrodisiac. If that is not reason enough, scientists today insist that the compounds that give some vegetables their bitter taste are *the* most beneficial for our health!

Make the lentil soup as described above. Instead of home-pickled cabbage, add a few pickled or roasted *volvoi*. Greeks used to export them, but you are more likely to find Italian *lampascioni*, a traditional product of Puglia, the region at the heel of the Italian "boot" (see Sources, page 244).

Tunisian Chickpea Soup (*Leblebi*)

½ pound (225 g) dried chickpeas, soaked overnight in water to cover with a pinch of baking soda added, or precooked chickpeas (page 35)

2 cups (480 ml) vegetable broth or water, plus more as needed

4 cloves garlic

3 tablespoons olive oil

Salt

Freshly ground black pepper

TOPPINGS (PER PERSON):

1 poached egg

Barley *paximadia* (page 214) or ½ cup (about 50 g) cubed day-old, whole-wheat bread

1 tablespoon *h'rous* (page 62) or harissa, thinned with some water

1 sun-dried tomato, soaked in warm water for 30 minutes and drained

Diced roasted red or green bell peppers (optional)

1 pinch of Aegean Herb and Hot Pepper Mix (page 55) or ground cumin

Freshly ground black pepper

4 to 5 black olives, preferably Kalamata

1 tablespoon rinsed capers

Good, fruity olive oil

1 lemon wedge

Leblebi is yet another ingenious combination of legumes and all kinds of readily available vegetables, herbs, and spices that create an irresistibly satisfying dish. Slowly cooking the chickpeas in the oven, inside a clay pot, as Paula Wolfert suggests, makes a wonderfully flavored, silky base. But precooked frozen chickpeas, simmered briefly with garlic in their broth, will make excellent *leblebi*, flavored with homemade *h'rous* and sprinkled with Aegean Herb and Hot Pepper Mix.

If you are using dried chickpeas, preheat the oven to 225°F (110°C). Drain the soaked chickpeas and place them in a clay casserole with a lid (a Dutch oven will work, too). Add the broth, garlic, olive oil, and salt and pepper to taste, and extra broth as needed to cover the peas by 1 inch (2.5 cm). Bring to a boil over medium heat, cover, and place in the oven for at least 3 hours, until the chickpeas are soft and silky.

If you are using cooked chickpeas, warm the olive oil in a saucepan, add the garlic, and sauté for 1 minute. Add the chickpeas, turn a few times, pour in the broth, and add salt and pepper to taste. Bring to a boil, reduce the heat, and simmer for at least 30 minutes, until the chickpeas are very tender.

You can make the soup up to this point and store it in the refrigerator for up to 3 days.

When you are ready to serve, reheat the chickpeas in their liquid while you poach the eggs. You should have one egg for each bowl of soup (see Note).

Place a few pieces of *paximadia* in the bottom of a bowl and cover with some of the chickpeas and their cooking liquid. Set an egg on top and cut it so that the yolk runs. Drizzle some *h'rous* over the top, add sun-dried tomato and roasted pepper (if using), and sprinkle with the herb mix and black pepper. Top with olives and capers. Drizzle good, fruity olive oil on top and squeeze the lemon wedge over the soup. Repeat for each serving.

NOTE: *Paula Wolfert's method of egg poaching: Fill a bowl with ice water. In a pan of boiling water, add the eggs (still in their shells), cover with the lid, and turn off the heat. After 6 minutes, slip the eggs into the ice water to cool. Once they are cool, peel them carefully.*

Old-fashioned Bean Soup (*Fassoláda*) VEGAN GLUTEN-FREE

SERVES 4

2 cups (400 g) dried white beans, soaked overnight in water and drained, or 4 cups (680 g) precooked white beans (page 34)

½ cup (120 ml) olive oil

2 onions, halved and thinly sliced (about 2 cups/320 g)

3 large cloves garlic, sliced

2 to 3 carrots, thinly sliced (about 1½ cups/ 180 g)

1 (16-ounce/455-g) can diced tomatoes, with their juices, or 2 cups (240 g) grated ripe tomatoes (see page 27)

1 tablespoon ground turmeric

Peel from ½ orange, in 2 strips

1 teaspoon salt, or more to taste

1 to 2 teaspoons Maraş pepper, or a pinch of crushed red pepper flakes, to taste, plus more for serving

2 cups (200 g) coarsely chopped celery, preferably "wild" (see page 51, and Note)

2 teaspoons Dijon mustard

Good, fruity olive oil, for drizzling

1 lemon, quartered

My addition to this traditional family recipe is the inclusion of turmeric, which deepens the flavor of all legumes. My mother added orange peel, when available, to most dishes with tomatoes, inspired by the days she had spent in Sparta in the southern Peloponnese, an area filled with orange and olive groves. She later started to add mustard to her *fassoláda*, claiming that it made the beans easier to digest. I have my doubts about this claim, but mustard certainly enhances the soup's flavor. Serve with feta cheese, smoked fish, or with a simple bowl of olives, plain or smoked (page 47), as is the custom in Greece during Lent.

If you are using dried white beans, place the beans in a large pot and cover with plenty of water. Bring to a boil, reduce the heat to a simmer, and cook for 5 minutes. Drain, discarding the cooking water. If you use cooked beans, omit this step.

In the same pot, warm the olive oil over medium heat. Add the sliced onion and sauté for 3 minutes. Add the garlic, sauté for 1 minute more, then add the carrots and the beans. Toss a few times and add the tomatoes (with juice), turmeric, orange peel, salt, Maraş pepper, celery, and 2 cups (480 ml) water.

Bring to a boil, lower the heat, and simmer for 30 to 40 minutes, adding water as needed, until the beans are very tender. Add the mustard, taste, and adjust the seasoning. Simmer for 5 minutes more, until the beans are just covered with broth. Remove from the heat and serve, drizzled with good, fruity olive oil. Pass the lemon quarters so people can add a fresh, bright squeeze at the table, and also pass Maraş pepper to sprinkle over the beans.

NOTE: *If you use common celery, add an extra ½ cup (30 g) coarsely chopped, fresh flat-leaf parsley with the mustard toward the end of cooking.*

Tomato Soup with *Trahana*

¼ cup (60 ml) olive oil

3 to 5 cloves garlic, minced, to taste

4 cups (480 g) fresh or frozen vine-ripened tomato pulp, or 4 cups (480 g) canned tomatoes pureed in a blender with 4 to 5 sun-dried tomatoes

1 teaspoon Maraş pepper or a good pinch of crushed red pepper flakes, plus more for sprinkling

1 cup (120 g) *trahana* or *ksinohondros* (page 31)

2 to 4 cups (480 ml to 1 L) vegetable broth or water

Salt

Good, fruity olive oil, for drizzling

1 tablespoon dried mint or fresh or dried oregano (optional)

1 cup (120 g) crumbled feta (optional)

3 slices day-old country bread, diced, fried in olive oil, and drained on paper towels (optional)

Made with the traditional eastern Mediterranean "pasta," this soup used to be the quintessence of comforting peasant winter dinner fare. Pounded wheat grains are combined with yogurt or soured milk and left to ferment; the longer the fermentation, the tangier and more pungent the "pasta." The basic soup I suggest here is made with the milder, homemade *trahana* or *ksinohondros*. It is based on the soup I remember from my childhood, which my mother served topped with olive oil–fried bread croutons. Instead of *trahana*, you can also make the soup with toasted bulgur or oat grits (steel-cut oats). It is a different but equally enticing tomato soup (see Variation).

Warm the olive oil in a medium, heavy-bottomed pot over medium heat. Add the garlic and sauté very briefly, 1 minute or less, just until fragrant. Pour in the tomato, add the Maraş pepper, and bring to a boil. Reduce the heat and simmer for about 10 minutes, until the soup starts to thicken. Add the *trahana* and 2 cups (480 ml) broth, bring to a boil, reduce the heat, and simmer, stirring every now and then, for 15 to 20 minutes, adding water or broth as needed. The *trahana* should be cooked and mushy, and the soup will have thickened. Add some salt—keeping in mind that if you plan to top the soup with feta, it may not need any; taste and adjust the seasoning.

Serve, drizzled with fruity olive oil and sprinkled with mint, more Maraş pepper, and crumbled feta or fried-bread croutons, if you like.

VARIATION

TOMATO SOUP WITH TOASTED OAT GRITS AND FETA GLUTEN-FREE

For a gluten-free variation, substitute 1 cup (90 g) oat grits (steel-cut oats) for the *trahana*. Add the grits to a dry, heavy-bottomed pan or skillet and toast over medium-high heat, tossing with a spatula, for about 4 minutes, until fragrant and starting to color. Transfer to a bowl and set aside.

Sauté the garlic, cook the tomato, and add the grits, as described above. Adjust the amount of broth needed as the grits simmer and cook until soft, but not completely mushy—about 20 minutes. Serve with crumbled feta, Maraş pepper, and any herbs you like.

Warm Yogurt Soup with Grains and Greens

SERVES 6

1 bunch Swiss chard (see Note)

⅓ cup (80 ml) olive oil, plus more for drizzling

1 onion, chopped

3 scallions, white and most of the green parts, finely chopped

3 large cloves garlic, coarsely chopped

½ cup (50 g) medium-grain rice, or 1 cup (160 g) precooked wheat berries or pearl barley (page 35)

1 cup (240 ml) white wine

5 cups (1.2 L) water or 3 cups (720 ml) vegetable broth and 2 cups (480 ml) water, or more if needed

Salt

1 tablespoon cornstarch

2 cups (480 ml) natural yogurt

Freshly ground black pepper

2 teaspoons dried tarragon or mint, or more to taste

Good, fruity olive oil, for drizzling

Maraş pepper or crushed red pepper flakes, for sprinkling (optional)

Sprigs of fresh tarragon or mint, for serving (optional)

Pazili Lebeniye Çorbasi (Swiss chard–yogurt soup) is part of a large category of similar soups that are popular not just in Turkey, but all over the eastern Mediterranean. You can substitute broccoli stems—reserving the florets for salads—for the chard or make the soup with spinach or kale (see Note).

Wash and drain the chard, cutting off and discarding only the hard stem ends. Separate the leaves and set aside. Chop the stems into about ½-inch (1.3-cm) pieces.

Heat the olive oil in a medium, heavy-bottomed pot over medium heat. Add the onion and scallions and sauté for 3 minutes. Add the chard stems and continue to sauté for 5 minutes more, or until they start to soften. Add the garlic and toss for 2 minutes more. Add the rice, wheat berries, or barley, toss for 1 minute, pour in the wine, stir, and add the water. Add salt to taste, bring to a boil, reduce the heat to medium-low, and cook for 10 minutes. Coarsely shred the chard leaves and add them to the pot. Simmer for 10 minutes more, or until the rice and greens are very tender. Remove from the heat.

In a cup, dilute the cornstarch with 3 tablespoons cold water to make a slurry. In a medium bowl, whisk the yogurt with the cornstarch mixture. Continue whisking and pour in 1 ladle of the hot broth. After it is incorporated, slowly add 2 to 3 more ladles of broth, whisking until the yogurt mixture gets quite hot. Pour the yogurt mixture into the pot with the rest of the soup, return to low heat, and cook, stirring, until the soup almost boils. Add black pepper and tarragon to taste, stir, and remove from the heat. Taste and adjust the seasoning. Cover and let stand for 10 minutes.

Serve, drizzling each bowl with some good, fruity olive oil and sprinkling with Maraş pepper and fresh tarragon or mint, if you like.

NOTE: *You may substitute 2 to 3 cups (200 to 300 g) chopped broccoli stems for the Swiss chard, but cook them with the onion. If you like, pulse the broccoli soup with a stick blender to make a coarse puree before adding the yogurt. You may also use a bunch of tender kale (any kind), chopping the stems and cooking them first, as described for the chard, then adding the shredded leaves.*

Cold Yogurt Soup with Cucumber, Herbs, and Rose Petals GLUTEN-FREE

SERVES 6

¼ cup (15 g) dried rose petals, crushed

⅓ cup (40 g) almonds, preferably not skinned

⅛ preserved lemon, rinsed briefly

2 cups (500 g) Greek-style yogurt, preferably full-fat

1½ cups (360 ml) ice water

½ cup (80 g) golden raisins, finely chopped

1½ cups (180 g) finely diced, peeled, and seeded cucumber (1 small or two-thirds of a large cucumber)

¼ cup (15 g) finely chopped fresh mint

¼ cup (15 g) finely chopped fresh dill

¼ cup (25 g) finely chopped fresh chives or scallions, white and most of the green parts

Salt and freshly ground black pepper

Sumac

3 tablespoons coarsely chopped pistachios (optional)

Unlike the boldly flavored *cacik*, the Turkish yogurt-cucumber-garlic soup common throughout the Mediterranean and an ancestor of *tzatziki*, this older, hauntingly aromatic Persian soup has no garlic. Adapted from a recipe by Iranian-American chef Hoss Zaré, this dish combines nuts and raisins with dill, mint, chives, and dried rose petals, all suspended in yogurt, creating a delicate, refreshing, and crunchy soup. I use almonds instead of the walnuts the original recipe calls for, and I add preserved lemon, which enhances the soup with its salty fragrance. I suggest you double the recipe and enjoy it the next morning for breakfast.

Preheat the oven to 350°F (175°C).

In a small bowl, soak the rose petals in lukewarm water until softened and cold, about 20 minutes. Drain and pat dry with paper towels.

Spread the almonds on a baking sheet and toast in the oven for 8 minutes, or until fragrant and lightly colored. Let cool and then chop finely in a food processor together with the preserved lemon.

In a large bowl, whisk the yogurt with the ice water. Add the raisins, cucumber, mint, dill, chives, soaked rose petals, and toasted almonds. Season with salt and pepper.

Cover and refrigerate for at least 1 hour.

Taste the soup and adjust the seasoning, then serve in glasses or in shallow bowls, sprinkling generously with sumac and pistachios, if desired.

Youvarlakia with Mushrooms, Eggplant and Walnuts in Egg-and-Lemon Broth

SERVES 6

3 large eggplants (about 2½ pounds/ 1.2 kg total)

1 cup (100 g) walnut halves or almonds, preferably not blanched

½ cup (120 ml) olive oil

1 cup (160 g) coarsely chopped onion

4 cloves garlic, coarsely chopped

1 cup (about 80 g) packed dried porcini mushrooms

1 cup (100 g) toasted bread crumbs, or more as needed

2 large eggs, lightly beaten

Salt

1 teaspoon Maraş pepper, or a good pinch of crushed red pepper flakes (½ to 1 teaspoon freshly ground black pepper also works well)

½ teaspoon ground allspice

1 teaspoon ground cumin

⅔ cup (65 g) uncooked rice

1½ cups (90 g) chopped fresh flat-leaf parsley leaves

½ cup (30 g) chopped fresh dill

4 scallions, white and most of the green parts, thinly sliced

1 cup (240 ml) white wine

1 quart (1 L) vegetable broth (page 60), plus more as needed

FOR THE EGG-AND-LEMON SAUCE:

2 eggs

1 teaspoon cornstarch

¼ cup (60 ml) fresh lemon juice

Fresh lemon juice

Salt and freshly ground black pepper

Meatballs made with ground veal and rice, simmered in broth and finished with *avgolemono* (egg-and-lemon sauce), are a popular Greek comfort food—the kind of winter one-pot meal that both adults and children enjoy. My vegetarian *youvarlakia* look exactly like the dish my mother used to make, but they are made from completely different ingredients; they are inspired by Domenica Marchetti's Eggplant and Porcini "Meatballs" in Tomato Sauce, an ingenious Sicilian recipe from her book *The Glorious Vegetables of Italy.*

Preheat the oven to 375°F (190°C). Line a baking sheet with aluminum foil.

Using a fork, prick the eggplants all over, especially close to the stem, and place them on the baking sheet. Roast in the center of the oven for 45 minutes, or until very soft. Don't turn the oven off. Let the eggplants cool slightly.

Spread the walnuts on a baking sheet and toast in the oven for 10 minutes, or until they start to color. Remove and set aside to cool. Turn off the oven.

Peel the eggplants and chop the flesh coarsely. You will have about 2 cups (200 g)—set aside in a bowl.

In a small skillet, warm 3 tablespoons of the olive oil over medium heat and sauté the onion for 4 minutes. Add the garlic and sauté for 2 minutes more. Remove from the heat.

In the bowl of a food processor, combine the toasted nuts, half of the dried porcini, and the bread crumbs, pulsing several times to grind. Add the eggplant flesh and the sautéed onion and garlic and pulse to chop and mix. Transfer to a bowl and add the eggs, 1½ teaspoons salt, the Maraş pepper, allspice, and cumin. Fold in the rice, stirring to distribute evenly. Cover and refrigerate the *yovarlakia* for 1 hour or overnight.

Mix the parsley and dill together and spread on a dish. Scoop out ¼ cup (25 g) of the eggplant mixture, halve this portion, and shape it into 2 walnut-size balls; roll each one on the herbs and then roll tightly in your palms to incorporate the herbs. Transfer to a baking dish and repeat with the remaining eggplant mixture. Refrigerate, uncovered, while you prepare the broth.

In a medium pot, warm the rest of the olive oil over medium heat and sauté the scallions for 4 minutes, or until soft. Add the rest of the mushrooms and toss, pour in the wine and bring to a boil. Add the broth, return to a boil, and add any leftover herbs

on the plate. Reduce the heat and carefully add the *youvarlakia* to the broth, a few at a time. Add 2 to 3 cups (480 to 720 ml) water and more broth, if needed, to cover them. Simmer for 10 minutes or more, until cooked. Taste a "meatball" to make sure.

Make the egg-and-lemon sauce: In a medium bowl, whisk together the eggs and 2 tablespoons water. In a cup, dilute the cornstarch with the lemon juice and whisk the mixture into the eggs. Whisking constantly to avoid curdling, slowly pour 2 to 3 cups (480 to 720 ml) of the hot broth in which you cooked the *youvarlakia* into the eggs. Slowly pour the egg mixture back into the pot, carefully stirring, again to prevent curdling. Taste and adjust the seasonings with more lemon juice, salt, and pepper, if needed. Simmer for 2 minutes more, but do not boil. Serve hot.

MAIN COURSES

The Western notion of a three-course meal is foreign to most Mediterranean countries. Dishes are rarely plated and served to individuals. Instead, a medley of food is brought to the middle of the table in large platters, family-style, or served on a buffet. There is no clear distinction between what is considered a main course and what is a meze. Some of the dishes in this chapter could also be served as meze, just as a few of those in the meze chapter can be served as a main course.

Frugal cooks around the Mediterranean were limited to a small variety of vegetables and greens for months on end, so they devised an incredible number of ways to prepare them differently. They stew vegetables with aromatics, stuff them with bulgur or rice, grate them, and mix them with cheese to make the filling for pies, or fry them and serve them with *tarator* or *skordalia* (page 70).

The most beloved of all summer dishes are the vegetable stews called *ladera* in Greek, *zeytinyagli* in Turkish. Green beans, okra, eggplants, and zucchini are cooked in an onion-tomato sauce, often accompanied by potatoes, bulgur, or homemade pasta. Or they may be served on their own, with a side of feta or local cheese and plenty of crusty bread to soak up the wonderful juices. These dishes may also appear as side dishes to meat or fish. Peas, artichokes, fresh favas, zucchini, and carrots taste particularly delicious when cooked in olive oil that is brightened with fresh lemon and scented with fennel or dill.

Stuffed vegetables and grape or other leaves, rolled around a stuffing, are another important group of traditional vegetarian dishes. Vegetables suitable for stuffing include tomatoes, peppers, zucchini, squash, eggplants, and onions; quince, a much-loved winter fruit used in both savory and sweet dishes throughout the region, also lends itself to a spicy stuffing (page 156). Rice, bulgur, barley, and other grains are cooked with onion, garlic, and herbs and are often complemented with nuts, then stuffed into hollowed-out vegetables, which are either baked or cooked on the stovetop.   *(continued)*

In the winter, when freshly harvested garden vegetables are scarce, Mediterranean cooks turn to greens. The wild leafy plants, called *horta* in Greek, grow in the hills or as weeds among the crops. Braised and complemented with grains or potatoes, leafy greens are a winter staple. They are also the basic filling for traditional *hortopita* or *spanakotyropita* (page 168). Eastern Mediterranean pies (*pites* or *börek*) are the kind of convenient, seasonal food that only resourceful cooks with limited ingredients could invent. Besides being irresistibly delicious, *pites*—especially those made with foraged plants—contain antioxidants and other nutrients that promote good health, scientists have discovered.

Legumes of all kinds, often complemented by grains, have been Mediterranean staples since antiquity. Cooked by themselves or combined with seasonal vegetables, legumes form the base of family meals. Chickpeas, sealed in clay pots and left to cook overnight in the receding heat of the wood-burning oven, were a Sunday dish throughout the Greek islands. Falafel and the immense popularity of hummus (the word for "chickpeas" in Arabic) have given an international leading role to the once humble chickpea—my favorite legume. Dried favas were *the* ancient Mediterranean bean. When more refined white beans came from the New World, they often replaced dried favas, which take longer to cook. Fresh favas have been rediscovered recently by creative chefs, but in the Mediterranean they have always been used in some of the most popular spring dishes. In our garden we plant favas in October to enrich the soil for the tomatoes, eggplants, and peppers that we plant in April and hopefully enjoy all through the summer.

Olive Oil and Yogurt Béchamel Sauce

MAKES 2 CUPS (480 ML)

3 tablespoons olive oil

3 tablespoons all-purpose flour

1 cup (240 ml) milk plus 1 cup (240 ml) plain yogurt (not thick), or 2 cups (480 ml) whole milk

Many years ago I created a lighter version of béchamel, the ubiquitous heavy sauce used in moussaka, *pastitsio*, and other Greek dishes. I replace the butter base with olive oil and maintain the creamy consistency with 1 part yogurt to 1 part milk. My recipe was included in the seventh revised edition of the *Joy of Cooking* (1997).

In a saucepan, heat the olive oil over medium-high heat. Add the flour and cook, stirring with a whisk, until frothy. Remove from the heat and continue stirring for 30 seconds. Add the milk-and-yogurt mixture, stir a few times, and return to medium-high heat. Stir continuously until thickened. Remove from the heat and continue stirring for a few more seconds.

Cauliflower Gratin with Garlic and Feta

SERVES 4 TO 5

1 head cauliflower (about 3 pounds/1.5 kg)

Salt

3 large cloves garlic, sliced

½ cup (120 ml) whole milk

Olive Oil and Yogurt Béchamel Sauce (opposite page)

½ pound (225 g) feta cheese, crumbled

Freshly ground black pepper, to taste

About ½ cup (120 ml) olive oil

¼ cup (25 g) whole-grain bread crumbs or Bread Crumbs with Olives or Capers (page 59)

¼ cup (35 g) hulled sunflower seeds, coarsely ground

We are addicted to this comforting winter dish that uses all parts of the cauliflower, not just the florets. The first time I made it with anchovies to spice up the cauliflower's sweetness (see Variation). I liked it a lot, but Costas definitely prefers the feta version, so I begin there. It is inspired by a broccoli-and-potato gratin from Provence described by Guy Gedda in *La Table d'un Provençal*.

Preheat the oven to 400°F (205°C).

Pare the hard stem of the cauliflower, discarding only the outer layers along with any wilted green leaves. Quarter the cauliflower, separate the florets from the stem, and arrange the florets in a steamer basket or colander that can be fitted over a pot.

Place the stems in a pot and add water to cover. Sprinkle with some salt and bring to a boil. Place the florets on top, cover, and steam for about 15 minutes, until the florets are tender. The stems should be tender, too. If they are not, boil for a few minutes more.

Drain the stems and pat dry with paper towels. Drop them in a food processor together with the garlic and milk and process to get a smooth paste. Mix with the béchamel, and add the feta and plenty of freshly ground pepper. Stir, taste, and adjust the seasoning.

Brush a 9-by-8-inch (23-by-20-cm) clay baking pan (or a 9- or 10-inch/23- or 25-cm square or round baking pan) with olive oil and sprinkle with half of the bread crumbs and sunflower seeds. Lay the cauliflower florets over the crumb-and-seed mixture and drizzle lightly with olive oil. Top with the béchamel mixture, sprinkle with the rest of the crumbs and seeds, drizzle with the remaining olive oil, and bake for about 30 minutes, until golden and sizzling. Let cool slightly, and serve warm or at room temperature.

VARIATION

CAULIFLOWER GRATIN WITH GARLIC AND ANCHOVIES

Omit the cheese and add 5 to 6 drained anchovy fillets with the garlic and cauliflower stems in the food processor.

Roasted Potatoes with Garlic, Orange, and Mustard VEGAN GLUTEN-FREE

SERVES 4 TO 6

⅔ cup (160 ml) olive oil

4 to 6 cloves garlic, minced, to taste

2 tablespoons Dijon mustard

1½ tablespoons dried oregano or thyme, crumbled

1½ teaspoons salt, or more to taste

2 teaspoons Maraş pepper or a good pinch of crushed red pepper flakes (plenty of freshly ground black pepper will also suffice)

1 teaspoon ground cumin

1 teaspoon ground turmeric

2 tablespoons fresh lemon juice

½ to 1 cup (120 to 240 ml) fresh orange juice, as needed

3 pounds (1.5 kg) fingerling potatoes, halved, or any baking potatoes, peeled and cut into 1½-inch (4-cm) cubes

2 oranges, washed, halved, and cut into thick slices

3 teaspoons chopped fresh oregano and/or 5 thyme sprigs

As with many of the new dishes my mother added to her repertoire, this dish entered our house via an acquaintance at the hairdresser's salon—a place of serious culinary exchange in Greece. This is my mother's variation on the classic lemon-oregano potatoes that traditionally accompany roasted meat and poultry; I always preferred these to the main dish. I make the potatoes spicier with the addition of hot red pepper, cumin, and turmeric, and I often mix the potatoes with fruit or other root vegetables (see Variation).

Serve with a green salad, feta, any aged cheese, or grilled halloumi.

Preheat the oven to 400°F (205°C).

In a food processor or blender, combine the olive oil, garlic, mustard, dried oregano, salt, Maraş pepper, cumin, turmeric, lemon juice, and ½ cup (120 ml) orange juice. Pulse to get a thick sauce.

Place the potatoes and orange slices in a single layer in a 13-by-9-inch (33-by-23-cm) baking dish and pour the sauce over them. Using two spatulas, toss well to coat the pieces generously.

Cover loosely with a piece of parchment paper and bake in the lower part of the oven for 40 minutes. Take out of the oven, uncover, and toss. The potatoes should be bubbly and easily pierced with a fork. Taste and adjust the seasoning. If the pan is dry, add a bit more orange juice and toss.

Bake, uncovered, for 20 minutes more, or until the potatoes are cooked through, with nicely browned edges. If the potatoes are fully cooked but lack color, place the pan under the broiler for 2 to 3 minutes, until the potatoes turn golden brown. Sprinkle with fresh oregano and/or thyme sprigs. Serve at once.

VARIATION

ROASTED ROOT VEGETABLES AND QUINCE WITH GARLIC, ORANGE, AND MUSTARD

Prepare the sauce as directed above. Substitute a couple of large carrots and/or parsnips for a few potatoes. Cut the carrots in 1½-inch (4-cm) slices. Halve or quarter 2 to 3 turnips, depending on their size—the pieces should all be consistent in size with the potatoes. If available, add 1 to 2 quinces. Halve each quince horizontally and then quarter and core them (but keep the skin). I find that the firm-fleshed, tart fruit beautifully complements the sweet medley of root vegetables. Arrange the vegetables and quince in the pan, cover with the sauce, toss and proceed as directed.

Potatoes and Olives in Onion-Tomato Sauce (*Patates Yahni*) VEGAN GLUTEN-FREE

SERVES 2 TO 3 AS A MAIN COURSE,
OR 4 TO 6 AS A SIDE DISH

About ⅔ cup (160 ml) olive oil

2 pounds (1 kg) medium potatoes, peeled and quartered

3 medium onions, thickly sliced

5 cloves garlic, sliced

1 to 2 teaspoons Maraş pepper or a good pinch of crushed red pepper flakes (plenty of freshly ground black pepper will also suffice)

½ cup (120 ml) dry white wine

1 teaspoon dried oregano

2 cups (240 g) chopped fresh or good-quality canned tomatoes

1 cup (180 g) Kalamata or other juicy but firm black olives, rinsed and pitted

Sea salt

½ cup (30 g) finely chopped fresh flat-leaf parsley

For Greeks this is a classic Lenten or vegan dish, cooked on the days that all foods derived from animal products are prohibited. Although in my family we didn't follow a religious menu, so to speak, I remember my grandmother saying that *patates yahni* was especially suited for the summer Lent before the Assumption (August 15).

My mother cooked the potatoes on the stove, stirring them every now and then; she kept the water in the pan to a minimum in order to concentrate the flavors, but often the potatoes collapsed even from the light stirring.

In my version, I finish the cooking in the oven, which keeps the pieces intact. This is one of the very few Mediterranean stews that needs to be consumed the day it is cooked. Its flavor and texture deteriorate if you refrigerate and reheat.

Serve with feta cheese, *shanklish* (page 82), or a flavorful spread like Syrian Eggplant Dip with Tahini and Yogurt (page 89).

Heat the olive oil in a heavy-bottomed pan over medium heat. Add the potatoes and sauté until they turn golden brown on all sides, about 15 minutes. They don't need to cook through because they will continue cooking in the sauce.

Preheat the oven to 375°F (190°C).

Using a slotted spoon, remove the potatoes from the skillet and place them in a clay or glass ovenproof pan that can hold them in one layer. Set aside. Add the onions to the oil and sauté until soft, about 10 minutes, then add the garlic and Maraş pepper. Pour in the wine and add the oregano, tomatoes, and olives. Cook for 1 minute and remove from the heat.

Pour the sauce over the potatoes, and bake, uncovered, for 30 to 45 minutes—adding a little water if needed—until the potatoes are tender. Taste after 20 minutes and add salt if necessary. Keep in mind that the olives are quite salty.

Remove from the oven, sprinkle with the parsley, and serve hot, warm, or at room temperature.

Creamy Eggplant Puree (*Hünkar Beğendi*)

SERVES 4 AS A MAIN DISH,
OR 8 TO 10 AS AN APPETIZER

4 large eggplants (about 2½ pounds/
    1.2 kg total)

2 tablespoons fresh lemon juice

¼ cup (60 ml) olive oil

3 tablespoons all-purpose flour

⅔ cup (160 ml) whole milk, or more as needed

2 cups (240 g) grated Gruyère or cheddar,
    or a combination of 1 cup (120 g) crumbled
    feta and 1 cup (120 g) grated smoky
    provolone or cheddar

Freshly ground pepper, preferably white

Salt

An Ottoman Sultan, a French Princess . . . and *Hünkar Beğendi*—all the necessary ingredients for romance, intrigue, and culinary invention. According to legend, this rich and creamy eggplant puree was created in the eighteenth century by one of the Sultan's cooks. The occasion was a dinner given in honor of a French princess visiting the palace of the Ottoman ruler in Istanbul. The French were known for their love of vegetable purees, so the cook paid homage to the princess by presenting an Oriental version, using the Empire's most admired vegetable. The dish was a great success.

In Turkey and in Greece *hünkar* traditionally accompanies a tomato meat stew. You can also serve it with braised kale or other greens (page 151). *Hünkar* also makes a great appetizer. Serve it with toasted pita triangles to scoop up the creamy puree or spread it on toasted, garlic-rubbed multigrain bread.

Using a skewer, toothpick, or fork, pierce each eggplant in several places around the stem. Place on a rack about 1 inch (2.5 cm) from the coals on a gas or charcoal grill, or under a very hot broiler. Turn the eggplant methodically, exposing all sides to the heat. The skin will char evenly and the flesh will soften in about 10 minutes (see Note, Syrian Eggplant Dip, page 89). The slower and longer you roast the eggplant, the smokier the taste. If using an electric stove, roast the eggplants over medium to low heat on a ridged stovetop grill (which allows liquid to drain), turning as above, for 20 to 30 minutes.

Transfer the eggplants to a colander. Using a sharp knife, halve them lengthwise and let them drain for 10 minutes. Scoop out the flesh, discarding the skin and hard seeds. Mash the flesh with a fork and transfer to a medium bowl. Toss with the lemon juice to keep the flesh white.

In a heavy-bottomed saucepan or skillet, warm the olive oil over medium heat. Add the flour, stirring continuously until it starts to foam. Remove from the heat and add the eggplant puree and milk, stirring continuously. Return to the stove and cook over medium-low heat, stirring, until the mixture becomes thick and creamy. If it is too thick, add some more milk. Remove from the heat, fold in the cheese, and add several grindings of pepper. Taste and only then add salt, as the cheeses may be salty enough. Serve immediately.

You can cool and refrigerate the *hünkar* for up to 5 days, but reheat it before serving.

Pseudo-Moussaka with Spicy Tomato Sauce, Walnuts, and Feta

SERVES 6

Sea salt

2 large eggplants (about 1½ pounds/680 g total), cut lengthwise into ¼-inch (.6-cm) slices

Olive oil, for frying

2 tablespoons bread crumbs

1⅔ cups (200 g) coarsely chopped walnuts

1 pound (500 g) potatoes, peeled and cut into ¼-inch (0.6-cm) slices

3 large green bell peppers, seeded, quartered lengthwise, and cut into about 1-inch (2.5-cm) pieces

1½ cups (240 g) chopped onions

1 to 2 teaspoons Maraş pepper or a good pinch of crushed red pepper flakes, to taste (freshly ground black pepper works as well)

⅓ cup (80 ml) red wine

½ cup (70 g) black currants, preferably Zante

1 cinnamon stick

1 pound (500 g) chopped red, ripe tomatoes, any juices reserved, or 2½ cups (300 g) imported canned tomatoes, with their juices

1 to 2 teaspoons Lebanese Seven-Spice Mixture (baharat; page 54)

1 cup (120 g) crumbled feta cheese

FOR THE TOPPING:

2 cups (240 g) grated aged cheddar, Gruyère, or graviera cheese

2 cups (480 ml) Olive Oil and Yogurt Béchamel Sauce (page 130)

"Pseudo-Moussaka" is a meatless version of the iconic Greek dish my mother often prepared in the summer. In my adaptation of the family recipe, the eggplants, bell peppers, and potatoes are spiced up with an oriental-inspired tomato sauce that is enriched with walnuts and feta. This meatless version of moussaka resembles a gratin, with just a thin layer of light béchamel. Don't expect to cut perfect rectangular pieces when you serve. If you are concerned about serving at the table, bake this dish in six individual heatproof dishes for a more elegant presentation. And plan ahead, because the dish tastes even better the second day, when the flavors have had time to meld. Pseudo-Moussaka should be served warm or at room temperature.

Preheat the broiler to 400°F (205°C). Line a baking sheet with parchment paper.

Salt the eggplant slices and leave them in a colander for at least 30 minutes and up to 3 hours. Rinse the eggplants and pat dry with paper towels. Brush the eggplant slices lightly with oil on both sides, lay them on the prepared baking sheet, and grill under the broiler, turning as needed, until golden on both sides, about 20 minutes. Set aside; leave the oven on. (You can broil the eggplants a day before and refrigerate them. You can also make a batch well in advance and freeze in zip-top bags, to use in this or any other dish; see Note page 89.)

Sprinkle the bottom of a 9-by-12-inch (23-by-30-cm) glass or clay baking dish—at least 2½ inches (6 cm) deep—with the bread crumbs and 2 tablespoons of the walnuts.

Heat about 1 inch (2.5 cm) olive oil in a deep, heavy skillet and fry the potato slices until golden brown and cooked about halfway through. Remove with a slotted spoon and layer them in the baking dish over the bread crumb mixture.

Sauté the bell peppers in the same oil, stirring often, until they start to color, about 10 minutes. Remove with a slotted spoon and set aside.

Carefully pour off all but ⅔ cup (160 ml) of the frying oil from the pan and reserve the rest to make the béchamel. Sauté the chopped onions in the skillet, stirring often, for about 10 minutes, until soft. Add Maraş pepper and the red wine. When it starts to boil, add the currants, cinnamon, and tomatoes (with juice). Reduce the heat and simmer for about 10 minutes, until the sauce thickens. Add the spices and remove from the heat. Add the rest of the walnuts and the feta. Taste and correct the seasoning with more salt or Maraş pepper—the mixture should be quite spicy.

Arrange the eggplant slices over the potatoes. It doesn't matter if they overlap. Place the sautéed peppers over the eggplants and top with the tomato sauce.

Make the topping: Prepare the béchamel as directed on page 130, using the reserved oil. Remove from the heat, and fold in the cheese, reserving 2 tablespoons. Pour the béchamel over the dish, sprinkle with the reserved cheese, and bake for about 1 hour, until the moussaka is bubbly and the top colors.

Let cool for at least 15 minutes before serving. You can also cool the moussaka completely, refrigerate, and reheat just before serving. It will keep in the refrigerator for 4 to 5 days.

Potato Pie (*Patatopita*)

SERVES 8 TO 10

1 cup (240 ml) olive oil, plus more for oiling the pan

¼ cup (25 g) toasted whole-wheat bread crumbs

5 pounds (2.5 kg) medium baking potatoes, cut into ¼-inch (0.6-cm) slices

3 to 4 cups (720 ml to 1 L) water or vegetable broth (page 60)

1 cup (240 ml) plain full-fat yogurt, preferably sheep's milk

5 eggs, lightly beaten

1 pound (500 g) feta cheese, crumbled

1 teaspoon freshly ground black pepper

Salt (optional)

3 tablespoons milk

This very rustic version of a *gratin dauphnois*—with olive oil, feta, eggs, and yogurt—originates from Volos in central Greece. It is my husband's childhood comfort food, baked by his mother, Athanasia Moraitis, following a recipe from her mother-in-law. We try to bake it only when we have guests, hoping that they will eat most of it. We can't help ourselves and will guiltily devour any leftovers. Serve with just a light salad, as this is quite a substantial dish.

Preheat the oven to 400°F (205°C).

Oil a 13-by-9-inch (33-by-23-cm) pan and sprinkle with half the bread crumbs.

In a large pot, cook the potatoes for 10 minutes in water or broth that just covers them, then drain.

Spread half the potatoes over the bread crumbs in the baking pan.

In a bowl, whisk the oil with the yogurt and eggs, setting aside 3 tablespoons of the mixture. Add the feta and plenty of pepper to the mix. Taste and add salt if necessary—feta is usually quite salty.

Pour a little less than half the egg-and-cheese mixture over the layer of potatoes. Arrange the remaining potatoes on top and pour the rest of the mixture over them. In a bowl, mix the milk with the reserved egg mixture and pour over the potatoes, sprinkling with the rest of the bread crumbs.

Bake for 10 minutes, then reduce the oven temperature to 375°F (190°C) and continue baking for at least 45 minutes, until the potatoes are golden brown and firm.

Serve hot, warm, or at room temperature.

Classic Caponata: Eggplants, Olives, and Capers in Sweet-and-Sour Sauce

SERVES 4 AS A MAIN COURSE,
OR 6 TO 8 AS AN APPETIZER

Salt

3 to 4 large eggplants (about 2½ pounds/
1.2 kg total), cut into 1-inch (2.5-cm) cubes

About ⅔ cup (160 ml) olive oil, as needed

2½ cups (400 g) thinly sliced onions

2 teaspoons honey, or more to taste

1½ cups (180 g) fresh tomato pulp, liquid
and seeds removed, or canned tomatoes
pureed in a blender

⅓ cup (80 ml) good-quality red wine vinegar,
or more to taste

2 celery stalks, coarsely sliced

1 cup (140 g) capers, preferably salt-cured,
rinsed under running water for 1 minute
and drained on paper towels

1 cup (180 g) pitted green olives, chopped,
rinsed, and drained on paper towels

¼ cup (40 g) sultanas (golden raisins)

1 to 2 teaspoons Maraş pepper, or a good
pinch of crushed red pepper flakes, to taste
(freshly ground black pepper works as well)

Leaves from 3 to 4 fresh basil sprigs

⅔ cup (65 g) bread crumbs, preferably from
whole-grain bread, or more as needed

¼ cup (25 g) pine nuts

¼ cup (25 g) slivered almonds

FOR SERVING:

Toasted Bulgur Pilaf (page 183) or cooked
pasta of your choosing, tossed with garlic
and olive oil

Grilled halloumi cheese or slices of manouri or
ricotta salata (optional)

From the Sicilian region of Catania, this caponata is not the moist mixture to which you are probably accustomed. Rather, it is an almost dry and crunchy vegetable medley, mixed with toasted bread crumbs, pine nuts, and almonds, that soaks up the sweet-and-sour tomato sauce. It was inspired by a recipe from Sicily in a book of regional recipes from The Silver Spoon collection. Traditionally caponata is an antipasto, but I like it as a main course with bulgur pilaf or with pasta. It is a lovely complement to grilled halloumi cheese, or slices of creamy manouri or ricotta salata.

Generously salt the eggplant, toss, and let drain in a colander for at least 30 minutes and up to 3 hours, tossing once. Rinse under cold running water and pat dry with paper towels.

Preheat the broiler. Line a baking sheet with parchment paper and arrange the eggplant cubes in a single layer. Drizzle with ¼ cup (60 ml) oil, toss, and place the baking sheet about 5 inches from the broiler. Broil, tossing twice, until golden, 10 to 15 minutes. You may need to do this in batches. (Alternatively, you can stir-fry the eggplant cubes in olive oil, then drain on paper towels and proceed.)

Heat 3 tablespoons of the olive oil in a heavy-bottomed pan over medium heat. Add the onions and sauté for about 10 minutes, until they have a light golden color. Add the honey and sauté for 8 minutes more, or until the onions have caramelized. Remove from the heat.

In a small saucepan, combine the tomatoes and vinegar, bring to a boil, and simmer for 5 minutes to reduce.

Reheat the onions, add 2 tablespoons of the olive oil and the celery, and toss for 2 minutes. Add the capers, olives, and sultanas and toss for 2 minutes more. Pour in the tomato sauce, add the eggplant and some Maraş pepper, and cook, tossing carefully, for 5 minutes.

Remove from the heat, taste, and add more honey, vinegar, or Maraş pepper as needed. Transfer to a large platter. Coarsely chop the basil, add to the eggplant mixture, and toss.

Heat 2 tablespoons of the olive oil in a skillet and sauté the bread crumbs over medium-low heat for 2 minutes. Add the pine nuts and almonds and sauté until golden. Add the bread crumb mixture to the eggplant, reserving 2 tablespoons for serving, and toss to mix. Let come to room temperature and sprinkle with the reserved bread crumb–nut mixture before serving with bulgur pilaf and grilled halloumi, if desired.

Braised Greens and Potatoes with Lemon and Fennel VEGAN GLUTEN-FREE

SERVES 4

½ cup (120 ml) olive oil

2 medium onions, halved and thinly sliced

3 to 4 small carrots, halved or quartered lengthwise

4 to 5 scallions, white and most of the green parts, thinly sliced

1 fennel bulb, trimmed and coarsely chopped, fronds and tender stalks reserved

4 medium-small potatoes, quartered or cut into ½-inch (1.3-cm) slices

1 teaspoon fennel seeds, crushed with a mortar and pestle or freshly ground

2 pounds (1 kg) mixed greens—spinach, sorrel, Swiss chard, outer leaves of romaine lettuce, pea shoots, nettle tops (see page 24), or any combination of sweet leafy greens—washed, large leaves coarsely chopped

½ cup (120 ml) white wine

¼ preserved lemon, flesh discarded, rinsed and cut into strips

½ to 1 teaspoon salt, or more to taste

3 to 5 tablespoons fresh lemon juice

½ cup (30 g) chopped fresh dill or wild fennel

1 to 2 teaspoons Maraş pepper or a good pinch of crushed red pepper flakes, to taste (freshly ground black pepper works as well)

Good, fruity olive oil, for drizzling

I love braising potatoes with seasonal leafy greens and vegetables of all kinds—artichokes, fresh fava, string beans, peas, and carrots. The potatoes soak up the flavorful juices released by the greens and herbs—each bite of this dish is delicious. Fresh lemon juice is the traditional flavoring, and I also add preserved lemon, which beautifully complements this simple dish, found with slight variations throughout the Mediterranean. Serve with creamy ricotta or feta cheese and fresh crusty bread.

Heat the olive oil over medium heat in a large, deep skillet or sauté pan. Add the onions and sauté for 5 minutes, or until soft. Add the carrots, scallions, fennel bulb, potatoes, and fennel seeds, stir to coat with the oil, and sauté for about 3 minutes, coating the vegetables and potatoes with oil on all sides.

Add the greens in batches, starting with the larger leaves and gradually adding the smaller, more tender ones. Stir a few times to help the leaves wilt and reduce in size, then add the wine and cook for 1 minute; add 1 cup (240 ml) water, the preserved lemon, and salt to taste.

Reduce the heat to low and simmer for about 10 minutes, until the greens and potatoes are tender and most of the juices have been absorbed. If there is too much liquid, cook for 2 to 3 minutes over high heat to reduce.

Add 3 tablespoons lemon juice, half of the dill, and sprinkle with Maraş pepper; toss, taste, and adjust the seasonings. Cook for 2 minutes more, then sprinkle with the remaining dill.

Serve warm or at room temperature, drizzled with good, fruity olive oil.

VARIATION **BRAISED ARTICHOKES AND FAVA WITH LEMON AND FENNEL**
(Pictured on page 65)

Omit 2 of the potatoes and all of the greens. Add 4 to 6 artichokes (depending on their size) and 1 pound (500 g) tender fava pods, washed and drained. Prepare the artichokes as described on page 97 and halve or quarter each one (again, depending on the size). Shell only the large fava pods. Trim the ends of tender pods and chop into 2-inch (5-cm) pieces. Sauté the artichokes and fava with the carrots, fennel, and potatoes for 5 minutes, then add the wine, the preserved lemon, and 2 cups (500 ml) water, and simmer for 10 to 15 minutes, or until the artichokes and fava are tender; finish the dish as above.

EGGAH, KOOKOO, AND NAKED PIES

The Arab *eggah* and the Persian *kookoo* (*kuku* or *kukuye*) are often likened to the Italian frittata. But they are very different: As much as I love a frittata, both *eggah* and *kookoo* are more complex than Italian open-faced omelets; they have no cheese and use just enough egg to bind the vegetables.

There are as many different versions of *kookoo* as there are cooks. One of the most common is the dark green *kookoo-ye sabzi*, the traditional Iranian New Year's Day dish. The richly flavored *Kookoo Bademjan* (with eggplants, page 143) is my favorite, and I suggest you try my variations, the Green Bean *Kookoo* and the Cauliflower *Kookoo*, which will help you take a fresh look at some of your kitchen staples.

The Arab *eggah* and the Balkan "naked pies"—pies that are not wrapped in phyllo—are very similar dishes. There are many names for crustless pies; *batzina* and *mamaliga* (from the Romanian word for polenta-like dishes) are just a couple of examples. Like the *kookoo*, these Balkan pies are mixtures of vegetables, onions or scallions, and herbs, with even less eggs than those used in the Persian dish. Cooks add either bread crumbs or yellow cornmeal as a binding agent, and cheese is often included. My favorite naked pie is the one we make in the summer with zucchini (opposite).

All these egg-vegetable mixtures "can be turned into small fritters (tiny *eggahs*) by dropping tablespoons into hot oil and turning them to brown on the other side," according to Claudia Roden. With slight variations, the mixture used for the crustless zucchini pie can be turned into *kolokythokeftedes* (zucchini fritters, page 77).

"Naked" or Crustless Zucchini Pie GLUTEN-FREE

SERVES 5 TO 6 AS A MAIN COURSE (OR MAKES 8 TO 10 APPETIZER PORTIONS)

⅓ cup (80 ml) olive oil, plus more for drizzling

2 pounds (1 kg) zucchini, coarsely grated on a box grater or on a mandoline fitted with the julienne attachment

Salt

1 onion (about ½ pound/225 g), finely chopped or grated

1¼ cups (100 g) ground quick-cooking rolled oats

¾ pound (340 g) feta cheese, crumbled

1 teaspoon Maraş pepper or freshly ground black pepper, to taste

3 tablespoons chopped dill

½ cup (about 50 g) packed fresh mint leaves, chopped

3 eggs

1 cup (140 g) hulled sunflower seeds or pepitas

3 to 4 tablespoons grated pecorino or *kefalotyri*

A French guest once called it "flan," but this rustic Balkan dish is too hearty for such a dainty description. This pie has no cream and uses only two eggs and toasted bread crumbs as a binding agent for the raw grated zucchini, which is scented with fresh mint and dill. If you don't have zucchini, squash is a wonderful substitute. Once I found myself without stale bread and substituted rolled oats, ground in a blender. I have also used sunflower seeds and pecorino to top the pie, giving it a nice crunchy crust. I usually serve it as main course, with a generous tomato salad. But it can also be an appetizer and is our guests' favorite picnic food, as we often bring it with us to the beach, precut into bite-size pieces.

Preheat the oven to 375°F (190°C). Lay a piece of parchment paper on a baking sheet and drizzle with olive oil.

Toss the zucchini with 1 teaspoon salt and let wilt in a colander for about 10 minutes.

Press handfuls of the zucchini over the sink to extract most of the juices and transfer to a large bowl. Add the onion, oats, feta, Maraş pepper, dill, and mint. Combine and add the eggs, one at a time, mixing well with your hands or with a large spatula. Add ⅓ cup (80 ml) olive oil and stir well.

Sprinkle the oiled baking sheet with a few sunflower seeds, and carefully pour the zucchini mixture over them. Spread and level the surface with a spatula, drizzle with olive oil, and sprinkle with the rest of the sunflower seeds and the grated cheese.

Cover loosely with aluminum foil and bake for 30 minutes. Remove the foil and bake for 10 to 15 minutes more, until the mixture is set and deep golden on top.

Let cool on a rack for at least 20 minutes. Cut into pieces and serve warm or at room temperature.

Eggplant "Cake" with Onions and Walnuts (*Kookoo Bademjan*)

SERVES 4 TO 6

3 to 4 tablespoons olive oil, plus more as needed

5 medium eggplants (about 2½ pounds/ 1.2 kg total), washed and dried

1 leek, white and light-green parts, washed and thinly sliced

1 medium red onion, thinly sliced

Salt

3 cloves garlic, minced

1 tablespoon ground turmeric

1 teaspoon ground cumin, or to taste

½ cup (40 g) ground walnuts

2 cups (80 g) fresh flat-leaf parsley, chopped

1 to 3 teaspoons Maraş pepper or a good pinch of crushed red pepper flakes, to taste (freshly ground black pepper works as well)

3 large eggs, lightly beaten

2 tablespoons all-purpose flour (see Note)

2 medium tomatoes, thinly sliced

2 teaspoons fresh oregano or thyme (optional)

Crusty bread, for serving

Greek-style yogurt, for serving

This is a basic recipe and my favorite *kookoo*, as few vegetables can rival the allure of eggplant. If you like a smoky taste, rub the eggplants with olive oil and char under the broiler until their skins blacken and crack. Then lower the heat, move the eggplants to the middle of the oven, and continue baking until they are cooked through. Instead of baking a round *kookoo* you can make it in four or six ramekins, or make bite-size "cakes" in small muffin tins if you plan to serve it as finger food.

Preheat the oven to 350°F (175°C). Oil the bottom and sides of a 9-inch (23-cm) round baking dish or line with parchment paper.

Using a fork, pierce the eggplants in several places and bake for 30 to 40 minutes directly on the oven rack, until soft. Transfer to a colander, slice in half, and let the eggplants drain. When cool enough to handle, remove the skin and chop the eggplant flesh.

Heat 3 tablespoons olive oil in a skillet over medium heat, add the leek and onion, sprinkle with salt, and sauté for about 8 minutes, until the onions and leeks soften and start to color. Add the garlic, turmeric, and cumin. Stir and sauté for 1 minute more. Remove from the heat and add the walnuts, parsley, and Maraş pepper and stir well to mix.

In a large bowl, combine the chopped eggplant with the onion-leek mixture. Taste and adjust the seasoning. Add the eggs and flour and mix thoroughly. Pour the mixture into the prepared baking dish, flatten, and arrange the tomato slices evenly on the surface. Drizzle with olive oil, and sprinkle with salt, Maraş pepper, and oregano or thyme, if you like. Loosely cover with aluminum foil and bake for 40 minutes. Remove the foil and bake for 15 to 20 minutes more, until set. If you like, place the *kookoo* under the broiler for 2 to 3 minutes to caramelize the tomatoes. Serve warm or at room temperature with crusty bread and yogurt.

NOTE: *For a gluten-free version, substitute cornmeal for the all-purpose flour.*

VARIATIONS

CAULIFLOWER *KOOKOO* (*KOOKOO GOL-KALAM*)

Instead of eggplant, steam the florets and boil the stems of a cauliflower as described for Cauliflower Gratin (page 131). Drain well and chop the stems and florets finely, then combine with the onion-leek mixture and proceed as described above.

GREEN BEAN *KOOKOO* (*KOOKOO LOOBIA-SABZ*)

Instead of eggplant, steam 1 pound (500 g) green beans (fresh or frozen), drain on paper towels, and finely chop. Combine with the onion-leek mixture, adding ½ to 1 bunch chopped fresh cilantro, if you like. Proceed as described above.

Okra and Zucchini in Harissa-Tomato Sauce

VEGAN GLUTEN-FREE

SERVES 4 TO 6

1 pound (500 g) small okra (no longer than 3 inches/7.5 cm), tops trimmed, if you like

1½ tablespoons salt, plus more as needed

⅓ cup (80 ml) red wine vinegar

½ cup (120 ml) olive oil

2 pounds (1 kg) small zucchini, trimmed and halved vertically or cut into 1-inch (2.5-cm) rounds

1½ cups (240 g) coarsely chopped onions

1½ cups (180 g) grated ripe tomatoes or canned diced tomatoes, with their juices

1 tablespoon ground turmeric

1 cinnamon stick

2 tablespoons *h'rous* (page 62) or harissa, or 2 to 3 teaspoons Maraş pepper, or a good pinch of crushed red pepper flakes

Pinch of sugar

2 cups (120 g) chopped fresh flat-leaf parsley

Bulgur (page 183) or rice pilaf, couscous, polenta (page 193), or bread for serving

Labne or feta cheese for serving (optional)

Okra is braised in thick tomato sauce throughout the Mediterranean. But the thick sauce poses a problem: Stirring during cooking crushes the pods to mush, defeating the point of all the hard work that was once done in paring the stems. In Egypt women found a way to cook the pods to silky tenderness without letting them get mushy—they bake the okra, often together with meat or poultry in a rich tomato sauce (see Note). Adopting this method, I spice up my dish with homemade *h'rous* or harissa, inspired by traditional North African slow-cooked vegetables. Even people who claim to hate okra can't stop eating this dish.

Serve on its own, with fresh, crusty bread and feta cheese, or with bulgur, rice, or any grain pilaf; it is also a great topping for polenta.

Preheat the oven to 200°F (90°C). Line a baking sheet with parchment paper.

Place the okra in a single layer on the baking sheet. Sprinkle with the salt, drizzle with the vinegar, and toss well. Place in the oven and bake for 20 minutes. Transfer to a 9- to 10-inch (23- to 25-cm) round baking dish and set aside.

Increase the oven temperature to 400°F (205°C).

In a large skillet, heat ¼ cup (60 ml) of the oil over high heat. Add the zucchini and sauté until they start to color, 5 to 10 minutes. Transfer to the baking dish with the okra and set aside.

Add the remaining ¼ cup (60 ml) oil to the skillet and heat over medium heat. Add the onions and sauté until soft, about 8 minutes. Add the tomatoes (with juice), turmeric, cinnamon, *h'rous*, and salt to taste. Cook the sauce until it starts to thicken, about 10 minutes. Add the sugar and all but ¼ cup (15 g) of the parsley. Taste and adjust the seasonings, adding more *h'rous*, if desired.

Pour the sauce over the okra and zucchini and bake until the vegetables are cooked through and tender, 30 to 40 minutes.

Let cool for 15 minutes. Sprinkle with the reserved ¼ cup (15 g) parsley and serve warm or at room temperature, accompanied by crusty bread and *labne,* if you like; you can also serve with pilaf or couscous, or as a topping for polenta.

NOTE: *In Crete and in the Peloponnese, fish steaks or fillets are sometimes baked together with the okra in the rich tomato sauce.*

Braised Green Beans and Potatoes in Tomato Sauce (*Fassolakia Ladera*) VEGAN GLUTEN-FREE

SERVES 4 TO 6

⅔ cup (160 ml) olive oil

2 cups (320 g) coarsely chopped onions

1 tablespoon sea salt, or to taste

3 cloves garlic, coarsely chopped

2 pounds (1 kg) fresh runner beans or young green beans, ends trimmed

1 to 2 teaspoons Maraş pepper or a good pinch of crushed red pepper flakes to taste

1 pound (500 g) potatoes, cut into 1½-inch (4-cm) cubes

Freshly ground black pepper

1½ cups (90 g) chopped fresh flat-leaf parsley

4 to 5 vine-ripened tomatoes, quartered and pureed in a blender (yields about 3 cups/720 ml), or 3 cups (720 ml) canned diced tomatoes, with their juices

Fresh country bread, for serving (optional)

Feta cheese, for serving (optional)

Stringless green beans (probably the only kind you can get in the United States) became widely available in Greece only in the last few years. As far back as I can remember, before we could cook this very popular summer dish, we had to slave for hours trimming each one of the flattish beans—a kind of runner bean—that we cooked. Tender green beans are so much easier to prepare, but their taste lacks the meatiness of those old beans we called *barbounia*—"red mullet," likened to the dainty and most expensive of all Mediterranean fish.

I shouldn't lament, though; *fassolakia ladera* made with any kind of seasonal green beans, even with frozen ones, is an amazing dish! The potatoes take on a wonderful flavor cooked together with the beans in a rich tomato sauce, and I can't resist eating them while still warm.

Heat ½ cup (120 ml) of the olive oil in a deep, heavy-bottomed skillet or sauté pan over medium heat. Add the onions, sprinkle with the salt, and sauté for 5 minutes. Add the garlic, beans, and Maraş pepper. Sauté for 5 to 6 minutes more, until the beans are well coated with olive oil.

Arrange the potatoes on top of the beans in one layer, pressing to submerge them slightly in the beans. Season with salt and black pepper to taste, sprinkle with the parsley—reserving 2 tablespoons for serving—and pour in the tomatoes (with juice). Bring to a boil, cover, reduce the heat, and simmer for 15 minutes. Check periodically to see that there is enough liquid in the pan, adding just a little water if the sauce becomes too dry. Taste, correct the seasonings, and continue cooking for about 10 minutes, occasionally shaking the pan.

When the beans and potatoes are cooked, use a slotted spoon to transfer them to a serving platter. Raise the heat to high and cook the sauce until it thickens. Pour the sauce over the beans and potatoes, sprinkle with the reserved 2 tablespoons parsley, and serve warm or at room temperature with fresh country bread and feta cheese, if desired.

VARIATION

Add 1 pound (500 g) tender zucchini, cut into ⅔-inch (1.5-cm) slices, and sauté with the beans before arranging the potatoes on top and pouring the sauce over.

Roasted Summer Vegetables with Garlic and Herbs VEGAN GLUTEN-FREE

SERVES 4 TO 6

2 medium eggplants, cut into 1½-inch (4-cm) chunks

Salt

⅔ cup (160 ml) olive oil

2 heads garlic, halved horizontally, plus 4 cloves garlic, halved

1 tablespoon ground turmeric

1 teaspoon ground cumin

2 teaspoons Maraş pepper or a good pinch of crushed red pepper flakes, to taste

2 tablespoons dried Greek oregano or thyme, crumbled

1 small fennel bulb, trimmed (fronds and tender stalks coarsely chopped and reserved), halved and cut into thin wedges

5 small zucchini, cut into 1-inch (2.5-cm) rounds

2 green and 2 red bell peppers, cored, quartered, seeded, and cut into ½-inch (1.3-cm) pieces

2 medium tomatoes, cored and chopped

3 medium red onions, cut into eighths

3 medium carrots, halved lengthwise and cut into 1½-inch (4-cm) chunks

1 tablespoon Za'atar (page 56) or Aegean Herb and Hot Pepper Mix (page 55)

Leaves from 3 to 4 fresh thyme sprigs or a handful of shredded fresh basil leaves

I bake all or some of the vegetables on the ingredient list, depending on what my garden produces. For example, I omit the eggplants and increase the amount of zucchini in June, when I harvest more zucchini than I could otherwise cook. Needless to mention, again, that simple dishes like this one depend on the quality of the vegetables. Pick the freshest vegetables from your local farmers' market and your summer roast will always be spectacular, no matter what vegetables you choose.

Leftovers are great as a topping for polenta or grain pilaf. You can also spoon them on toasted pita or bread to make a bruschetta, topped with crumbled ricotta or feta; they also make a great inclusion in a frittata, or add them to a Crispy Cheese Pie (page 172).

Place the eggplants in a colander and sprinkle generously with salt. Let stand for at least 30 minutes and up to 3 hours. Rinse and pat dry with paper towels.

Meanwhile, preheat the oven to 400°F (205°C). Line a large baking dish that can hold the vegetables in one layer with parchment paper.

In a food processor or blender, combine the olive oil, garlic cloves, turmeric, cumin, Maraş pepper, oregano, reserved fennel fronds, and salt to taste. Pulse to get a thick sauce.

In a large bowl, combine the drained eggplant, zucchini, bell peppers, tomatoes, onions, fennel bulb, carrots, and garlic halves. Pour the sauce over and toss well, using your hands or two spatulas.

Transfer to the baking dish, cover with parchment paper, and bake for 30 minutes. Remove the parchment paper, toss with two spatulas, sprinkle with the za'atar, and bake for 10 minutes more, or until all the vegetables are tender. The tops should char a bit as they caramelize. Sprinkle with fresh thyme and serve warm or at room temperature.

Fresh Fava Beans with Coriander Seeds, Garlic, and Cilantro VEGAN GLUTEN-FREE

SERVES 3 TO 4

2 pounds (1 kg) tender fava pods, washed and drained (see Note)

½ cup (120 ml) olive oil

4 to 6 cloves garlic, sliced, to taste

2 teaspoons freshly ground coriander seeds, or more to taste

Salt

Freshly ground black pepper

1 bunch fresh cilantro, coarsely chopped

1 lemon, quartered (optional)

Fresh bread, for serving (optional)

We are blessed with an abundance of fava beans, which forces me to seek new and exciting ways to cook the jewels of my garden's fresh pods. In my search for variety I came across a perfectly simple, yet luscious recipe on Deborah Gardner's blog. The preparation originates from the old Jewish community of Aleppo, Syria. "Be generous with coriander; it should make the dish brownish," she writes. I followed her basic instructions, but decided to add fresh cilantro at the end, as well as some lemon juice. The lemony sourness definitely complements the creamy sweetness of favas.

Shell only the large fava pods. Trim the ends of the small, tender pods and chop them into 1½-inch (4-cm) pieces.

Heat the olive oil in a sauté pan or deep skillet over medium heat. Add the fava and garlic; sauté for a few minutes, until the garlic starts to sizzle. Add the coriander and sauté for about 3 minutes more. Pour in 1 cup (240 ml) water and continue tossing often, until the fava are just tender. Add a little water, if necessary, just to keep the fava cooking, but be careful not to overcook because they will become unpleasantly mushy and stringy. Most of the water should have evaporated when the favas are done cooking. Remove the pan from the heat.

Sprinkle with salt and pepper, add the cilantro, toss, and serve hot, warm, or at room temperature. Squeeze some lemon juice over the dish, if you like. Accompany with fresh bread, if desired, to soak up the delicious juices.

NOTE: *I freeze fresh, tender fava pods as well as shelled fava beans in zip-top bags. I cooked both this and the variation with the frozen fava and the results were wonderful. Nevertheless, if fava is not available you can make a "perfectly honest dish," as M. F. K. Fisher would say, with green beans.*

VARIATION **FAVA BEANS WITH CORIANDER SEEDS AND YOGURT (*FISTUQIA*)**

(Inspired by a recipe in Claudia Roden's *Book of Middle Eastern Food*)

Cook the fava pods as described above, until almost done.

In a bowl, beat 2 cups (480 ml) full-fat natural yogurt (not thick) with 1 egg. Add the mixture to the fava, together with ½ cup (75 g) cooked rice or ½ cup (70 g) coarse bulgur (soak the bulgur in warm water for 30 minutes and drain).

Cook for 5 to 8 minutes, stirring often, until the favas are tender and the sauce thickens. Add salt, pepper, and chopped fresh cilantro or mint. Toss and serve.

Tomato and Olive Oil Scrambled Eggs GLUTEN-FREE

SERVES 2 TO 3 AS A MAIN COURSE, OR
5 TO 6 AS PART OF A MEZE SPREAD

8 to 10 pieces Tomato Confit (page 27),
   or 6 canned plum tomatoes (best quality),
   drained, plus 6 sun-dried tomatoes,
   coarsely chopped

2 to 3 tablespoons olive oil (less if you
   use Tomato Confit)

5 eggs

Salt

¼ cup (65 g) Greek-style yogurt

Good pinch of Maraş pepper or crushed
   red pepper flakes, to taste

Feta cheese, for serving

Good, fruity olive oil, for drizzling

1 tablespoon chopped fresh oregano
   or thyme (optional)

Toasted whole-wheat bread slices,
   for serving (optional)

We called it *strapatsada,* from the Italian *uova strapazzate* (scrambled eggs); it was the comfort food my mother cooked for my sister and me on summer evenings. Plain scrambled eggs are not a common Greek dish, but a huge egg-and-tomato scramble, as you might find in a Greek diner in America, is still a national institution. Some people add crumbled feta in the pan, but I much prefer to sprinkle it at the end. Serve with toasted multigrain or whole-wheat bread and a green salad, or with roasted vegetables (page 147). I often serve it with Toasted Bulgur Pilaf (page 183), but simple sliced potatoes fried in olive oil are still my favorite complement.

If you use Tomato Confit, place the tomatoes in a skillet together with their oil and cook over medium-high heat, stirring often to thicken.

If you use canned and sun-dried tomatoes, warm the olive oil in a skillet, add the tomatoes, and cook over medium-high heat, stirring often, for 10 minutes, or until thickened.

In a bowl, beat the eggs lightly with a pinch of salt and the yogurt.

Reduce the heat and add the eggs to the tomatoes, sprinkle with the Maraş pepper, and cook, tossing often with a wooden spatula, until the eggs are just set. Be careful not to overcook the eggs.

Transfer to a shallow bowl and serve warm or at room temperature. Sprinkle with feta, drizzle with fruity olive oil, and add fresh oregano, if you like.

Alternatively, you can spread tablespoons of the *strapatsada* on toast and serve as bruschetta.

VARIATIONS

TURKISH TOMATO AND PEPPER SCRAMBLED EGGS (*MENEMEN*)

Sauté 1 seeded and diced red or green bell pepper until soft. Add the tomatoes to the pan and proceed as above.

SCRAMBLED EGGS FROM ARLES (*BRUILLADE À L'ARLÉSIENNE*)

Grate a small zucchini and sauté in 1 tablespoon olive oil until soft. Add a small minced garlic clove and the tomatoes and proceed as above.

Braised Kale with Peppers   VEGAN GLUTEN-FREE

SERVES 3 TO 4

1 pound (500 g) tender kale (about 2 bunches: curly, Italian cavolo nero, Russian, or any kind), only the very tough ends discarded

1 tablespoon olive oil

2 red bell peppers, seeded, quartered, and cut into ½-inch (1.3-cm) strips

3 scallions, white plus most of the green parts, thinly sliced

4 cloves garlic, thinly sliced

½ cup (120 ml) white wine

Good pinch of Maraş pepper or crushed red pepper flakes, to taste

1 tablespoon fresh lemon juice or balsamic vinegar, to taste

½ teaspoon salt, or to taste

Freshly ground black pepper

Good, fruity olive oil, for drizzling

Hearty and flavorful, kale is the ideal green for braising. If you want more variety in the dish, a mixture of chard, mustard greens, chicory, and the outer leaves of romaine lettuce can also be cooked the same way. My take on this classic dish is inspired by *tsigarelli*, the braised mixed greens from the island of Corfu that are seasoned with plenty of hot paprika. I add sweet red peppers to enrich the flavor of the greens, and I brighten the dish with fresh lemon juice or vinegar.

Serve on its own, or with multigrain bread and ricotta, feta, or fresh goat cheese. As pictured on page 192, use as a topping for polenta (page 193) or serve with any rice or bulgur pilaf, as well as with boiled, fried, or scrambled eggs with tomatoes (opposite).

Wash the kale. Chop the stems and set aside, then chop the leaves coarsely.

In a large skillet or sauté pan, heat the olive oil over medium-high heat. Add the bell peppers and sauté with the scallions until they start to soften. Add the garlic and sauté for 1 minute, then add the kale stems and sauté for 2 minutes more. Add the kale leaves and toss for 1 minute more, then add the wine, Maraş pepper, and ½ cup (120 ml) water. Cover and cook for 5 to 8 minutes, until the kale is tender.

Stir in the lemon juice and remove from the heat. Add salt and black pepper to taste, and finish with a drizzle of fruity olive oil.

Laurent Gras's Ratatouille Niçoise   VEGAN GLUTEN-FREE

How perfectly liberating to read the celebrated chef's description of his mother's ratatouille! In his beautiful online cookbook, *My Provence*, Gras gives the recipe for a dish very different from traditional ratatouille. His Ratatouille Niçoise—chosen for the cover of *My Provence*—is very similar to the Turkish *Türlü* (*tourlou* in Greek), a family favorite all over the Mediterranean that relies on the same principle: a medley of cooked vegetables. The rustic versions (as shown above) combine any summer vegetable the garden offers plus a few potatoes to give the dish body. Note that you need end-of-summer vegetables and tomatoes that burst with flavor; otherwise there is no point in making the dish because the stew will be flavorless.

Serve with feta cheese and fresh, crusty bread to sop up the luscious sauce, or complement it with Toasted Bulgur Pilaf (page 183).

About ½ cup (120 ml) olive oil

1 large onion, halved and sliced into half-moons

Salt

3 cloves garlic, thinly sliced

1 red and 2 green bell peppers, halved, seeded, and cut into 1-inch (2.5-cm) dice

2 to 3 elongated eggplants (about 1½ pounds/680 g total), sliced in strips and cut into 1½-inch (4-cm) cubes

2½ cups (300 g) grated or briefly pulsed vine-ripened tomatoes (3 to 4 medium-large tomatoes)

1 tablespoon tomato paste (optional)

2 medium zucchini, quartered lengthwise and cut into 1½-inch (4-cm) pieces, or ½ pound (225 g) tender green beans, cut into about 2-inch (5-cm) pieces (see Note)

1 to 2 teaspoons Maraş pepper or a good pinch of crushed red pepper flakes (plenty of freshly ground black pepper will also suffice)

10 to 12 fresh basil leaves, chopped

Good, fruity olive oil, for drizzling (optional)

Pistou (see below; optional)

Heat ⅓ cup (80 ml) of the oil in a heavy-bottomed pan over medium-high heat. Add the onions and sprinkle with 1 teaspoon salt. Sauté for 5 minutes, or until the onions soften. Add the garlic and sauté a minute longer, then add the bell peppers and continue to cook, tossing often, for 8 minutes more, or until the peppers soften. Add the remaining oil, and as it starts to sizzle, add the eggplant. Cook, tossing, for 10 minutes more before you pour in the tomato and the tomato paste (if using).

Add the zucchini, toss, and cook for 10 to 15 minutes more, until the zucchini is done. Stir in the Maraş pepper.

Remove from the heat, fold in the basil, and taste to adjust the seasoning. Cover and let cool before serving warm or at room temperature, drizzled with some good olive oil. Top with a spoonful of *pistou*, if you like.

NOTE: *If you use green beans instead of zucchini, add them to the pot after you add the tomatoes: Bring the juice in the pan to a boil and add the green beans. Toss, reduce the heat to medium, and add the pepper. Cover and simmer for 15 minutes, tossing every now and then, and continue with folding in the basil.*

Pistou VEGAN GLUTEN-FREE

4 small cloves garlic, quartered

Sea salt

Leaves from 1 bunch fresh basil (about 2 ounces/55 g)

½ cup (120 ml) good, fruity olive oil

1 ounce (28 g) grated Parmesan or pecorino cheese (optional)

This French version of pesto contains no pine nuts—or any other nut, for that matter. Chef Gras insists on pounding the ingredients in a mortar, and the wonderful pictures of the bruised basil in the large marble mortar are mouthwatering. I have heard all the arguments before in Genoa, *the* capital of pesto. If you have the patience and strength, by all means follow his instructions! (I still use my blender.)

In the bowl of a blender or food processor, combine the garlic, a good pinch of salt, the basil, and the olive oil. Pulse a few times. Scrape down the sides with a spatula, add the cheese if you are using it, and pulse for one more second. Transfer to a bowl and bring to the table with the ratatouille.

Grape Leaf–Wrapped Pies with Yogurt and Herb Filling (*Asmapita*) GLUTEN-FREE

In this recipe, the cornmeal-thickened yogurt with scallions and herbs, baked or fried and wrapped in tangy grape leaves, develops into an unexpectedly sophisticated "pie" with complex flavor. In an earlier version, I made a large pie that I baked in the oven. It was good, but difficult to divide into portions. Paula Wolfert suggested small fried "packets," which worked much better. Now I propose something in between: individual little pies, baked in tartlet pans or shallow muffin tins. When finished under the broiler, the grape leaves caramelize beautifully!

Serve with risotto or any grain pilaf, with red lentils, with Old-Fashioned Bean Soup (page 122), or with a *friselle* (page 217).

SERVES 6

About ⅓ cup (80 ml) olive oil, as needed

15 to 20 grape vine leaves, fresh or frozen, or brine-packed grape leaves, drained and rinsed with boiling water

3 cups (750 g) thick, full-fat Greek-style yogurt

⅓ cup (50 g) cornmeal

⅔ cup (65 g) finely chopped scallions

⅔ cup (40 g) finely chopped fresh dill

⅔ cup (40 g) finely chopped fresh mint leaves

Salt

½ to 1 teaspoon minced jalapeño or other fresh chile or freshly ground black pepper, to taste

Preheat the oven to 375°F (190°C). Oil six 4-inch (10-cm) mini tartlet pans or shallow muffin tins. Line each pan or tin with 1 large or 2 small grape leaves, making sure they amply cover the bottom and sides. Brush liberally with olive oil.

In a bowl, combine the yogurt and the cornmeal; add the scallions, herbs, and salt, and jalapeño to taste and stir well.

Divide the yogurt mixture among the prepared pans. Top each with a leaf, tucking the edges inside to make a neat package, and brush liberally with olive oil. Bake for about 30 minutes, until the mixture is set and a knife inserted in the center comes out clean.

Preheat the broiler. Line a baking sheet with parchment paper and invert the pans onto it. Place the pies under the broiler for a few seconds to caramelize the leaves.

Serve hot, warm, or at room temperature.

Quince Stuffed with Wheat Berries, Nuts, and Raisins VEGAN

SERVES 4

4 quinces (about 3 pounds/1.5 kg total)

FOR THE STUFFING:

⅓ cup (80 ml) olive oil

2 cups (240 g) coarsely chopped onions

Salt

2 cups (about 200 g) almonds (with skins) or walnuts, coarsely ground, plus a few whole nuts, for garnish

½ cup (120 ml) fresh orange juice

1½ cups (240 g) precooked wheat berries or farro (page 35)

1½ teaspoons Lebanese Seven-Spice Mixture (*baharat*, page 54), or more to taste

1 cup (140 g) raisins

1 cup (60 g) finely chopped dill (1 tablespoon reserved for garnish)

FOR THE SAUCE:

¼ cup (60 ml) olive oil

3 tablespoons tomato paste

2 cinnamon sticks

2 bay leaves

1 to 2 teaspoons Maraş pepper, or a good pinch of crushed red pepper flakes, to taste, plus extra for sprinkling

1 cup (240 ml) sweet dessert wine, such as Marsala or Mavrodaphne

All through the winter, I keep a basket of fragrant quinces on the table. As they ripen, it is like watching the winter change slowly on my kitchen table. Quince is so versatile and adds flavor and texture to both savory and sweet dishes. I cut quinces to roast with root vegetables (page 147), braise them with greens or grains, or prepare this dish, stuffing them with a sweet and spicy filling of walnuts, grains, and raisins. The filling for this recipe is inspired by the classic, sumptuous Turkish meat-stuffed quince. With nuts, chewy wheat berries, raisins, and a very aromatic Lebanese spice blend, I think I have created an equally enticing meatless dish.

Preheat the oven to 400°F (205°C) and line a baking sheet with parchment paper.

Rub the fuzz off each quince, wash, and dry. Halve each fruit through the equator, using a good chef's knife. Don't peel. Arrange them on the baking sheet, cut side down, and bake for 30 minutes, or until easily pierced with a fork. Let cool; leave the oven on.

(You can bake the quince up to 4 days in advance and keep, covered, in the refrigerator until needed. Bake more and freeze them to use later in savory or sweet dishes.)

Using a grapefruit knife or spoon, very carefully remove as much flesh as possible from each quince half without piercing the skin. If, while removing the core and pips, you prick the bottom, don't worry; simply patch it with a piece of the removed flesh. Discard the pips and core (see Note, opposite), place the quince flesh in a blender, and pulse to chop—you will have about 2 cups (240 g).

Make the stuffing: In a large skillet, heat the olive oil over medium-high heat, add the onions, and sprinkle with salt. Sauté until soft, 8 to 10 minutes. Add the almonds, orange juice, wheat berries, and 1½ cups (180 g) of the quince pulp—reserve about ½ cup (60 g) pulp for the sauce—and toss. Remove from the heat and add the spices, raisins, and dill; stir well to mix. Taste and correct the seasoning.

Arrange the quince, hollow side up, in an ovenproof clay or glass pan that holds them snugly. Fill each fruit with the stuffing, using all of it.

Make the sauce: In a skillet, heat the olive oil over medium-high heat, add the tomato paste, and stir for a few seconds. Add the reserved quince pulp, the cinnamon, bay leaves, and Maraş pepper to taste. Pour in the wine and cook for 2 minutes. Remove from the heat.

Spoon the sauce over each stuffed quince, tucking the cinnamon sticks and bay leaves between the quinces (see photo above). Cover loosely with aluminum foil and bake for 40 minutes. Remove the foil, stick an almond half on top of each quince, and bake for 5 to 10 minutes more, to brown the tops. Sprinkle with the reserved dill and serve hot, warm, or at room temperature.

NOTE: *In the old days quince pips were dried and stored in jars for use in tisanes— with or without other herbs. My grandmother was convinced that a few quince pips, steeped for at least 5 minutes in boiling water, were the best remedy for colds and sore throats. It certainly doesn't hurt, and it makes a delicious infusion.*

Eggplants *Imam Bayeldi*, Stuffed with Onions, Peppers, Cheese, and Nuts GLUTEN-FREE

SERVES 4

4 eggplants (1½ to 2 pounds/680 g to 1 kg total)

Salt

¼ cup (60 ml) olive oil, plus extra for drizzling

3 medium onions (about ⅔ pound/300 g total), halved and thinly sliced

3 green or red bell peppers, halved, seeded, and cut into ¼-inch (0.6-cm) strips

1 tablespoon coarsely chopped garlic

1 to 3 teaspoons Maraş pepper or a good pinch of crushed red pepper flakes, to taste

1 teaspoon ground cumin

1 cup (80 g) walnuts, coarsely ground

1 cup (100 g) coarsely grated *graviera* or good quality pecorino (aged cheddar works well, too)

1 large beefsteak tomato, cut into 8 slices

1½ cups (360 ml) Basic Tomato Sauce (page 61)

2 to 3 fresh parsley sprigs (optional)

My version of the famous Turkish *Imam Bayeldi* (literally "the Imam fainted") is based on my mother's recipe. I have enriched the stuffing of onions, garlic, and peppers by adding walnuts and cheese, and I top with tomato sauce just before baking. These additions and the extra sauce, as well as the tomato slices I place under the eggplants, are my take on the classic dish.

Slice the eggplants in half lengthwise, keeping part of the stem. Score the flesh with a knife, salt generously, and let drain in a colander for 1 hour. Rinse under cold running water and pat dry with paper towels.

Preheat the oven to 400°F (205°C) with a rack in the middle. Line a baking sheet with parchment paper and place the eggplants cut side up on the sheet. Brush liberally with olive oil on both sides. Bake until the eggplants are golden, about 20 minutes. Keep the oven warm.

(You can bake the eggplants 2 to 3 days in advance, cool them, and refrigerate until needed, or you can freeze them for up to 6 months. Bring to room temperature before cooking.)

Warm the olive oil in a deep skillet over medium heat, add the onions, and sprinkle with 1 teaspoon salt. Sauté until soft, 8 to 10 minutes. Add the bell peppers and sauté for 8 minutes more, or until soft. Add the garlic, sauté for 1 minute, then remove from the heat. Add the Maraş pepper, cumin, walnuts, and cheese. Toss to mix and taste to adjust the seasoning.

Choose a baking dish that will hold the eggplants snugly. If you like, line with parchment paper. Brush the pan (or paper) with olive oil and line with the tomato slices. Place the eggplants on the tomatoes. Using a spoon, press into the softened flesh to create indentations for the stuffing. Fill each eggplant half with the onion-pepper mixture and top with 2 to 3 tablespoons of the tomato sauce. Pour any remaining sauce around the eggplants. Drizzle the stuffed eggplants with 2 to 3 tablespoons olive oil and bake for 40 minutes, or until bubbling and somewhat charred on top. Let cool for at least 20 minutes. Transfer the eggplants to a serving dish and top each one with a tomato slice from the pan. Garnish with parsley (if using) and serve warm or at room temperature.

Zucchini Rolls Stuffed with Halloumi

SERVES 4 AS A MAIN COURSE,
OR 6 TO 8 AS AN APPETIZER

3 large zucchini (each about 11 ounces/310 g),
or 3 to 4 medium-long eggplants (about
2 pounds/1 kg total)

3 to 4 tablespoons olive oil

Salt

1 tablespoon minced garlic

¼ cup (20 g) ground walnuts

½ teaspoon ground allspice

1 teaspoon Maraş pepper or a good pinch of
crushed red pepper flakes, to taste (freshly
ground black pepper works as well)

10 fresh mint leaves, chopped

½ pound (225 g) halloumi cheese (see Note)

Toasted freekeh or bulgur pilaf (page 183), for
serving

2 cups (480 ml) Basic Tomato Sauce (page 61),
warmed, for serving

They are called *rulos* or *revoltinos*, these "mock" stuffed vegetables, writes Claudia Roden in her *Book of Jewish Food*. Stuffed with lean ground meat combined with bread crumbs and allspice, *rulos de berengena* (eggplant rolls) are on the list of every Istanbul caterer, she writes, served at Jewish celebrations in Istanbul and beyond. Here I substitute halloumi cheese in my zucchini or eggplant rolls, adding chopped walnuts and garlic. I like them as a main course, with toasted bulgur or freekeh pilaf and a rich tomato sauce on the side. Each roll can also be served as finger food as part of a meze table.

Trim the zucchini and cut each lengthwise into 5 to 6 slices (about ¼ inch/0.6 cm thick or a bit less). If you like, peel the skins of the first and last slice using a vegetable peeler. Heat the broiler or a ridged stovetop grill. Brush the zucchini slices with olive oil on both sides and broil or grill for 3 to 4 minutes on each side, until tender and lightly charred.

If you use eggplant, cut them lengthwise into slices about ⅔ inch (1.5 cm) in width. If the eggplants are quite round, halve the slices lengthwise. Using a vegetable peeler, peel only the skins of the first and last slice. Place the eggplant slices in a colander, salt liberally, and let stand for 30 minutes. Rinse and pat dry with paper towels. Brush with olive oil on both sides and broil or grill for 3 to 4 minutes on each side, until tender and lightly charred.

In a small bowl, mix the garlic, walnuts, allspice, Maraş pepper, and mint.

Cut the halloumi into 15 or 18 pieces, equal to the number of zucchini or eggplant slices. Keep in mind that halloumi is a folded, pressed cheese, so slice accordingly. Spread some garlic-walnut mixture on each zucchini or eggplant slice. Place a piece of cheese about 1 inch (2.5 cm) from the end of the slice and roll the vegetable around the cheese, securing each roll with a toothpick, or threading a skewer through 3 or 4 rolls.

(You can prepare the rolls up to 3 days ahead, cover them, and refrigerate until ready to use. Bring to room temperature before proceeding.)

Preheat the broiler. Line a baking sheet with parchment paper and arrange the zucchini or eggplant rolls standing on one of the cheese sides—you want the cheese exposed to the broiler. Broil for 3 to 4 minutes, until the cheese turns a crackling golden brown. Flip and broil on the other side. Serve hot or warm with freekeh or bulgur pilaf, and tomato sauce.

NOTE: *You can substitute provolone—preferably* affumicato *(smoked) or* picante *(sharp)—for the halloumi, if you like.*

Chard Leaves Stuffed with Rice, Vegetables, and Herbs VEGAN GLUTEN-FREE

SERVES 6

⅔ cup (160 ml) olive oil

2 leeks, white parts plus some of the tender greens, thinly sliced

2 cups (320 g) coarsely chopped onions

3 bunches large chard (see Note), leaves and stems separated and reserved

4 large cloves garlic, coarsely chopped

1 to 2 teaspoons Maraş pepper or a good pinch of crushed red pepper flakes, to taste

1 cup (100 g) medium-grain rice, such as Arborio, soaked in hot water for 10 minutes and drained

½ cup (120 ml) dry red or rosé wine

1 cup (120 g) ripe tomatoes, cored and diced, or canned diced tomatoes, with their juices

1 pound (500 g) zucchini, coarsely grated, sprinkled with salt, and left in a colander to drain

2 medium carrots, grated

1 cup (about 70 g) packed coarsely chopped fresh flat-leaf parsley

1 cup (60 g) finely chopped fresh dill

1 teaspoon ground allspice

2 teaspoons ground turmeric

1½ teaspoons salt, or more to taste

Juice of 1 lemon, plus 1 to 2 lemons, quartered, for serving

Good, fruity olive oil, for drizzling

Greek-style yogurt or *labne*, for serving (optional)

Grape and cabbage leaves are the traditional vehicle for all wrapped foods. But any kind of green—the leaves of beans, cherry trees, mallows, collards, and sorrel, to name a few—can be stuffed to great effect with rice, bulgur, any grain combination, and often with small amounts of meat. Try to plan and cook a day ahead—these stuffed leaves always taste better the next day. I avoid blanching and use the leaves raw, breaking and tenderizing the central stem with the back of a knife. My stuffing is inspired by the filling of a traditional pie from Cephalonia that has a well-balanced blend of vegetables and herbs.

Heat ¼ cup (60 ml) of the oil in a large skillet over medium heat. Add the leeks and onions and sauté until soft, 8 to 10 minutes. Finely chop 1½ cups (135 g) of the tender chard stems and add to the leeks and onions. Sauté for 3 minutes, then stir in the garlic, Maraş pepper, and rice. Turn a few times. When the mixture starts to sizzle, pour in the wine and tomatoes (with juice), stir a couple of times, remove from the heat, and transfer to a large bowl.

Press the zucchini to drain and add it to the onion mixture, together with the carrots, parsley, dill, allspice, turmeric, and salt. Stir, cover, and let stand for 10 minutes.

Line a pot with the remaining chard stems and any leaves that are torn.

Place a whole chard leaf, shiny side down, on your work surface, with the stem toward you. Press and slide the back of a knife along the middle core of the leaf to crush the inner stem and to tenderize the leaf. Depending on the size of the leaf, place about 2 tablespoons of the filling in a vertical line near the stem. Fold the two adjacent sides of the leaf over the filling, then begin to fold and roll from the bottom. Roll up the leaf like a cigar, not too tightly, making sure to bring the side edges in as you roll up from the bottom. This will create a neat package. Place the stuffed leaf, seam side down, on top of the stems in the pot. Continue with the remaining leaves and stuffing, placing the stuffed chard leaves tightly next to each other in the pot. When the bottom of the pot is full, make a second layer.

Pour the remaining olive oil into the pot, along with the lemon juice and enough water to almost cover the stuffed leaves. Place an inverted heatproof plate over the stuffed leaves to keep them from rising and unrolling as they cook. Bring to a boil, cover, reduce the heat to low, and simmer for 30 minutes, or until the rice is cooked. To check, remove one stuffed leaf and taste.

Remove from the heat and let cool for at least 20 minutes in the pot. Carefully transfer to a serving platter, including the stems at the bottom, which are delicious! If there is too much broth, raise the heat and boil until it has reduced. Pour it over the stuffed leaves.

Cool, and if you can, refrigerate the stuffed chard leaves overnight. They taste better the next day. To serve, bring to room temperature and drizzle with fresh lemon juice and good, fruity olive oil. If you like, accompany with thick yogurt or *labne*.

NOTE: *Use any kind of large chard leaf: white, yellow, or red. You can also stuff the outer leaves of romaine lettuce or the leaves of Chinese cabbage.*

Grape Leaves Stuffed with Rice, Tomatoes, and Pomegranate Molasses VEGAN GLUTEN-FREE

The traditional Greek stuffed grape leaves are prepared in the spring, with fresh leaves picked from the garden or bought at the farmers' market. We call them *dolmades*, adopting the Turkish word for "stuffed." This recipe is adapted from the fragrant stuffed grape leaves chef Mohammad Antabli serves at Al Waha in London. If you can, prepare them a day before, as they taste so much better the next day. Instead of potatoes, you can cook beans at the bottom of the pan. With the same mixture, you can also stuff zucchini or squash.

About 60 tender fresh grape leaves, or an 8-ounce (240-ml) jar brine-packed grape leaves, drained and rinsed

1 cup (240 ml) olive oil

1½ cups (150 g) medium-grain rice, such as Arborio

¼ cup (25 g) pine nuts

½ teaspoon ground allspice

5 tablespoons (75 ml) pomegranate molasses

1 teaspoon sea salt, or more to taste

1 to 1½ teaspoons freshly ground black pepper, to taste

3½ cups (560 g) finely chopped onions

2 cinnamon sticks

2½ cups (300 g) grated ripe tomatoes (about 1½ pounds/680 g), or 2½ cups (300 g) canned diced tomatoes, with their juices

1½ cups (90 g) chopped fresh mint, plus a handful of leaves for lining the pan

1 teaspoon dried mint (optional)

2½ cups (150 g) finely chopped fresh flat-leaf parsley

2 large or 3 medium potatoes, thinly sliced

3 cloves garlic, thinly sliced

¼ to ⅓ cup (60 to 80 ml) fresh lemon juice, to taste

Labne or Greek-style yogurt, for serving (optional)

Bring a large pot of water to a boil. Carefully separate the grape leaves and blanch them, in batches, for about 1 minute. (If using leaves from a jar, rinse them well with boiling water.) Rinse with cold water and spread the leaves carefully on a towel.

Heat ½ cup (120 ml) of the olive oil in a deep skillet or sauté pan over medium-high heat. Add the rice and sauté for 5 minutes. Add the pine nuts and continue to sauté for 3 minutes more, or until the rice and pine nuts turn a light golden color. Be careful not to let the pine nuts burn. Remove from the heat. Place a sieve over a large bowl and transfer the rice and pine nuts to drain for a few seconds. Pour the oil from the bowl back into the skillet and transfer the rice and pine nuts to the bowl. Add the allspice, pomegranate molasses, and salt and pepper to taste to the bowl and toss to mix.

Reheat the oil in the skillet over medium heat, add the onions and cinnamon, and sauté for about 6 minutes, until the onions soften. Discard the cinnamon sticks and transfer the onions to the bowl with the rice, adding 1½ cups (180 g) of the tomatoes (with juice), the fresh mint, the dried mint (if using), and the parsley. Toss well to mix.

Line the bottom of a pot with any smaller and/or torn grape leaves, add the potato slices to cover the bottom, and scatter the garlic cloves and mint leaves over the potatoes.

Place a large grape leaf, shiny side down, on your work surface, with the stem toward you. Cut off the stem with scissors. Place about 2 teaspoons of the filling in a vertical line near the stem. Fold the two adjacent sides of the leaf over the filling, then begin to fold and roll from the bottom. Roll up the leaf like a cigar, not too tightly, making sure to bring the side edges in as you roll up from the bottom. This will create a neat package. Place the stuffed leaf, seam side down, in the pot. Continue with the remaining leaves, placing the stuffed grape leaves tightly next to each other in the pot. When the bottom of the pot is full, make a second layer.

Pour 1 cup (240 ml) water, the remaining ½ cup (120 ml) olive oil, remaining 1 cup (120 g) tomatoes (with juice), and ¼ cup (60 ml) lemon juice over the stuffed leaves. The liquid should almost cover them; if it does not, add a little more water. Place an inverted heatproof plate over the stuffed leaves to keep them from rising and unrolling as they cook. Bring to a boil, cover, reduce the heat to low, and simmer for 40 minutes, or until the rice is cooked. To check, remove one stuffed leaf and taste. When cooked, remove from the heat.

Let the stuffed grape leaves cool in the pot and then carefully transfer them to a serving platter. The potatoes at the bottom are delicious; I suggest you eat them while still warm.

If you can, refrigerate the stuffed leaves overnight. To serve, bring to room temperature and serve drizzled with fresh lemon accompanied by *labne,* if you like.

Stuffed Summer Vegetables with Rice, Farro, and Pine Nuts VEGAN

SERVES 6

2 or 3 small eggplants

Salt

5 to 7 medium ripe but firm tomatoes (as many as the pan can hold), plus 1 medium tomato, thinly sliced

2 to 3 medium white onions, blanched in salted water for 8 minutes and drained (optional)

5 medium green bell peppers

1 cup (240 ml) olive oil

3 cups (480 g) chopped onions

1½ cups (150 g) Arborio rice

¼ cup (25 g) pine nuts, toasted

½ cup (80 g) precooked farro or wheat berries (page 35)

⅔ cup (90 g) black raisins

1 cup (60 g) chopped fresh flat-leaf parsley

1 cup (60 g) chopped fresh dill

½ cup (30 g) chopped fresh mint

1½ teaspoons salt, plus more to taste

1 to 2 teaspoons Maraş pepper or freshly ground black pepper, plus more for sprinkling

1 to 2 medium potatoes, scrubbed, halved crosswise, each half quartered

Greek oregano, for sprinkling

Feta cheese or *labne*, for serving (optional)

Eggplants, peppers, onions, and tomatoes—with herbs, grains, pine nuts, and raisins, plus the bits and pieces removed to make room for the stuffing—cook slowly in the oven for an hour or more. Once cooled completely, their flavors meld together and make the perfect summer lunch.

Start by choosing a pan that will hold, somewhat snugly, the vegetables you plan to stuff. Don't worry if you have leftover stuffing; transfer to a saucepan, add some water, and simmer, stirring every now and then, to make a delicious risotto.

This dish is time-consuming but worthwhile, and you can prepare it in stages. Tomatoes take longer to hollow than peppers or eggplant, so you can start them a day in advance. Once emptied, keep the tomatoes upside down over paper towels in the refrigerator and complete the preparation the next day.

Cut about one-third, lengthwise, from the side of each eggplant, and set it aside, leaving the stem attached to the larger part, but peeling the green leaves that surround it. Score the flesh of the larger of the asymmetrical eggplant pieces with a knife, salt generously, and let drain in a colander for at least 30 minutes and up to 3 hours. Rinse under cold running water and pat dry with paper towels.

Using a spoon, remove most of the flesh from the larger part of each eggplant and chop the flesh. Chop the reserved eggplant slice and set aside together.

Cut off the top ½ inch (1.3 cm) of each whole tomato. Set aside the tops. Using a grapefruit spoon, very carefully remove as much pulp as possible from each tomato, without piercing the skin. Chop the pulp or puree in a blender and reserve. If you are stuffing onions, cut off the top 1 inch (2.5 cm) of each and, using a grapefruit spoon or a curved grapefruit knife, carefully remove most of the inner part, leaving about ¼ inch (0.6 cm) of onion shell. Chop the onion heart and add it to the chopped onions. Cut off and reserve the tops of 4 bell peppers, discarding the seeds and any inner membranes. Seed and finely dice 1 bell pepper and add it to the chopped eggplant pulp.

Arrange the tomatoes, eggplants, onions (if using), and bell peppers in a baking dish that holds them snugly. Preheat the oven to 375°F (190°C).

In a large skillet, heat ⅔ cup (160 ml) of the oil over medium-high heat. Add the chopped onions and sauté for 4 minutes. Add the chopped eggplant and bell pepper and sauté for 10 minutes more, or until soft. Add the rice, pine nuts, and farro and sauté for 2 minutes. Add the tomato pulp—reserving ½ cup (60 g)—and the raisins. Reduce

the heat to low and cook, stirring, for 3 minutes more. Stir in the parsley, dill, and mint and cook for 1 minute more. Remove from the heat and add the salt and Maraş pepper.

Stuff the tomatoes, bell peppers, onions (if using), and eggplants with the rice mixture. Cover the tomatoes and bell peppers with the reserved tops, and arrange the tomato slices over the stuffed eggplants. Distribute the potato pieces in the gaps between the vegetables.

Pour the remaining tomato pulp over everything and drizzle the remaining ⅓ cup (80 ml) oil over the stuffed vegetables. Sprinkle with salt, Maraş pepper, and oregano. Bake for 1 hour, or until the rice is tender (lift the cover of a tomato and check). Turn off the heat and let stand in the oven for 10 minutes, then let cool to room temperature.

Serve one or half of each stuffed vegetable per person, with a couple of potato pieces on each plate. Accompany with feta cheese, if you like.

Spinach and Cheese Pie (*Spanakotyropita*)

This is my version of the traditional "green" pie made with raw chopped spinach or other leafy greens, herbs, and onions. Spinach leaves are perfect, but any combination of spinach, chard, dandelion greens, arugula, and mesclun will be delicious. The chopped greens are rubbed with salt and olive oil to wilt; they are always complemented by feta. In my version I like to go beyond feta alone and add a mixture of more pungent cheeses that enhance the flavor of the pie. The fragrant filling cooks slowly inside the crunchy, homemade phyllo and the resulting pie is excellent eaten warm or at room temperature. If you use frozen phyllo, brush the top with egg wash (see Note, page 170); this small addition makes the commercial, ordinary crust much more interesting.

FOR THE PHYLLO DOUGH:
(see Note, page 170):

4 cups (500 g) all-purpose or bread flour

1 teaspoon salt

⅓ cup (80 ml) olive oil, plus more for brushing

2 tablespoons vinegar, preferably white wine

Cornstarch, for rolling

3 tablespoons fine bulgur or dried whole-wheat bread crumbs

FOR THE SPINACH-CHEESE FILLING:

10 cups (about 1 kg) packed shredded spinach leaves (not baby spinach), trimmed; you will need about 1½ pounds (680 g) spinach

1 cup (120 g) finely chopped shallots

1 cup (120 g) finely chopped scallions, white plus most of the green parts

1½ cups (90 g) finely chopped fresh parsley

1 cup (60 g) finely chopped fresh dill

½ cup (30 g) chopped fresh mint leaves

3 tablespoons chopped fresh thyme or oregano, or 2 teaspoons dried

1 teaspoon sea salt

1 cup (240 ml) olive oil, or as needed

2 cups (240 g) crumbled feta

1 cup (120 g) aged cheddar or a mixture of aged and smoked cheddar

½ teaspoon freshly ground black pepper

2 eggs, beaten lightly

Make the phyllo dough: In the bowl of a stand mixer fitted with the dough hook attachment, combine the flour and salt, make a well in the center, and pour in the olive oil and vinegar. With the machine running slowly, pour in about 1 cup (240 ml) water, as needed, and work the mixture for about 6 minutes to get a smooth, elastic dough. Cover the bowl with plastic wrap and let the dough rest for at least 15 minutes and up to 2 hours.

Make the spinach-cheese filling: In a large bowl, combine the spinach, shallots, scallions, parsley, dill, mint, and thyme. Add the salt and olive oil. Rub the mixture with your hands to mix and wilt the spinach and herbs; it will reduce to about half its volume. Add the feta, cheddar, pepper, and eggs. Stir well to combine and set aside.

Roll the phyllo and assemble the pie: Divide the dough into thirds. Divide two of the pieces into thirds again, shape each into a ball, cover, and set aside. Divide the remaining piece of dough into quarters, shape each into a ball, and set aside, covered, separately from the 6 large balls of dough.

Line a 10-by-15-inch (25-by-38-cm) baking pan with parchment paper and brush liberally with olive oil.

Take one of the 6 larger pieces of dough to roll a bottom sheet. Sprinkle your work surface and the dough with cornstarch and roll to make an almost round sheet, about 16 inches (40.5 cm) in diameter (for detailed instructions on rolling phyllo, see page 36). Stretch the dough carefully to extend it and set it in the baking dish with about 1½ inches (4 cm) hanging over the edges. Brush with olive oil and roll the remaining 5 larger pieces of dough in the same manner, brushing the surface of each sheet lightly with olive oil.

Sprinkle the top sheet of phyllo with the bulgur and pour in the prepared filling. Spread and level the filling with a spatula and drizzle about ⅓ cup (80 ml) olive oil over the filling.

Preheat the oven to 375°F (190°C).

Roll the remaining phyllo and place it over the filling inside the pan, brushing each sheet lightly with olive oil. Fold the overhanging bottom phyllo sheets over the top sheets without crimping—they will seal as they bake. Using a sharp knife, score the surface and bake for about 1 hour, until golden brown on the top and bottom; the pie will shrink somewhat and will completely detach from the pan. Lift it out of the pan carefully, using the parchment paper as "handles," and transfer to a wire rack. Slide the parchment paper out from underneath the pie to prevent the bottom crust from becoming soggy. Let cool for at least 20 minutes before sliding the pie back into the pan, onto a serving platter or, preferably, onto a wooden board to take to the table to cut and serve.

(continued)

Leftover pie keeps, covered, in the refrigerator for 3 to 4 days; it can be frozen for up to 6 months. Reheat the pie directly from the freezer, loosely wrapped in aluminum foil, in a preheated 375°F (190°C) oven, for about 15 minutes. Open the foil and heat for 5 to 10 minutes more, turning once, to crisp the phyllo on both sides.

NOTE: *To make the pie with commercial frozen phyllo: Use the thickest phyllo you can find and thaw it following the instructions on the package. Lay one more than half of the sheets in the package on the bottom of the pan, brushing each sheet lightly with olive oil. Sprinkle with bulgur, pour in the filling, and top with the rest of the sheets, brushing them with olive oil. Crimp the border and press it with the tines of a fork to prevent burning. I suggest you brush the top with egg wash, just before baking, to make the crust more interesting. To make egg wash, whisk together 1 small egg yolk with 3 tablespoons milk or natural yogurt (not thick).*

GASTRA, PEKA, OR SAÇI: THE PORTABLE OVEN

We heat our ovens with the turn of a dial, with no advance thought or preparation. Not long ago the difficulty for most cooks around the Mediterranean was not rolling phyllo, but finding an oven for baking the pie. On the nearly treeless islands, wood for the oven was probably the most valuable of the ingredients needed. Firing an oven is a lengthy process and in the past was done only once a week. The cook had to plan ahead to bake a series of dishes, besides the family's bread, in order to use every bit of the oven's precious heat. Pies were usually baked after the bread, as the oven started to cool. Lower temperatures were essential to allow both crust and filling to cook evenly.

Convenience and a scarcity of wood led people to invent portable makeshift ovens. One such device is a convex clay cover. The fragile clay devices, used from ancient times up until the mid-twentieth century, were replaced by more robust metal, though many families in rural villages continue to use clay. What we call a *gastra* in Greece—a *saçi* in Albania and a *peka* in Croatia—is roughly the same domed cover with a ledge around the outer edge to hold charcoal. Placed atop a few charcoals on the ground or in the fireplace, the underside of the lid preheats before food is placed beneath it and the charcoal above it. Before placing coals on the *gastra* it is important to add a layer of sand or cold ashes.

The families of friends in southern Albania continue to use a *saçi* regularly, bypassing their electric ovens—electricity can be unpredictable in the villages, and the pie waits for no one. Pies like the Crispy Cheese Pie (page 172), breads, and even plain vegetables baked with live fire under the dome acquire a unique, addictive, smoky aroma. Like pies made with home-rolled phyllo, once you taste the difference it is difficult to go back to the convenience of frozen phyllo or the sterility of electric heat.

Crispy Cheese Pie (Lazy Woman's Pie)

SERVES 3 TO 4 AS A MAIN COURSE,
OR 6 TO 8 AS PART OF A MEZE SPREAD

Olive oil, for brushing the baking sheet
   and the phyllo

⅔ cup (160 ml) milk

2 eggs

2 sheets homemade phyllo (page 36), or
   4 sheets thick frozen phyllo, thawed
   according to the package instructions

2 cups (240 g) crumbled feta (see Note,
   page 174)

½ cup (50 g) grated Parmesan (optional—
   for when using frozen phyllo)

2 tablespoons chopped fresh oregano,
   thyme, or marjoram

1 to 2 teaspoons Maraş pepper or a good
   pinch of crushed red pepper flakes (optional)

This is my adaptation of the cheese pies Balkan women prepare whenever they fire the wood ovens. They are easy and fast to make. The thin, crackerlike cheese pastry is called *tis tembelas* ("lazy woman's pie") in Epirus, at the northwestern edge of Greece, no doubt because it is not a proper pie with several sheets of phyllo and stuffing; often it is a simple batter of flour, eggs, crumbled feta, and milk, spread on a sheet pan and browned instantly to crispy perfection in a blazing-hot wood-fired oven. My version, even the one with commercial frozen phyllo—which I rarely use—is extremely simple and highly addictive! A handful of roasted vegetables or wilted greens is sometimes added, if you are feeling ambitious. Serve as a main course with soup, or accompany with a large salad of steamed or fresh vegetables. Cut into bite-size pieces and serve as finger food.

Preheat the oven to 430°F (220°C). Line a baking sheet with parchment paper and brush the paper with olive oil. In a bowl, whisk together the milk and eggs.

If using homemade phyllo: Stretch or crimp one sheet of phyllo as necessary to fill the baking sheet. Brush with olive oil and sprinkle with half of the feta. Pour half of the egg mixture over the feta and sprinkle with the herbs and Maraş pepper, if you like. Lay the second sheet of phyllo over the egg mixture and brush with olive oil. *(continued)*

Crumble more feta on top and drizzle with the remaining egg mixture. Sprinkle with more Maraş pepper, to taste. Proceed to baking.

If using frozen phyllo: Lay one sheet of frozen phyllo on the baking sheet, brush with olive oil, and sprinkle with half of the Parmesan, then lay another sheet of phyllo on top and brush with olive oil. Sprinkle half of the feta over the second sheet and pour half of the egg mixture over the top. Sprinkle with the herbs and Maraş pepper, if you like. Place a third sheet on top, brush with olive oil, sprinkle with the remaining Parmesan, then lay the last sheet on top and brush with olive oil. Sprinkle the remaining feta on top and drizzle with the remaining egg mixture. Sprinkle with more Maraş pepper, to taste. Proceed to baking.

Bake in the lower part of the oven for 25 minutes, or until golden brown and crisp. Check to make sure the pie is well browned on the bottom. If the top browns too quickly, cover the pie loosely with foil and continue baking. If it is well browned underneath but the top is not yet crispy enough, heat the broiler and bake for a few minutes right under the broiler. Serve at once, cutting the pie into pieces with a pizza wheel.

NOTE: *If the feta is too salty, mix it with some ricotta; I often use equal amounts of feta and ricotta in this recipe.*

Orange–Olive Oil Pastry Rolls with Olives and Scallions VEGAN

SERVES 4 TO 6 AS A MAIN COURSE,
OR 8 TO 10 AS PART OF A MEZE SPREAD

FOR THE PASTRY:

4 cups (500 g) all-purpose flour

1½ teaspoons baking powder

1 teaspoon salt

1 cup (240 ml) olive oil

1 cup (240 ml) fresh orange juice

FOR THE FILLING:

3 tablespoons olive oil

2 cups (240 g) finely chopped scallions, white
and most of the green parts

3 cups (540 g) juicy black olives, pitted and
coarsely chopped

1 teaspoon dried oregano

¼ cup (15 g) chopped fresh mint leaves

Freshly ground black pepper

⅓ cup (50 g) sesame seeds, soaked in 1 cup
(240 ml) water

Many years ago, during a wine tasting at my friend Roxani Matsa's estate in Kantza, I tried an olive pie with an unusual orange–olive oil crust. It was prepared by Zoe Evangeliou, one of Roxani's neighbors, an exceptional cook. I published the recipe in my newspaper column, adapting it and merging it with a Cypriot olive pie that adds sautéed leeks and plenty of mint to the olives. I used Mrs. Evangeliou's crust, which complemented the filling beautifully. At some point Vali Manouelides, a friend and accomplished cook, created her own variation, basically forming smaller rolls to increase the ratio of crust to filling. I prefer to use scallions instead of leeks in this, my latest version.

Serve as a main course with a salad or soup, like the Nettle Soup with Mushrooms and Yogurt on page 112, or with braised vegetables, like Ratatouille Niçoise (page 152) or okra. You can also cut the pies into bite-size pieces and serve them as an addictive meze.

Make the pastry: In a large bowl, stir together the flour, baking powder, and salt. In another bowl, whisk together the olive oil and orange juice. Add the liquid to the flour mixture and knead briefly to make a soft dough. Cover and let rest while you prepare the filling.

Make the filling: Heat the olive oil in a heavy-bottomed pan over medium heat. Add the scallions and sauté for 4 minutes, or until the scallions soften. Add the olives and the oregano and sauté for 1 minute more. Remove from the heat and stir in the mint and plenty of pepper. Let cool, taste, and adjust the seasoning.

Preheat the oven to 400°F (205°C).

Divide the dough into 4 pieces. Roll out each piece to make a rectangle, about 16 by 4.5 inches (40.5 by 11 cm). Place one-quarter of the filling on each sheet, forming a line in the center of the rectangle. Fold the two long sides to the center to cover, pinching to enclose the stuffing and forming a log.

Drain the sesame seeds and spread them on a tray. Carefully, roll one stuffed log on the sesame seeds so that it gets a seed crust, then transfer to a baking sheet, seam side down. Repeat with the remaining 3 logs.

Bake for about 30 minutes, until the logs are a light golden color. Let cool completely before slicing with a good serrated knife, as it is quite crumbly.

Rolled Pie with Fermented Cabbage, Peppers, Walnuts, and Raisins

Fermented cabbage is a staple in every Balkan home, so using it in a pie filling comes as no surprise. I added sweet peppers and raisins to complement the cabbage's tartness. Instead of the traditional round pie, I prefer to roll it into logs that are sliced into neat pieces with the right combination of crust and filling. I hope you will make the effort to roll your own phyllo, but in case you don't, I give you a trick I learned from Turkish women (see Note); it transforms even the tasteless commercial sheets into an interesting crust.

FOR THE PHYLLO DOUGH (SEE NOTE):

3 cups (375 g) all-purpose or bread flour

1 teaspoon salt

¼ cup (60 ml) olive oil

1½ tablespoons white wine vinegar or cider vinegar

Cornstarch, for rolling

FOR THE FILLING:

¼ cup (60 ml) olive oil, plus more, for brushing

4 scallions, white and most of the green parts, thinly sliced

Salt

2 large red bell peppers, quartered, seeded, and cut into ½-inch (1.3-cm) pieces

2 cups (300 g) Pink Fermented Cabbage (page 40)

1 teaspoon ground turmeric

1 cup (120 g) coarsely chopped walnuts

⅔ cup (100 g) sultanas (golden raisins)

1 cup (60 g) chopped fresh dill

1 to 2 teaspoons smoked paprika

1 to 2 teaspoons Maraş pepper, or a good pinch of crushed red pepper flakes (plenty of freshly ground black pepper works as well)

Greek-style yogurt, for serving

NOTE: *If you make the pie with commercial frozen phyllo, use 6 sheets of the thickest phyllo you can find and thaw it following the instructions on the package. Use 2 sheets for each roll, as described above, brushing them with olive oil. Spread the filling and brush the border with egg wash (see below), then fold and roll. Place the rolls on the pan, prick with a knife or skewer, and brush each roll liberally with egg wash just before baking.*

To make egg wash, whisk together 1 small egg yolk with 3 tablespoons milk or natural yogurt (not thick).

Make the phyllo dough: In the bowl of a stand mixer fitted with the dough hook attachment, combine the flour and salt, make a well in the center, and pour in the olive oil and vinegar. With the machine running slowly, pour in ½ to ⅔ cup (120 to 160 ml) water, as needed, and work the mixture for about 6 minutes to get a smooth, elastic dough. Cover the bowl with plastic wrap and let the dough rest for at least 15 minutes and up to 2 hours.

Divide the dough into 6 pieces, shape each piece into a ball, cover, and let rest for 10 minutes.

Sprinkle your work surface and one piece of dough with cornstarch. Roll the dough out to make an almost round sheet, about 16 inches (40.5 cm) in diameter (for detailed instructions on rolling phyllo, see page 36). Move the sheet onto a cloth and roll a second sheet. Keep the unrolled dough covered.

Make the filling: Heat ¼ cup (60 ml) of the olive oil in a deep skillet over medium heat. Add the scallions, sprinkle with 1 teaspoon salt, and sauté for 3 minutes. Add the bell peppers and sauté for 6 minutes, or until they soften and start to color. Add the cabbage and turmeric. Sauté for 3 minutes more. Remove from the heat and add the walnuts, sultanas, and dill, stirring to mix. Add as much paprika, Maraş pepper, or any other pepper as you like; taste and correct the seasoning, probably adding more salt.

Preheat the oven to 375°F (190°C). Line a baking sheet with parchment paper.

Brush one rolled phyllo sheet with olive oil and stretch it a little from the top and bottom to make it oval. Place the second sheet over it, stretch it to take the form of the previous sheet, and brush with olive oil. Spread one-third of the filling evenly over the phyllo, leaving about 1 inch (2.5 cm) between the filling and the edge of the oval. Fold the border on the two longer sides over the filling. Starting from the bottom, fold and roll, brushing the top with olive oil as you roll the sheet, to make a log about 13 inches (33 cm) long. Place it on the lined baking sheet, seam side down.

Roll two more pieces of phyllo dough into sheets. Stretch and oil them as for the first roll and proceed to fill and roll as before. Place the finished second roll on the baking sheet at least 1½ inches (4 cm) from the first, then repeat with the remaining dough and filling to make a third log. Using the tip of a knife or a skewer, prick the logs in several places.

Bake for 30 minutes, or until golden brown. Let cool at least 10 minutes before cutting crosswise into slices.

Serve warm or at room temperature, with thick yogurt.

You can freeze the uncut cooled pie logs in a zip-top bag. Reheat them right from the freezer, wrapped loosely in aluminum foil, in a preheated 350°F (175°C) oven, for about 20 minutes. Unwrap and bake for 10 to 15 minutes more, until crisp.

Spinach, Herb, and Feta Skillet Pies (*Gözleme*)

SERVES 6

FOR THE PHYLLO DOUGH:

3 cups (375 g) all-purpose flour

1 teaspoon salt

¼ cup (60 ml) olive oil

1½ tablespoons white wine vinegar or cider vinegar

Cornstarch, for rolling

FOR THE STUFFING:

1 cup (30 g) wilted spinach leaves, squeezed dry and finely chopped (see Note)

1 cup (30 g) finely chopped fresh parsley leaves

½ cup (15 g) finely chopped fresh dill

1 teaspoon dried Greek oregano

2 tablespoons olive oil, plus more to brush the phyllo

1 cup (120 g) crumbled feta

Freshly ground black pepper

Olive oil, for brushing

Greek-style yogurt, for serving (optional)

Next to the popular markets in Istanbul, and in most other Turkish cities and villages, there is usually a lady preparing *gözleme*. She sits on the floor, rolling phyllo (or *yufka*, as it is called in Turkish) on a *sofra*—a large, low, round wooden table. Next to her burns a makeshift charcoal stove with a piping-hot *saç* griddle, a large concave drum blackened and shiny from years of constant use. With these humble instruments she creates the most tempting street food the market has to offer. My version of *gözleme*, a delicious skillet pie, is simple to make, provided you can roll phyllo. If you have a pasta machine it is easy to make your own thin phyllo strips and to create rectangular or square *gözleme*. They may look different than the traditional pies, but they will be equally delicious.

Make the phyllo and divide as described on page 177.

Make the stuffing: Squeeze small handfuls of spinach to extract all the moisture and transfer to a medium bowl. Add the parsley, dill, oregano, and olive oil and rub the mixture with your fingers for a couple of minutes to combine and wilt the herbs. Add the feta and pepper to taste, toss well to mix, cover, and set aside.

Assemble the *gözleme*: If rolling by hand, take one of the 6 balls of dough, keeping the rest covered, and sprinkle your work surface and the dough with cornstarch. Roll out the dough with a long rolling pin to make an almost round sheet, about 16 inches (40.5 cm) in diameter (for detailed instructions on rolling phyllo, see page 36).

Heat a ridged stovetop grill pan or a large skillet over medium heat. Line a baking sheet with paper towels.

Cut the rolled sheet of phyllo in half. Starting with one of the pieces, brush both sides lightly with olive oil. Spread about 2 tablespoons of the filling evenly over half the surface and then fold the other half over it. Press to extract air bubbles and to smooth the filling. With the help of a large spatula, carefully transfer to the heated grill and toast, cooking for about 4 minutes or until golden and crisp; lift carefully with the spatula to check. Press often with the spatula if it puffs up. Turn over and cook on the other side for 3 to 4 minutes, until golden brown and crisp. Transfer to the lined baking sheet and continue rolling out the phyllo, stuffing it, and toasting all the *gözleme*.

If using a pasta machine: Halve each ball of dough to get 12 pieces and roll each piece through the pasta machine as thin as possible, according to the manufacturer's instructions. Transfer to a large tray lined with a kitchen towel.

Depending on the size of your grill or skillet, cut each long sheet into two or three pieces. Take one piece and brush with olive oil on both sides. Spread the filling over half the surface, fold, press and toast as described above, one or two pieces at a time.

Serve the *gözleme* hot, warm, or at room temperature, accompanied by thick yogurt, if desired.

NOTE: *Instead of spinach you can use any green or a combination of greens: beet greens, arugula, chard, pea shoots, etc.*

Chickpeas and Toasted Bread with Yogurt-Tahini Sauce (*Fattet Hummus*)

SERVES 4 TO 6

FOR THE CHICKPEAS:

¼ cup (60 ml) olive oil

3 cloves garlic, minced

1 teaspoon ground turmeric

3 cups (600 g) precooked chickpeas, preferably not canned (page 35)

½ to 1 teaspoon ground cumin

1 to 2 teaspoons Maraş pepper or a good pinch of crushed red pepper flakes, to taste

1½ cups (360 ml) chickpea cooking broth, or ½ cup (120 ml) white wine and 1 cup (240 ml) vegetable stock or water, plus more as needed

Salt

FOR THE SAUCE:

1½ cups (275 g) Greek-style yogurt

⅔ cup (160 ml) tahini

1 clove garlic, minced

Salt

3 tablespoons fresh lemon juice, or to taste

FOR SERVING:

3 to 4 stale pita breads, preferably whole-grain

2 to 3 slices stale multigrain bread, diced, or barley *paximadia* (page 214)

Good, fruity olive oil, for drizzling

¼ cup (25 g) pine nuts, toasted

Dried oregano, mint, or any dried or fresh herb you like

Maraş pepper or crushed red pepper flakes, for sprinkling

1 or 2 lemons, quartered

Fattet Hummus is "one of the many exquisite Arabic dishes that revolve around day-old bread," writes Annia Ciezadlo in *Day of Honey. Fattet* means "crushed" or "crumb" and refers to the bread pieces that form the base of several ingeniously delicious and frugal dishes. Pieces of stale pita are given new life when toasted. Spread on a platter, they absorb the juices of the chickpeas (*hummus* in Arabic) and complement their earthy flavor. Meat, poultry, fried or stuffed eggplants, and many other combinations of ingredients go well with the chickpeas. After countless experiments, I've settled on a combination of pita and cubes of toasted multigrain bread—the combination yields a crunchier, more robust base. This is one of the few dishes in the book that needs to be finished just before serving. But most of its elements—the chickpeas as well as the yogurt-tahini sauce—can be prepared in advance.

Make the chickpeas: Heat the olive oil in a skillet over medium heat. Add the garlic, turmeric, chickpeas, cumin, and Maraş pepper. Toss a few times until the garlic starts to sizzle. Add the broth and salt to taste. Bring to a boil, reduce the heat, and simmer for 15 minutes, or until the chickpeas are tender and about 1 cup (240 ml) broth is left in the pan. Remove from the heat, taste, and adjust the seasoning. Cover and set aside until needed.

Make the sauce: In a bowl, stir together the yogurt and the tahini. Add the garlic, salt to taste, and lemon juice. Taste and adjust the seasoning. Stir in 2 to 3 tablespoons water to thin the sauce just to the point that it is pourable. Cover and store in the refrigerator until needed.

To finish and serve: Preheat the broiler.

Open the pita (divide them horizontally) and crumble into large pieces or cut them in triangles or ribbons. Spread them on a baking sheet with the cubed bread. Place under the broiler and toast for 2 minutes, toss, and broil for 1 to 2 minutes more, until deep golden brown. Line the bottom of a deep serving dish with most of the toasted pita and bread, reserving a handful to garnish.

Meanwhile, gently reheat the chickpeas, adding more broth if they look dry. There should be ⅔ to 1 cup (160 to 240 ml) broth in the pan. Spoon the chickpeas and broth evenly over the toasted bread. Stir the yogurt-tahini sauce and pour it over the chickpeas. Drizzle with good, fruity olive oil; sprinkle with pine nuts, oregano, and Maraş pepper and garnish with the reserved pita and bread. Serve immediately in soup plates or bowls, passing a bottle of good, fruity olive oil and additional herbs, Maraş pepper, and lemon quarters at the table.

Milk, Herb, and Scallion Baked Rice (Stamatia's Greek-Albanian *Briani*) GLUTEN-FREE

SERVES 6

½ cup (120 ml) olive oil, plus more for drizzling

1½ cups (160 g) finely chopped scallions, white and most of the green parts

1 to 2 jalapeños, seeded and finely chopped (optional), or ½ teaspoon freshly ground black pepper

1 cup (60 g) chopped fresh dill

2 quarts (2 L) whole milk

2 cups (200 g) medium-grain rice, such as Arborio or any risotto rice

Salt

You never quite outgrow this Balkan comfort food. I make it often, following the recipe of my friend Stamatia, who comes from an ethnic Greek village in southern Albania. Our friends love it as much as her young grandsons, who ask her to make it for them every time they visit. What follows is the "poor-man's" version, but the flavors are rich despite their humble origins. *Briani* was also made with chopped lamb's liver; Stamatia's grandmother even made it with eel, whenever they happened to catch one in the local stream! It was customary to flavor the meat versions with chervil and green fenugreek instead of dill. The chiles are my humble addition. I always prepare it well in advance and let it cool before serving, which allows the flavors to come together.

Preheat the oven to 375°F (190°C) with a rack in the middle.

In a large skillet, heat the olive oil over medium heat. Add the scallions and jalapeños (if using) and sauté until just soft, about 4 minutes. Add the dill and toss for 30 seconds, then remove from the heat.

Heat the milk in a small saucepan to just below boiling.

Spread the rice in a 13-by-9-inch (33-by-23-cm) glass or clay baking dish and add the scallions, dill, and 1½ teaspoons salt. Add about half the hot milk and stir to mix.

Transfer the dish to the oven and carefully stir in the remaining milk.

Bake for 15 minutes, then reduce the oven temperature to 300°F (150°C). Continue baking for 15 minutes more. Most of the milk will have been absorbed, but the rice will be quite wet. Remove from the heat and let cool for at least 20 minutes. It will set, but will be quite creamy. Serve warm or at room temperature.

Toasted Bulgur Pilaf VEGAN

SERVES 3 TO 4

2 medium tomatoes, quartered, or 1 cup (120 g) canned tomatoes with their juices

1 small onion, quartered

¼ cup (60 ml) olive oil

1 teaspoon Maraş pepper, or a good pinch of crushed red pepper flakes, to taste

1½ cups (210 g) coarse bulgur

Salt

Freshly ground black pepper (optional)

Good, fruity olive oil, for drizzling

Bulgur was once the predominant grain of the eastern Mediterranean. It was used for all kinds of pilafs, as a thickener for soups and stews, and in salads and stuffings, much like rice today. Bulgur is a precooked and dried cracked wheat, so it cooks fast and is ideal if you want to prepare a quick and nourishing main course or side dish. You have to use coarse bulgur for pilaf and for any stuffing, while classic Lebanese *tabouleh* is made with fine bulgur.

Freekeh or *fireek* (see Sources, page 246)—the bulgurlike cracked grains from green, unripe wheat—are cooked in a similar way. The immature grains are roasted over an open fire to remove the chaff; the process gives freekeh its subtle and smoky flavor. Unlike bulgur, freekeh is not precooked, so it takes longer to prepare. Freekeh and bulgur pilaf can be used interchangeably. Millet is another grain that you can cook in the same way.

Serve with Okra and Zucchini in Harissa-Tomato Sauce (page 144) or with any braised vegetable dish, with Eggplants *Imam Bayeldi* (page 159), or serve the pilaf with slices of grilled halloumi, if you like.

In a blender, puree the tomatoes, onion, olive oil, and Maraş pepper. Measure and add about 1 cup (240 ml) water, as needed, to make a 2½-cup (600-ml) liquid mixture.

Heat a medium saucepan over medium-high heat and add the bulgur. Toast in the pan, stirring frequently, for about 3 minutes, until it starts to color and smell nutty. Reduce the heat to low, pour in the tomato mixture, and stir. Add some salt and simmer for about 7 minutes, until the bulgur is al dente. Add a little more water if the bulgur is too dry. Remove from the heat, cover, and let rest for 7 to 10 minutes more.

Taste and correct the seasoning with salt, Maraş pepper, and black pepper, if desired. Fluff with a fork and serve, drizzled with good, fruity olive oil.

Camargue Risotto with Leeks, Mushrooms, Fresh Fava Beans, and Cilantro VEGAN GLUTEN-FREE

SERVES 3 TO 4

⅓ cup (80 ml) olive oil

1 leek, white and tender green parts, thinly sliced

½ cup (35 g) chopped dried porcini mushrooms, soaked in warm water for 30 minutes

2 cups (200 g) red rice, preferably from Camargue

2½ cups (600 ml) boiling vegetable broth or water

Salt

½ to 1 teaspoon Maraş pepper or a good pinch of crushed red pepper flakes, to taste

Freshly ground black pepper (optional)

3 cups (360 g) fresh (or frozen) shelled fava beans, blanched for 1 minute, drained, and peeled (see Note)

1 cup (60 g) chopped fresh cilantro or ½ cup (30 g) chopped fresh flat-leaf parsley

Good, fruity olive oil, for drizzling

¼ cup (25 g) pine nuts, toasted, or coarsely ground walnuts

South of Arles, in Provence, the legendary wetlands of Camargue produce a superb red long-grain rice. Grown in Europe's largest delta, the rice tastes incredibly nutty and lends itself to all kinds of dishes, warm or cold. Less known than the Italian Arborio or the Spanish Calasparra and Bomba—all medium-grain rices—the red long-grains of Camargue are easier to cook. They don't require constant stirring and retain their shape and bite beautifully. This recipe is simple, and you can use it as the base to create your own variations with seasonal vegetables, greens, and herbs, or with dried fruits and nuts.

Heat the olive oil in a heavy-bottomed pan over medium heat. Add the leeks and sauté for 6 minutes, or until they soften. Drain the mushrooms, reserving their soaking water, and add them to the pan. Cook for 3 minutes more. Using a slotted spoon, transfer the leeks and mushrooms to a bowl and set aside.

Add the rice to the hot pan and sauté for 8 minutes. Pour in 2 cups (480 ml) of the broth, the leeks, mushrooms, and the reserved mushroom liquid. Reduce the heat, add salt and Maraş pepper, and simmer for 15 to 20 minutes. Check often and add more broth as needed until the rice is al dente. Taste and correct the seasoning, adding more salt and black pepper, if you like.

Stir in the fava beans and cilantro. Plate the risotto, drizzle with good, fruity olive oil, and sprinkle pine nuts over each serving.

NOTE: If fava beans are not available, you can use peas or flageolet beans.

Linguine with Spicy Lentils and Caramelized Onions VEGAN

SERVES 3 TO 4

½ cup (120 ml) olive oil, plus more for serving

2 large onions, halved lengthwise and thinly sliced into half-moons

3 cups (660 g) cooked green or brown lentils (see Note)

1 tablespoon ground turmeric

1½ cups (360 ml) dry red wine

2 tablespoons red wine vinegar

1 teaspoon freshly ground black pepper, plus more for serving

2 to 3 teaspoons Lebanese Seven-Spice Blend (page 54), to taste

Salt

1 pound (500 g) linguine

1 cup (60 g) chopped fresh cilantro

1 cup (120 g) crumbled feta or grated pecorino, for serving (optional)

Fried onions and lentils, scented with Lebanese Seven-Spice Mix, make for a fantastic pasta sauce. This recipe is inspired by *rishta-bil-adas* (Lebanese pasta with lentils) from Arto der Haroutounian's *Vegetarian Dishes from the Middle East*. In that traditional recipe, equal amounts of pasta and lentils are cooked together. The combination of pasta and lentils is less common than *mujadara* (rice with lentils), but equally enticing. Lebanese seven-spice blend is available from any Middle Eastern store, but you can easily make your own.

Serve with a green salad enriched with fermented cabbage (page 40) or with steamed spinach, chard, or a combination of greens, dressed simply with olive oil and lemon.

In a large, deep skillet with a lid, heat the olive oil over medium-high heat. Add the onions and sauté for 8 minutes, or until soft. Add the lentils and turmeric and sauté for 3 to 5 minutes more, until the onions start to color. Add the wine, ½ cup (120 ml) water, the vinegar, and pepper and stir. Reduce the heat to low, cover, and simmer for 8 to 10 minutes, until the lentils and onions are soft and the sauce has thickened. Add the seven-spice blend and stir.

Meanwhile, bring a large pot of salted water to a boil and cook the pasta according to the package directions until just al dente. Just before draining the pasta, add ½ cup (120 ml) of the cooking liquid to the onion mixture and bring to a boil. Drain the pasta in a colander and drizzle it with oil. Add the pasta to the onion and lentils and toss well. Remove from the heat, add the cilantro, and toss again. Cover and let stand for 2 minutes.

To serve, sprinkle with feta (if using), and pepper.

NOTE: *To prepare the lentils: Wash and drain 1½ cups (330 g) lentils. Add to a saucepan, pour in water to cover, bring to a boil, reduce the heat, and cook for about 20 minutes, until the lentils are almost cooked. Drain, and continue with the recipe instructions above.*

Eggplant and Walnut *Pastitsio* with Olive Oil and Yogurt Béchamel

SERVES 4 TO 5

3 long Japanese eggplants (about 1 pound/500 g total; see Notes)

Salt

½ cup (120 ml) olive oil, or as needed

1 medium onion, halved and thinly sliced into half-moons

3 tablespoons all-purpose flour

1 cup (240 ml) whole milk

1 cup (240 ml) full-fat natural yogurt (not thick)

1 teaspoon ground cumin, or more to taste

1 to 2 teaspoons Maraş pepper, or a good pinch of crushed red pepper flakes

1½ cups (150 g) *ditalini* pasta or small elbow macaroni

½ cup (60 g) coarsely chopped walnuts

1 cup (120 g) crumbled feta

Freshly ground black pepper

2 eggs, lightly beaten

3 tablespoons grated pecorino or aged cheddar

Pastitsio didn't enter my pantheon of dishes, ironically, until it left Greece. Faye Levy's recipe for Macaroni and Eggplant *Kugel*, on the *Jerusalem Post* website, helped me to reinvent a Greek classic as a simple and vegetarian *pastitsio*. She suggests making the béchamel together with the sautéed onions, which leaves one less pan to clean. But more important, Levy suggests baking the dish in a bain-marie, which creates a creamy and moist *pastitsio*, a far cry for the dry baked pasta that has become all too common with traditional *pastitsio*.

Serve with a tomato or mixed green salad and fermented cabbage (page 40).

Preheat the oven to 400°F (205°C). Line a baking sheet with parchment paper.

Cut 6 round slices, about ⅓ inch (0.8 cm) thick, from one of the eggplants (to use later in assembling the dish). Halve lengthwise the eggplant from which you cut the rounds. Cut the two halves into ⅓-inch (0.8-cm) slices. Halve the second and third eggplants lengthwise (you will not cut any rounds from these eggplants). Cut the eggplant halves into ⅓-inch (0.8-cm) slices. Transfer all the eggplant pieces, including the round slices, to a large bowl, sprinkle with 1 teaspoon salt and 3 tablespoons of the olive oil, and toss well to coat on all sides, adding more olive oil, if needed.

Spread the eggplant on the lined baking sheet. Roast in the lower part of the oven for 15 to 20 minutes, until golden brown and tender. Remove the eggplant from the oven, but leave the oven on. Set aside the round slices. (For a variation on cooking the eggplant, see Notes.)

In a deep, heavy-bottomed skillet, heat 3 tablespoons of the olive oil over medium heat. Add the onions and sauté for 10 minutes, or until the onions soften. Add the flour and stir with a wooden spoon until frothy—be careful not to let the flour burn. Pour in the milk, stir, and add the yogurt. Cook, stirring continuously, for about 5 minutes, until the yogurt béchamel thickens. Remove from the heat, add the cumin and Maraş pepper, toss to mix, and transfer to a large bowl.

Bring a large pot of salted water to a boil. Cook the pasta until al dente, about 30 seconds less than the package suggests. Drain the pasta and pass the colander under cold running water to stop the cooking—the pasta will finish cooking in the oven. Drain well and transfer to the onion-béchamel mixture. Add the eggplant pieces (excluding the round slices) and the walnuts. Stir in the feta, toss carefully but well, and taste to adjust the seasoning with more cumin, Maraş pepper, salt, and black pepper.

Oil a 9-inch (23-cm) round pan.

Fold the eggs into the pasta mixture, stir to combine, and pour into the oiled pan. Top with the reserved eggplant slices, drizzle with a little olive oil, and sprinkle with the grated pecorino.

Set the pan in a large, deep roasting pan and place in the lower half of the oven. Pour enough boiling water into the roasting pan to come halfway up the sides of the *pastitsio* dish. Bake for 35 to 40 minutes. The *pastitsio* should be set and golden brown and bubbling on top. Let cool for 10 minutes on a rack and serve hot.

NOTES: *I suggest long eggplants because the pieces will not fall apart as they bake with the pasta. Dice the round large eggplants; any kind of eggplant you find will work well and taste wonderful.*

Instead of baking, you can stir-fry the eggplants in batches.

VARIATION

PEPPER, MUSHROOM, AND WALNUT *PASTITSIO*

Omit the eggplants.

Soak 1 cup (70 g) dried porcini mushrooms in ½ cup (120 ml) hot water for 15 minutes. Halve, seed, and dice 5 green or red bell peppers, or a combination, and sauté in 2 to 3 tablespoons olive oil until soft. Chop the mushrooms with scissors and add to the peppers, together with their strained soaking liquid. Sauté for 2 minutes more.

Cook the onions, prepare the béchamel and pasta, and bake the *pastitsio* as described above.

Orzo Risotto with Garlic, Herbs, and Tomatoes

SERVES 4 TO 5

About ⅓ cup (80 ml) olive oil

1 cup (120 g) finely chopped onions

4 cloves garlic, thinly sliced

1 pound (500 g) orzo

½ cup (120 ml) white wine

Salt

7 to 8 cups (1.7 to 2 L) very hot vegetable
broth (page 60)

1 to 2 teaspoons Maraş pepper or a
good pinch of crushed red pepper
flakes, to taste

½ cup (30 g) chopped fresh flat-leaf parsley

3 tablespoons chopped fresh dill

½ cup (30 g) chopped fresh basil leaves

3 tablespoons chopped fresh mint

2 tablespoons chopped fresh oregano
or thyme

12 pieces Tomato Confit (page 27; see Note)

1 cup (120 g) crumbled feta cheese, plus
more for serving

Freshly ground black pepper

3 to 4 tablespoons chopped fresh cilantro
(optional)

You can cook almost any kind of pasta with vegetables in broth as if it were rice, but the pasta called orzo in the United States—from the Italian word for barley—is really ideal for that purpose. I often whip up this kind of pasta-risotto just before lunch, with any combination of herbs from the garden and the intensely flavored tomato confit I keep in the freezer. This dish is inspired by *skordomakarona*, a soupy, broken spaghetti cooked in garlicky tomato sauce, which was a frequent frugal staple of my youth. In the summer I make the orzo with fresh, vine-ripened tomatoes from the garden (see Note).

Serve with a green salad, roasted or fried vegetables, or steamed or braised greens.

In a saucepan, heat the olive oil over medium heat. Add the onions and sauté for about 5 minutes. Add the garlic and orzo and sauté for 5 minutes more, or until the orzo is shiny and sizzling. Pour in the wine, add salt to taste, and cook, stirring, for about 30 seconds. Pour in 3 cups (720 ml) of the hot broth and add the Maraş pepper, to taste. Cook, stirring often and adding more broth as the pasta absorbs the liquid, until the orzo is almost cooked, about 15 minutes more. Fold in the herbs and cook for 3 minutes more. Add the tomatoes, stir, and remove from the heat. Fold in the feta, taste, and correct the seasoning, finishing with black pepper and a sprinkle of cilantro, if you like.

Serve immediately with a bowl of feta on the side.

NOTE: *When they are in season, substitute 2 cups (240 g) fresh, diced, vine-ripened tomatoes for the Tomato Confit. I don't peel or seed my tomatoes; when tomatoes are in season, I don't dare to lose even a drop of their delicious flesh and flavor.*

Green Risotto with Garlic, Herbs, and Lime GLUTEN-FREE

SERVES 4 TO 6 AS MAIN COURSE,
OR 6 TO 8 AS A SIDE DISH

About ⅓ cup (80 ml) olive oil

1½ cups (240 g) finely chopped onions

3 cloves garlic, thinly sliced

2 cups (200 g) Arborio or other good-quality medium-grain rice

½ cup (120 ml) white wine

Salt

About 2 quarts (2 L) very hot vegetable broth (page 60; see Note)

1 cup (60 g) finely chopped fresh flat-leaf parsley

⅔ cup (40 g) finely chopped fresh dill

¼ cup (15 g) finely chopped fresh basil leaves

3 tablespoons finely chopped fresh mint

2 tablespoons finely chopped fresh oregano or thyme, or 1 teaspoon dried

3 tablespoons chopped fresh cilantro (optional)

½ to 1 teaspoon freshly ground black pepper, to taste

2 to 3 tablespoons lime or lemon juice, or more to taste

½ cup (50 g) grated Parmesan, grana, or aged *graviera*, plus more for serving

Good, fruity olive oil, for drizzling

1 lime or lemon, quartered

I fondly remember a light and delicious herb-lime risotto I enjoyed one sunny September day a few years ago. I was at La Fenière, Reine Sammut's celebrated hotel and restaurant in Loumarin, Provence, and it was one of the dishes on her Mediterranean olive oil tasting lunch. She served the risotto topped with thin strips of braised cuttlefish, drizzled with a few drops of its deep-black ink sauce. The seafood was excellent, but the fragrant, fruity rice was the real revelation for me. I didn't get Sammut's recipe, just a description, so this is my own rendition of the dish, using all or some of the herbs on the list, whatever my garden provides. When I don't have fresh herbs I use frozen ones or an herb paste (see page 29).

Serve with grilled halloumi or with fried or poached eggs. Also consider a nice salad like Steamed Zucchini and Roasted Peppers (page 100) or Orange, Olive, and Baby Leek Salad with *Verjus*-Tarragon Dressing (page 194).

In a saucepan, heat the olive oil over medium heat. Add the onions and sauté for about 5 minutes. Add the garlic and rice and sauté for 3 to 4 minutes more, until the rice is shiny and sizzling.

Pour in the wine, add salt to taste, and cook, stirring, for 30 seconds or so, until the wine has evaporated. Pour in 1 cup (240 ml) of the hot broth and cook, stirring frequently and adding more of the broth by the ladle as the rice absorbs the liquid, until the rice is almost cooked, about 15 minutes.

Fold in the herbs and cook for 4 to 5 minutes more, until the rice is al dente. Remove from the heat. Add the pepper and lime juice, fold in the cheese, and taste to correct the seasoning.

Finish with a drizzle of good, fruity olive oil and serve immediately with lime quarters and extra grated cheese on the side.

NOTE: *Instead of vegetable broth, soak ½ cup (35 g) dried porcini mushrooms in warm water for 20 minutes. Chop them finely with scissors and add to the rice with their strained liquid, after the wine has evaporated. Cook the risotto as described above, adding boiling water in place of stock as needed.*

MORE THAN JUST POLENTA:
MAMALIGA AND *KAÇAMAK*

Balkan polenta is made with a coarse yellow cornmeal, though still finer than the grains used for the Italian dish. Balkan *mamaliga*, as it is called, is usually served mixed with a rich dairy product: Sheep's-milk butter or a combination of buttermilk and feta are both common. The thickened porridge can also be baked, layered with a tomato or meat sauce and spicy cheese. Another popular preparation involves forming the *mamaliga* into balls, stuffed with cheese or sausage, which are then fried, much like Sicilian *arancini*.

Leftover cornmeal porridge can be cut into pieces and served with bean soups and stews. If you are feeling decadent, you can fry the pieces and serve them soaked in creamy homemade sheep's-milk yogurt, my Albanian neighbor's favorite dinner.

Called *kaçamak* in Turkish and *katsamaki* in Greece, cornmeal porridge used to be a common nourishing breakfast served to both kids and adults. In Greece it is usually eaten just with butter, while in Turkey it is topped with a tomato sauce spiced with pepper flakes and crumbled feta. In Bosnia and Herzegovina *kaçamak* is a main course of boiled potatoes mashed and cooked together with cornmeal, then flavored with olive oil or butter and feta chese.

Balkan Polenta with Feta GLUTEN-FREE

SERVES 4 TO 6

1¼ cups (200 g) yellow cornmeal

1 quart (1 L) vegetable broth
  (page 60)

½ cup (120 ml) olive oil

1 cup (240 ml) yogurt

2 cups (240 g) crumbled feta

Freshly ground black pepper

Salt

Good, fruity olive oil, for drizzling

Braised Kale with Peppers
  (page 151; shown opposite, optional)

I make polenta with yellow cornmeal following the Balkan tradition, but also because the Italian "polenta" I find in Greece is of the instant variety, which I find unacceptable for most dishes. I cook polenta in vegetable broth with olive oil, and as I take it off the heat I fold in some yogurt and crumbled feta. It is my favorite comfort food, and I love it cooked with slightly bitter, hearty greens like rapini or turnip tops (see Variation, below). I often enjoy it with a leftover vegetable or meat sauce.

Serve with braised kale or with tomato sauce (page 61) and roasted vegetables (page 147).

In a bowl, mix the cornmeal with 1½ cups (360 ml) cold water and let stand for 5 minutes.

Meanwhile, bring the broth to a boil. Add the cornmeal mixture and cook, stirring frequently, for about 12 minutes. Add the oil and cook for 5 minutes more, or until the mixture has thickened. Remove from the heat and fold in the yogurt and feta. Taste and adjust the seasoning with pepper and salt, if necessary—feta is quite salty, so the polenta may not need extra salt.

Serve immediately, drizzled with fruity olive oil and topped with braised kale, if you like.

VARIATION

POLENTA WITH RAPINI OR TURNIP TOPS (*POLENTA CON BROCCOLETTI*)

1 pound (500 g) broccoli rabe (rapini) or
  turnip tops, washed, drained, and
  coarsely chopped (stems included)

FOR THE TOPPING:

¼ cup (60 ml) olive oil

4 cloves garlic, halved and thinly sliced

1 to 2 teaspoons Maraş pepper or a good
  pinch of crushed red pepper flakes, to taste

4 to 5 anchovy fillets (optional)

½ cup (120 ml) white wine

Salt (optional)

2 tablespoons fresh thyme, marjoram, or
  oregano leaves

In a bowl, mix the cornmeal with 1½ cups (360 ml) cold water and let stand for 5 minutes. Bring 1 quart (1 L) water to a boil, and add the rapini or turnip tops and the cornmeal mixture. Cook as described above, adding the olive oil and folding in the yogurt and feta.

To make the topping, heat the oil in a small skillet. Sauté the garlic very briefly until fragrant, then add the Maraş pepper and the anchovy fillets (if using). Toss and mash together with a wooden spoon. Pour in the wine, and as it bubbles, remove the pan from the heat. Add salt if you have not used anchovies, and mix in the herbs. Drizzle the topping over the cooked polenta and greens and serve immediately.

Black-Eyed Peas with Greens, Tomatoes, and Toasted Olive Bread Crumbs VEGAN

SERVES 4 TO 5

1½ cups (240 g) dried black-eyed peas, picked over and rinsed

1 pound (500 g) tender greens (amaranth shoots, Swiss chard, or spinach), stems chopped, large leaves cut into 2-inch (5-cm) strips, stems and leaves kept separate

Salt

3 to 4 tablespoons fresh lemon juice

Good, fruity olive oil, for drizzling

1 tablespoon Aegean Herb and Hot Pepper Mix (page 55), or 1 tablespoon dried Greek oregano and 1 to 2 teaspoons Maraş pepper

2 cups (300 g) cherry tomatoes, halved or quartered

3 to 4 tablespoons toasted Bread Crumbs with Olives (page 59)

Today black-eyed peas (or beans) are often considered the black sheep of the bean family, overshadowed by more noble beans from the New World. Probably first cultivated in western Africa, then Asia and the Mediterranean, black-eyed peas are related to the yard-long beans of Asia. They are Old World legumes that were brought to the American South in the eighteenth century by settlers from Africa and Europe. To the traditional Cypriot recipe, *Louvia me Lahana* (black-eyed peas with greens), an earthy combination of peas or beans with sweet leafy greens, lemon, and fruity olive oil, I have added a few tomatoes for freshness and spicy toasted olive bread crumbs for zest and crunch.

Serve with feta, fresh goat's cheese, or grilled halloumi and toasted pita.

Place the peas in a medium saucepan, add cold water to cover by 3 inches (7.5 cm), and bring to a boil. Cook for 5 minutes, drain, and return the peas to the pan. Add fresh water just to cover the peas and return to a boil. Reduce the heat to low, cover, and simmer for 20 minutes, or until the peas are tender. Check often and add a little more water if necessary to keep the peas covered.

Add the stems of the greens and salt to taste and simmer for 4 minutes more. You should have about 1½ cups (360 ml) broth in the pan. If you have more, increase the heat and cook until it has reduced. Add the leaves of the greens and cook for 2 minutes more, or until just wilted. Add the lemon juice, stir, and remove from the heat.

Drizzle the *louvia* with olive oil and sprinkle with the spice blend. Transfer to a platter and serve warm or at room temperature, topped with the tomatoes and sprinkled with the bread crumbs.

BREADS & BISCOTTI

Prozymi is shrouded in secrecy. What goes into the starter for an excellent sourdough? You can ask around, but in Greece you're likely to receive evasive answers. Many Greek women believe that bread rises by divine intervention. They are certain that only the direct power of God can turn a mere flour batter into a leavening medium. Similar beliefs are shared all around the Mediterranean and have changed little through the ages. This is the reason why *prozymi*, the natural sourdough starter used in traditional baking, is always made either on September 14—the day the Greek Orthodox Church celebrates the discovery of the cross on which Jesus was crucified—or near the end of Holy Week, preceding Easter. On both occasions, some plants or flowers are added to the flour and water mixture.

I regularly bake the whole-wheat bread we consume, using a sour, old dough starter that I began a long time ago by fermenting honey with barley flour. Bread comes in many different forms from France to Croatia to Turkey, but everywhere, especially in the eastern Mediterranean, it still is the most basic food. Meze and main courses alike are always complemented with bread or pita—it is important to have good bread at all times. There is great artisanal bread readily available in the United States; still, I decided to offer a few of my favorite simple recipes to cooks who are not experienced bakers. Easy, hearty, whole-grain breads, scented with Mediterranean aromatics and flavored with olive oil, vegetables, fruit, and cheese, will increasingly find their way into your oven.

Besides bread, I have recipes for *paximadia* (barley rusks), *friselle*, and other savory biscotti. A favorite is the recipe for crunchy, twice-baked olive oil biscuits—savory and sweet flavored breads that can accompany coffee, drinks, meze spreads, salads, and soups.

LEFT: *Dough and toppings for Lagana with Dried Figs, Roquefort and Rosemary, and with Kumquat and Smoked Cheese (pages 202–203).*

Basic Bread Loaf, Baked in a Casserole VEGAN

MAKES 1 LARGE LOAF

3 cups (375 g) all-purpose flour, plus more as needed

1½ cups (210 g) bread flour or fine semolina

2½ cups (300 g) whole-wheat flour

½ cup (75 g) barley or rye flour

1½ envelopes (3¼ teaspoons/10 g) instant active-dry yeast

2 teaspoons coarse sea salt or kosher salt

1 tablespoon Spices for Bread (page 54), or 2 teaspoons ground coriander seeds and 2 teaspoons ground aniseeds

½ teaspoon ground black pepper

Olive oil

This is our everyday bread, which I like to bake inside a heated clay casserole or Dutch oven. The baking dish makes a big difference in the texture of the loaf. A Dutch oven keeps the moisture inside longer, and so the bread develops a nice chewy crumb and a thick crust. Preparing the dough the night before and leaving it to rise slowly in the refrigerator allows the bread to develop a fuller taste, even when made with instant yeast. I usually keep a piece of dough in the refrigerator to make sourdough starter, two days before baking. The spices I use, inspired by Greek festive breads, give it a very satisfying, slightly smoky aroma. Since it is a large loaf, I suggest you halve it after it cools, and if you are not going to eat it within three days, it is better to freeze one piece. The slices make delicious, hearty toasts, which I love to eat drizzled with good, fruity olive oil and topped with some of my bitter orange marmalade (page 238).

In the bowl of a stand mixer fitted with a dough hook or in a food processor, mix the flours, yeast, salt, spices, and pepper.

With the motor running, slowly add water, about 3½ cups (840 ml) or as needed, to make a soft dough. Work for about 6 minutes, until the dough is soft and slightly sticky and "cleans" the sides of the bowl.

Lightly oil a bowl and a piece of plastic wrap. With lightly floured hands, shape the dough into a ball and transfer to the oiled bowl. Cover with the oiled plastic wrap, place in the refrigerator, and let rise overnight.

Let the dough come to room temperature (about 2 hours) before proceeding further.

Lightly flour your work surface. Turn the dough out and knead briefly. Choose a bowl that is roughly the size of the casserole you will use to bake the bread in and line it with a large piece of parchment paper. Shape the dough into a ball and place it on the paper, inside the bowl; I usually put it seam side up. Cover loosely with plastic wrap and leave to rise for 40 minutes.

At least 20 minutes before baking the bread, place a 9-to-10-inch-deep (23-to-25-cm-deep) clay or cast-iron Dutch oven with a lid in the middle of the oven and preheat the oven to 400°F (205°C).

Very carefully, with thick oven mitts, transfer the hot casserole to a heatproof surface; uncover carefully, resting the lid on a heatproof surface as well. Discard the plastic over the dough and, holding the corners of the paper, lift the bread and transfer it to the hot casserole. Using scissors, cut a deep cross on the surface of the loaf, cover with the lid, and transfer back to the center of the oven.

Bake for 40 minutes. Uncover and bake for 15 minutes more. With a thermometer, check the temperature in the center of the bread—it should be 207°F to 212°F (97°C to 100°C).

Carefully remove the casserole from the oven and transfer the bread to a wire rack to cool, discarding the paper. Be very careful how you handle the casserole and the lid—they stay very hot for some time.

When completely cool, slice the bread and serve.

Leftover bread can be frozen. Reheat, directly from the freezer, loosely wrapped in aluminum foil, in a preheated 375°F (190°C) oven for at least 20 minutes, depending on the size of the piece. Open the foil and heat for 5 minutes more to crisp.

Olive Oil Bread and Savory Biscotti with Herbs

MAKES 2 LOAVES

⅔ cup (160 ml) plus 3 tablespoons olive oil, plus more for the bowl

1½ cups (about 100 g) packed coarsely chopped fresh flat-leaf parsley

1 cup (about 100 g) packed coarsely chopped fresh dill

2 tablespoons coarsely ground fennel seeds

4 cups (500 g) all-purpose flour, plus more for kneading

1 envelope (2¼ teaspoons/7 g) instant active-dry yeast

1½ teaspoons coarse sea salt or kosher salt

½ to 1 teaspoon freshly ground black pepper, to taste

⅔ cup (88 g) coarsely chopped walnuts (optional)

3 tablespoons milk or cream, for brushing (optional)

Think about this as an aromatic, fragrantly spicy olive oil brioche. It is an ideal bread for sandwiches that adds—and isn't merely a vehicle for—flavors. I often shape the dough into long baguettes, which I bake, slice, and bake again in a slow oven to dry completely and make crunchy, savory biscotti (see Rosemary-Scented Cornmeal Biscotti with Nuts, page 218).

Serve these biscotti as a snack or as an appetizer with drinks, ricotta, or any fresh or aged cheese. They also pair very well with coffee and quince preserves (page 236) as a dessert.

In a large skillet, heat 2 tablespoons of the oil over medium heat. Add the parsley and dill and sauté briefly, until just wilted, about 2 minutes. Transfer to a food processor, add ½ cup (120 ml) water and the fennel seeds, and process until smooth. Transfer the parsley mixture to a medium bowl and clean the bowl of the food processor.

Combine the flour, yeast, salt, and pepper in the food processor or in the bowl of a stand mixer fitted with the dough hook attachment and pulse or mix to blend. With the motor running, pour in the parsley mixture and ⅔ cup (160 ml) of the oil, then slowly add up to 1½ cups (360 ml) water, enough to form a soft dough. Process for about 5 minutes, until the dough "cleans" the sides of the bowl and forms a ball.

Oil a large bowl and a piece of plastic wrap. Lightly flour your work surface. Turn the dough out and knead, adding the walnuts, if using, and more flour if necessary, until smooth and elastic, about 2 minutes. Transfer the dough to the oiled bowl, cover with the oiled plastic wrap, and let rise until doubled in volume, 1½ to 2 hours.

Line 2 loaf pans with parchment paper. Oil 2 pieces of plastic wrap.

Lightly flour your work surface again. Turn the dough out and divide it into 2 pieces. Form each piece into a loaf, cover with oiled plastic wrap, and allow to rise for 30 minutes, until almost doubled in volume.

Alternatively, form the dough into small round, oval, or triangular buns. For the triangles, form two logs, 10 to 12 inches (25 to 35 cm) long, and cut into triangles with a spatula. Place buns on a parchment-lined baking sheet, 1½ to 2 inches (4 to 5 cm) apart. Cover with oiled plastic wrap and let rise for 30 minutes, until almost doubled in volume.

At least 20 minutes before baking, preheat the oven to 375°F (190°C). Brush the tops of the breads with milk or cream, if you like, and use scissors to make a few diagonal cuts 1 inch (2.5 cm) deep on the top of each bread. (Skip this step if you are making buns.) Bake for at least 40 minutes for the loaves, until golden brown and hollow sounding when you tap the bottom (a thermometer inserted in the center should read 205°F to 210°F/95°C to 100°C). The buns should be ready in 25 to 30 minutes. Remove from the oven and transfer the loaves or buns to a wire rack. Let cool completely before slicing to serve.

Flat Bread with Dried Figs, Roquefort Cheese, and Rosemary (*Lagana*)

Bits of zucchini or pepper sautéed with olive oil and garlic, onions, or scallions; shredded garden herbs with salt crystals, Maraş pepper flakes, and poppy or sesame seeds; feta or coarsely ground cheese with nuts or dried fruits: These are the various and versatile toppings for my flat breads—focaccia and *lagana*. The dried figs and Roquefort is one of my most popular toppings. Feel free to try almost any combination, keeping in mind a good blending of flavors. You can balance the tartness of dried apricots and cranberries with creamy *manouri*, ricotta salata, or a robust Gruyère. The possibilities are endless.

FOR THE BREAD DOUGH:

3 cups (375 g) all-purpose flour, plus more as needed

2 cups (280 g) bread flour or fine semolina

2½ cups (300 g) whole-wheat flour

1 envelope (2¼ teaspoons/7 g) instant active-dry yeast

2 teaspoons coarse sea salt or kosher salt

2 teaspoons ground coriander seeds

¼ teaspoon ground mastic

½ teaspoon ground black pepper

Olive oil

FOR THE TOPPING:

About ½ cup (120 ml) milk

About 30 dried figs, sliced

2 cups (270 g) crumbled Roquefort, gorgonzola, or any spicy blue cheese

¼ cup (15 g) chopped fresh rosemary leaves

VARIATION

FOR THE TOPPING:

About ½ cup (120 ml) milk

10 to 12 kumquats

2 cups (270 g) Gouda or another smoked cheese

Serve warm with drinks before the meal, as I usually do, or give the breads center stage for a lunch or dinner, complemented by soup and salad.

Make the bread dough: In the bowl of a stand mixer fitted with the dough hook or in a food processor, mix the flours, yeast, salt, and spices.

With the motor running, add 3 cups (720 ml) water or more to make a soft dough. Work the dough for about 6 minutes, until it is soft and slightly sticky, adding more water if needed.

Oil a large bowl and a piece of plastic wrap. With floured hands, shape the dough into a ball and transfer to the oiled bowl. Cover with the oiled plastic wrap, place in the refrigerator, and let rise overnight. Let the dough come to room temperature (about 2 hours) before proceeding further.

Preheat the oven to 375°F (190°C). Line 2 large baking sheets with parchment paper.

Shape the *laganes*: Lightly flour your work surface. Turn the dough out and knead briefly. Divide in two, cover one piece, and flatten the other to fill the first baking sheet. Stretch and dimple with wet fingers to expand the dough to cover the whole pan. Cover with oiled plastic while you shape and place the next *lagana* on the second baking sheet. Cover and let the dough rise for about 40 minutes.

To top the breads: Brush the breads with milk and divide the fig slices between them, pressing the figs to stick onto the surface of the breads. Sprinkle generously with the cheese and rosemary.

Bake for about 30 minutes, or until the breads are golden at the bottom. If they brown on top but still look uncooked at the bottom, cover loosely with aluminum foil and bake a bit longer.

Let cool on a rack, slice, and serve warm or at room temperature. Leftover bread can be frozen. Reheat directly from the freezer, loosely wrapped in aluminum foil, in a 375°F (190°C) oven for about 20 minutes. Open the foil and heat for 8 to 10 minutes more to caramelize the top.

FLAT BREADS WITH KUMQUAT AND SMOKED CHEESE

Make the dough as directed above. Wash, dry, and halve the kumquats. With a spoon remove and discard the bitter flesh (or use it to flavor the orange cake syrup, see page 230). Cut the skin into slivers.

Shape the flat breads as described above, brush the tops with milk, and sprinkle generously with the cheese. Scatter the kumquat slivers on top of the breads, cover, let rise, and bake as directed.

Olive Oil Crackers with Aniseed (*Tortas de Aceite*) VEGAN

MAKES 20 CRACKERS

FOR THE FIRST-STAGE DOUGH
(SEE NOTE):

3 cups (375 g) all-purpose flour

¼ teaspoon instant active-dry yeast

½ teaspoon salt

Olive oil

FOR THE SECOND-STAGE DOUGH:

3 tablespoons sesame seeds

3 tablespoons aniseeds

⅔ cup (160 ml) olive oil

Zest of 1½ lemons

2 tablespoons ouzo, Pernod, or any anise-flavored liqueur

⅔ to 1 cup (80 to 125 g) all-purpose flour

About ⅓ cup (65 g) granulated sugar, for sprinkling

The moment I first tasted these irresistible crackers from Seville, I knew that I had to make them. The expensive, imported *tortas de aceite* usually arrive shattered, despite the fact that they are each individually wrapped in waxed paper and packed in nice boxes. Before trying to get the traditional recipe I thought that I could make the crackers by just adding extra olive oil and aniseeds to my phyllo recipe (page 36), roll the dough into disks, sprinkle with sugar, and bake until golden. But I was mistaken. It took some time and a few more misses until I came across Penelope Casas's book *La Cocina de Mama: The Great Home Cooking of Spain*. My *tortas de aceite* are adapted from her recipe.

Serve *tortas de aceite* with coffee, herbal or regular tea, or sweet wine. They are great with refreshing, homemade lemonade and other fresh fruit juices and are a more interesting accompaniment than a sugar cone to any sorbet or ice cream.

Make the first-stage dough: In a food processor or in the bowl of a stand mixer fitted with the dough hook attachment, combine the flour, yeast, and salt and pulse to blend. With the motor running, slowly pour in enough water (about 1 cup plus 2 teaspoons/250 ml) to form a soft dough. Process for about 5 minutes, until the dough "cleans" the sides of the bowl and forms a ball. Transfer to an oiled bowl, cover with an oiled piece of plastic wrap, and let rise until doubled, about 1 hour.

Alternatively, you can refrigerate the dough overnight, but allow it to come to room temperature (about 2 hours) before proceeding further.

Make the second-stage dough: Preheat the oven to 400°F (205°C).

Toast the sesame seeds and aniseeds in a small skillet over medium heat, tossing frequently, until fragrant, about 5 minutes.

Transfer the dough, olive oil, lemon zest, toasted seeds, and ouzo to a food processor or the bowl of a standing mixer and work on a low speed, adding ⅔ cup (80 g) flour, or a little more as needed, until you get a soft, oily dough.

Halve the dough with a spatula, then halve both pieces. Divide each piece into quarters (you will have 16 pieces total), rolling each piece into a small ball. Let rest, covered with plastic wrap, for at least 30 minutes and up to 1 hour. You can also refrigerate the dough, covered, for up to 3 days.

Line a baking sheet with a piece of parchment paper. Flatten one ball of dough and stretch it to make a thin disk, about 4½ inches (11 cm) in diameter. Sprinkle with sugar and

press to make the sugar sticks to the dough. Shape 2 to 3 more disks, as many as fit on the baking sheet, then carefully slide the paper onto the oven rack, sprinkling the disks with more sugar, if you like. Bake for about 15 minutes, until golden. Continue shaping and baking the rest of the crackers as above. If you have enough racks and oven space, bake 2 or 3 sheets together in the oven, rotating the sheets so all the crackers bake evenly.

If you like your *tortas de aceite* sweeter, when all the crackers are baked, heat the broiler and arrange the crackers on one or two baking sheets, somewhat overlapping, sugared side down. Sprinkle with sugar and broil each batch about 5 inches from the broiler for a few seconds, until the sugar starts to melt. Be very careful, because they will burn quickly.

Let cool on a wire rack, and then store in an airtight container.

NOTE: *Instead of making the first-stage dough, you can buy 1½ pounds (680 g) bread or pizza dough and proceed to the next stage, adding the olive oil, seeds, and other ingredients.*

Lebanese Flat Breads with Za'atar and Other Toppings (*Man'oushé*) VEGAN

MAKES 8 THIN BREADS

FOR THE DOUGH:

1 cup (160 g) coarse semolina

3½ cups (420 g) whole-wheat flour

2 teaspoons salt

1 envelope (2¼ teaspoons/7 g) instant active-dry yeast

2 teaspoons Spices for Bread (page 54) or 1 teaspoon ground aniseeds and 1 teaspoon ground *mahlep* (see page 51)

Olive oil

FOR THE ZA'ATAR TOPPING (FOR EACH *MAN'OUSHÉ*; MULTIPLY BY AS MANY SERVINGS AS YOU PLAN TO MAKE):

1 tablespoon za'atar (page 56)

2 teaspoons good, fruity olive oil, or as needed to make a paste

Cornmeal, to spread on the baking surface

These flat breads, smeared with a thick paste of za'atar and olive oil, are the traditional Lebanese breakfast and snack, often complemented with *labne*—thick strained yogurt, similar to but creamier than Greek yogurt. They are not particularly photogenic, but they are deliciously aromatic and wholesome, a healthy street food. Vegetables—raw, sautéed, or pickled, as well as nuts and onions—are sometimes added to the thin, za'atar-topped bread, which is usually folded, wrapped in paper, and eaten while still warm, just out of the oven. In the photograph opposite, the toppings are slivered zucchini and cooked tomatoes, each sprinkled with feta cheese. Barbara Abdeni Massaad, who has written a book devoted to *man'oushé*, describes a regional variation from Nabatieh that uses whole-wheat flour and is scented with aniseeds and *mahlep*, much like my basic bread (page 198). But the interesting twist is the addition of cracked wheat or coarse semolina, soaked in warm water for 30 minutes before it is added to the flour. The resulting *manaeesh* (plural of *man'oushé*) are quite special, both crunchy and soft, ideal for any topping, especially my meatless *lahmaçun* (page 208).

Make the dough: Place the semolina in a small bowl and pour 1 cup (240 ml) warm water over the top. Stir and set aside to soak for 25 to 30 minutes.

In a food processor or in the bowl of a stand mixer fitted with the dough hook attachment, combine the flour, salt, yeast, and bread spice mix. Pulse to blend and aerate.

Stop the machine, add the soaked semolina, and pulse again. With the motor running, slowly pour in water, about ⅔ cup (160 ml) or as needed, until a dough forms. Work the dough for about 6 minutes on medium-low speed to make a soft dough that "cleans" the sides of the bowl.

Oil a large bowl and a piece of plastic wrap. Turn the dough out onto your work surface, shape it into a ball, then transfer to the oiled bowl. Cover with the oiled plastic wrap and let rise until doubled in size, about 1½ hours.

Turn out the dough and divide it into 8 pieces. Flatten each piece with your palm. Cut eight 13-inch (33-cm) square pieces of parchment paper and sprinkle lightly with some cornmeal. Using a lightly floured rolling pin, roll out each piece of dough on a piece of parchment paper to form a 10-inch (25-cm) disk, or a stretched oval about 6 by 11 inches (15 by 28 cm).

Place a pizza stone or a large, heavy baking sheet in the oven and preheat the oven to 450°F (230°C).

Make the za'atar topping: In a bowl, combine the za'atar with the fruity olive oil and blend to form a paste.

Smear the top of each *man'oushé* with the za'atar paste and slide them onto the heated stone or pan with the parchment, fitting as many pies in the oven as you can.

Bake for 12 to 15 minutes, until the filling sizzles and the crust is golden brown on both top and bottom. Repeat with any remaining pieces.

Cut each *man'oushé* into pieces, or score in the middle and fold. Wrap half of the folded pie with the parchment paper and serve warm or at room temperature.

Spicy Eggplant, Pepper, and Walnut *Lahmaçun* VEGAN

MAKES 8 PIES

FOR THE DOUGH:

1 cup (160 g) coarse semolina

3½ cups (420 g) whole-wheat flour

2 teaspoons salt

1 envelope (2¼ teaspoons/7 g) instant active-dry yeast

2 teaspoons Spices for Bread (page 54), or 1 teaspoon ground aniseeds and 1 teaspoon ground *mahlep* (see page 51)

Olive oil

FOR THE TOPPING:

About ⅔ cup (150 ml) olive oil, as needed

2 cups (320 g) chopped onions

4 medium eggplants (about 3 pounds/1.5 kg) finely diced, salted, and left in a colander to drain for 30 minutes or up to 3 hours

2 medium green bell peppers, diced

1 medium red bell pepper, diced

1 tablespoon tomato paste

1 tablespoon Maraş pepper, or a good pinch of crushed red pepper flakes, to taste

1½ cups (180 g) fresh tomato pulp or diced canned tomatoes, drained

2 teaspoons Lebanese Seven-Spice Mix (page 54), or ½ teaspoon ground allspice and 1 teaspoon ground cumin

½ cup (35 g) dried porcini mushrooms, coarsely ground in a blender

Salt

1½ cups (200 g) coarsely ground walnuts

½ cup (30 g) finely chopped fresh parsley

Cornmeal, to spread on the baking surface

8 small red chiles, for topping the pies (optional)

Traditionally topped with a spicy ground lamb filling, this irresistible street food of the Middle East is sometimes called "Arab pizza" in the West. My vegetarian take is very popular with our guests. You can make the pies with store-bought pizza dough, or with Basic Bread dough (page 198), but they are infinitely better with the Lebanese whole-wheat *man'oushé* dough from Nabatieh (page 206).

Make the dough as described on page 206 for *man'oushé*.

Make the topping: In a heavy-bottomed sauté pan, heat ⅓ cup (80 ml) of the olive oil over medium heat. Add the onions and sauté until translucent, about 3 minutes. Rinse the diced eggplant under cold water, pat dry with paper towels, and add to the skillet with the bell peppers. Sauté, stirring often, until all the vegetables wilt, 10 minutes or more (you may have to add the eggplants in batches, adding more olive oil as you do). When all the vegetables are wilted, add the tomato paste and toss for a minute, then add 2 teaspoons of the Maraş pepper and the tomatoes, the spices, ground mushrooms, and salt to taste. Toss and cook over medium-high heat, until almost all the juices have evaporated, 8 to 10 minutes. Remove from the heat and add the walnuts and parsley. Toss and taste to adjust the seasoning—the filling should be quite spicy.

In a small saucepan, combine 3 tablespoons of the olive oil and 1 teaspoon of the Maraş pepper and warm over low heat. Set aside.

Place a pizza stone or a large, heavy baking sheet in the oven and preheat the oven to 450°F (230°C).

On a lightly floured board, divide the dough into eight pieces and flatten each one with your palm. Cut eight 13-inch (33-cm) square pieces of parchment paper. Working with one at a time, sprinkle lightly with cornmeal. Roll out each piece of dough on the paper with a lightly floured rolling pin to form a 10-inch (25-cm) disk or a stretched oval. Brush with the peppered oil. Spread a thin layer of the filling, about ½ cup (125 g), on each pie. Add one chile (if using) to each pie and slide the pies onto the heated stone or pan with the paper, fitting as many pies in the oven as you can. Bake for 12 to 15 minutes or more, until the filling sizzles and the crust is golden brown on top and bottom. Repeat with any remaining pieces.

Cut each *lahmaçun* into pieces or score in the middle and fold. Wrap half the folded pie with parchment paper and serve warm or at room temperature.

Pumpkin, Tangerine, and Marmalade Bread

**MAKES 2 LOAVES OR
1 LARGE ROUND LOAF**

4 cups (500 g) all-purpose flour, plus more as needed

3 cups (360 g) whole-wheat flour

2 envelopes (4½ teaspoons/14 g) instant active-dry yeast

2 teaspoons salt

½ teaspoon freshly ground white pepper (optional)

3⅓ cups (800 g) fresh pumpkin-tangerine pulp (see Note)

1 cup (240 ml) marmalade, preferably homemade (page 238)

About ¼ cup (60 ml) light cream or milk, as needed, plus more to glaze the loaves

Olive oil, for brushing

Blanched almonds, for decorating (optional)

This bread is a sweet, festive treat that I like to make for New Year's breakfast. According to Greek tradition, on New Year's Eve or after the festive lunch on the first day of the year, the father of the family cuts into a rich, aromatic bread or cake that has the year written in almonds on top and a lucky coin hidden inside. Each family member gets a piece, starting with the elders, and whoever gets the symbolic coin is rewarded with a gift of money and good luck for the New Year.

This bread is great on its own or served with cheeses—the sharper the better.

Place the flours, yeast, salt, and pepper in the bowl of a stand mixer and stir with a spatula. Make a well in the center and pour in the pumpkin-tangerine pulp and the marmalade. Affix the dough hook to the mixer and beat the mixture on low speed for 1 minute. With the motor running, add the cream and work the dough on medium-low speed for about 5 minutes, occasionally stopping to turn the dough over with a large spatula. The dough should still be somewhat wet and sticky, but it will start to "clean" the sides of the bowl. If it is too dry, add a little more cream; if too wet, add 1 to 2 tablespoons more all-purpose flour.

Lightly oil a large bowl and a piece of plastic wrap. Lightly flour your work surface. Turn the dough out and shape into a ball. Transfer to the oiled bowl. Cover with the oiled plastic wrap and let rise until doubled in size, about 1½ hours.

Turn the dough out onto a floured work surface and press it to fit a 10-inch (25-cm) round pan lined with parchment paper, or halve it with a spatula and fill two loaf pans lined with parchment paper. Cover with oiled plastic wrap and let the bread(s) rest for 35 to 40 minutes more—they won't rise much.

Preheat the oven to 400°F (205°C).

Brush the breads with cream or milk and decorate with the almonds, if you like.

Bake for 5 minutes, then reduce the oven temperature to 375°F (190°C) and continue baking the breads for 35 minutes (or more, depending on their size), until golden brown and hollow-sounding when tapped at the bottom. A thermometer inserted into the center should read 205°F to 207°F (95°C to 96°C). Transfer to a wire rack to cool completely before you slice and serve.

NOTE: *To make the pumpkin-tangerine pulp, quarter 3 tangerines, without peeling, to remove the pips—place both the peel and the flesh in a blender. Add 3 cups (720 g) grated fresh or frozen pumpkin or squash. If you opt for canned pumpkin, first add just 1 cup (240 g) to the blender with the tangerines. Then mix in more canned pumpkin to get the amount needed.*

Cypriot Tahini, Cinnamon, and Walnut Cookies in Lemon Syrup (*Tahinopites*) VEGAN

FOR THE BREAD DOUGH:

4 cups (500 g) all-purpose flour, plus more as needed

3 cups (420 g) bread flour or fine semolina (see Note)

1 envelope (2¼ teaspoons/7 g) instant active-dry yeast

2 teaspoons coarse sea salt or kosher salt

1 teaspoon ground cinnamon

¼ teaspoon ground cloves

½ teaspoon ground black pepper

Olive oil

FOR THE SYRUP:

3 cups (600 g) granulated sugar

⅔ peel from large organic lemon

½ cup (120 ml) fresh lemon juice

FOR THE FILLING:

14 ounces (400 g) top-quality tahini paste (see Sources, page 244)

2 cups (400 g) granulated sugar

2 cups (160 g) medium-ground walnuts

2 tablespoons ground cinnamon

Traditionally made in Cyprus before Easter during Lent—when all foods deriving from animals are prohibited—*tahinopites* are round, syrupy breads, coiled and stuffed with a tahini mixture, much like the vegan *tsoureki* with preserves (see Variation on page 214). As the coiled *tahinopites* bake, the thin layer of dough cracks and the stuffing oozes out, caramelizing; these crunchy, darkened, sugary tahini bits are the best bites. Why not have more of the best parts of the pie? I decided to shape the dough differently in order to increase the caramelized area. The results are exquisite, bite-size *tahinopites*.

It is important to get the highest-quality tahini paste for these cookies. They taste best made a day in advance. As they cool, they absorb and fully incorporate the lemony syrup.

Make the dough: In the bowl of a stand mixer, combine the flours, yeast, salt, cinnamon, cloves, and pepper. Gradually work up to high speed to mix thoroughly. With the motor running on low speed, gradually add enough water, about 3½ cups (840 ml) or as needed, to form a soft dough. Mix at medium-low speed for 6 minutes, until the dough barely "cleans" the sides of the bowl. It should be soft and somewhat sticky.

Oil a large bowl and a piece of plastic wrap. Lightly flour your work surface. Turn the dough out, and with lightly floured hands shape into a ball. Transfer to the oiled bowl, cover with the oiled plastic wrap, and let rise at room temperature until doubled in size, about 1½ hours. Alternatively, place the dough in the refrigerator and let rise overnight.

Make the syrup: Bring the sugar and 2½ cups (600 ml) water to a boil over high heat, add the lemon peel, reduce the heat, and simmer for 5 minutes. Add the lemon juice and simmer for 2 minutes more. Remove from the heat and let cool completely.

Make the filling: In a bowl, whisk the tahini to incorporate any separated oil and paste. Add the sugar, walnuts, and cinnamon and stir well to combine.

Shape the cookies: Line 2 or 3 baking sheets with parchment paper.

Turn out the dough onto your floured work surface and knead briefly with floured hands. Divide the dough into 4 pieces. Cover the 3 pieces while you work the first piece. Flatten it to make a rectangle that is about 12 by 9 inches (30.5 by 23 cm). Spread generously with one-quarter of the filling to cover the surface of the dough.

With the help of a large dough scraper, roll up the dough like a jelly roll. Now stretch and roll carefully to extend and make a 14-inch (35.5-cm) log. With the scraper, cut 1-inch (2.5-cm) slices. Transfer the pieces, cut side up, to the lined baking sheet and shape each slice into a round "cookie," pressing gently to flatten. Shape all the *tahinopites* the same way. Set them on the baking sheets, leaving about ⅔ inch (1.5 cm) between cookies, because they will expand.

Cover loosely with plastic wrap and let rise for 45 minutes.

At least 20 minutes before baking, preheat the oven to 375°F (190°C).

Bake for about 25 minutes, until light golden and caramelized.

Discard the parchment paper and arrange the cookies snugly in two deep pans. Douse the cookies with syrup while they are still warm. Cover with fresh parchment paper or plastic wrap and let the cookies soak in the syrup for 20 minutes. Uncover and flip the cookies to soak on the other side. They will absorb most of the syrup. Leave them covered for at least 2 hours or overnight.

Flip again and transfer to a serving platter or place in a container, cover, and refrigerate. Let the cookies come to room temperature before serving.

NOTE: *I like the cookies somewhat chewy, but if you prefer softer ones, omit the combination of bread flour and semolina and make the dough with 7 cups (875 g) all-purpose flour.*

Orange and Saffron Olive Oil Bread (Vegan *Tsoureki*) VEGAN

MAKES 2 LARGE OR 4 SMALL LOAVES

4 cups (500 g) all-purpose flour

3 cups (360 g) whole-wheat flour

1 envelope (2¼ teaspoons/7 g) instant active-dry yeast

1½ teaspoons salt

1 tablespoon freshly ground *mahlep* (see page 51)

⅔ teaspoon saffron threads, diluted in ¼ cup (60 ml) boiling water and set aside for 15 minutes

1 tangerine, preferably organic, unpeeled, washed, dried, and quartered to remove any pips

Juice of 1 orange

3 tablespoons granulated sugar

5 tablespoons (80 g) thick almond butter

⅓ cup (80 ml) olive oil, plus more as needed

FOR BRUSHING THE BREADS (OPTIONAL):

2 tablespoons granulated sugar

3 tablespoons fresh orange juice

A friend asked me if I could get him a vegan recipe for *tsoureki*—the traditional festive Greek bread baked from a rich dough of milk, eggs, and butter, and usually braided, much like challah. No such recipe existed, so I set out to invent one, and here is the result. The dough is soft and easy to manipulate, so you can give it any shape you like. Inspired by a traditional wedding bread from Thrace, in the northeastern corner of Greece, I used part of the dough to make a coiled bread that is stuffed with fruit, pictured opposite (see Variation, page 214).

In the bowl of a stand mixer fitted with the dough hook attachment, combine the flours, yeast, salt, and *mahlep*; pulse to blend and aerate.

In a blender, combine the saffron water, tangerine, orange juice, sugar, almond butter, and olive oil. Pulse, periodically scraping down the sides with a spatula, to get a smooth pulp.

With the motor of the mixer running, pour the wet mixture into the dry ingredients and work the mixture on low speed for a couple of minutes, adding about 1½ cups (260 ml) water or as needed, to form a dough. Work the dough for about 5 minutes on medium-low to make a soft dough that "cleans" the sides of the bowl.

Oil a large bowl and a piece of plastic wrap. Turn out the dough onto your work surface and shape it into a ball. Transfer the dough to the oiled bowl and cover with the oiled plastic wrap. Let rise until doubled in size, about 1½ hours.

Turn out the dough and halve it, using one piece to make the stuffed bread (see Variation, page 214), if you like, or shape both pieces of dough to fit pan(s) lined with parchment paper. Cover loosely with plastic wrap and let rise again for 35 to 40 minutes, until almost doubled in size.

At least 20 minutes before baking, preheat the oven to 400°F (205°C).

If you like, dilute the sugar in the orange juice and brush the tops of the breads with the mixture just before putting them in the oven. Bake for 10 minutes, reduce the heat to 375°F (190°C), and continue baking for 20 minutes (or more, depending on the size of the breads), until golden brown in color and hollow sounding when you tap on the bottom. You may need to turn and change the position of the loaves halfway through baking to make sure they color evenly.

Let cool completely on a wire rack before cutting to serve.

2½ cups (about 400 g) drained and chopped "spoon sweets" (fruit preserves; I use green, unripe almonds, orange, bergamot, and some dried cherries)

2 to 3 tablespoons coarsely ground almonds, plus more for sprinkling

3 to 4 tablespoons sesame seeds

COILED WEDDING BREAD STUFFED WITH FRUIT PRESERVES

Use half of the dough from the recipe on page 212.

Shape the dough into a 35-inch (90-cm) long cord (or two 17-inch/43-cm cords, which you will then stick together). Flatten to a width of 4 inches (10 cm) and spread the fruit preserves in the middle of the dough, sprinkling with the almonds. Brush the edges with some of the orange juice–sugar mixture, roll, and pinch to cover the filling, creating a long, sausagelike bread. Coil the dough in a circle to make a round or oval bread. Transfer to a pan lined with parchment paper, brush with the remaining orange juice mixture, and sprinkle liberally with almonds and sesame seeds. Cover loosely with plastic wrap and let rise for 35 to 40 minutes, until almost doubled in size.

Preheat the oven and bake as on page 212, until well browned on the top and bottom. Let cool before cutting to serve.

Twice-Baked Barley Rusks (*Paximadia* or *Dakos*) VEGAN

MAKES 24 *DAKOS* (4-INCH/10-CM ROUND BISCUITS) OR ENOUGH SMALL *PAXIMADIA* TO FILL A 3-QUART (3-L) JAR

3 cups (375 g) all-purpose flour, plus more as needed

1½ cups (225 g) barley flour

1½ cups (about 225 g) fine malted barley (see Sources, page 246), ground in a coffee grinder

1 cup (about 150 g) coarse malted barley (see Sources, page 246), ground in the blender

2 envelopes (4½ teaspoons/14 g) instant active-dry yeast

2 teaspoons sea salt or kosher salt

2 tablespoons ground aniseeds

2 tablespoons ground coriander seeds

½ teaspoon freshly ground black pepper

3 tablespoons grape molasses, or 2 tablespoons honey and 1 teaspoon balsamic vinegar

½ cup (120 ml) olive oil, plus more as needed

Modern whole-grain barley flour is almost as white as unbleached all-purpose flour, made from the hull-less variety of barley with loosely attached outer hull that generally falls off during harvesting. I add malted barley grains—any of the aromatic whole grains used in beer making will do—to create the old-fashioned dark, rustic rusks, grinding them both fine and coarsely. Besides texture, malted barley adds flavor and aroma.

Following the tradition of Crete, I suggest you shape the dough into *dakos*, the round loaves that are sliced horizontally before they are baked for a second time to dry completely (see photo on page 66). Cutting the half-baked breads with a piece of wire creates a rugged, crunchy surface that better absorbs toppings. These barley rusks are very flavorful, somewhat hard but crunchy.

Place the flours, malted barleys, yeast, salt, aniseeds, coriander seeds, and pepper in the bowl of a stand mixer fitted with the paddle attachment and toss with a spatula to combine. Make a well in the center and pour in the grape molasses and olive oil. With the motor running, add cold water, about 2½ cups (600 ml) or as needed, and work the dough on medium-low speed for 6 minutes or more. The dough should still be somewhat sticky, but it will "clean" the sides of the bowl. If it is too dry, add a little more water; if too wet, add 1 to 2 tablespoons more all-purpose flour.

Lightly oil a large bowl and a piece of plastic wrap. Lightly flour your work surface. Turn out the dough and shape into a ball. Transfer to the oiled bowl. Cover with the oiled plastic wrap and let rise until doubled in size, 1½ to 2 hours.

To shape *dakos*: Turn out the dough onto your floured work surface. Divide the dough into 6 pieces. Work with 1 piece at a time, keeping the remaining pieces covered with plastic wrap. Roll each piece into a thick rope, about 18 inches (46 cm) long. Cut in half and then coil each half to form a round bagel-like bun, but without a hole in the middle. Shape the other half in the same manner, then press lightly to flatten both pieces and place about 1½ inches (4 cm) apart on parchment paper–lined baking sheets. Cover with plastic wrap and make the rest of the *dakos* in the same manner. Set aside for 30 minutes more—they won't rise much.

To shape small *paximadia*: Divide the dough into 4 pieces. Form each piece into a baguette and transfer to a baking sheet lined with parchment paper. Cover with plastic wrap and set aside for 30 to 40 minutes more—they won't rise much.

At least 20 minutes before baking, preheat the oven to 400°F (205°C). Bake the *dakos* or the *paximadia* for 10 minutes, then reduce the oven temperature to 375°F (190°C) and bake for 10 minutes more. Remove from the oven and let cool for 3 to 4 minutes. Reduce the oven temperature to 190°F (80°C). With a serrated knife, halve the *dakos* horizontally, while still warm. If you formed *paximadia*, slice them crosswise into about ½-inch (1.3-cm) pieces. Place the *dakos* halves or the slices, cut side up, directly on a rack in the middle of the oven and bake for 2 hours or more, until completely dry.

Let cool completely on the oven racks and store in airtight containers. They will keep for at least 6 months.

PAXIMADIA AND *DAKOS*: SAVORY BARLEY BISCUITS

In the 1950s, Ansel Keys and his colleagues studied the eating habits, health, and life expectancy of various peoples in seven countries, Greece being one of them. The inhabitants of Crete, in particular, were faring best of all. In those days twice-baked *dakos* or *paximadia* (barley rusks) were the staple food of the Cretans. But when the foods of Crete were recorded, and became the model for the Mediterranean Diet, the barley biscuits were translated as "whole-wheat bread" for northern Europeans and Americans unfamiliar with barley, *dakos*, and *paximadia*.

Since barley contains less gluten than wheat, bread made with barley is heavy and darker in color and dries out faster. So it is not surprising that it was baked twice in order to make it less perishable, especially when it was destined to feed sailors on long voyages.

Barley is now used almost exclusively in beer production and as animal fodder; barley flour has disappeared from the shelves of supermarkets, and one can find it only in specialty and health food stores, or at wholesale distributors. But it is worth seeking out. The Calabrian stores on Arthur Avenue in the Bronx, New York, sell barley biscuits similar to those from Crete.

Twice-Baked Semolina Breads (*Friselle*) VEGAN

MAKES 16 *FRISELLE* HALVES

3 cups (480 g) semolina flour

2 cups (240 g) whole-wheat flour

1 cup (125 g) all-purpose flour, plus more
  as needed

1 cup (160 g) yellow cornmeal

2 envelopes (4½ teaspoons/14 g) instant
  active-dry yeast

3 teaspoons sea salt

⅓ cup (80 ml) olive oil, plus more
  as needed

Traditionally these crunchy breads are shaped like fat bagels, the central hole of which almost disappears as they rise. Each bread is cut horizontally after an initial baking, then the pieces are baked again in a low oven until completely dry. Originally from Puglia, *friselle* were the food of the poor. Now they have spread all over Italy and are a chic summer appetizer. They are like large bruschetta, with a different, denser consistency. In Cyprus, similar breads are shaped into loaves, scored, and then cut into pieces and dried (see the photo, opposite). In my recipe I include a cup of yellow cornmeal to add even more crunch and flavor. Cutting the half-baked breads with a piece of wire creates a rugged, crunchy surface that better absorbs toppings.

Add the flours, cornmeal, yeast, and salt to the bowl of a stand mixer fitted with a dough hook and toss with a spatula to combine. Make a well in the center and pour in the olive oil. With the motor running on a low speed, gradually add water, about 2⅔ cups (640 ml) or as needed, and work the dough, increasing the speed to medium-low for 6 minutes. The dough should be only slightly sticky and will "clean" the sides of the bowl. If it is too dry, add a little more water; if too wet, add 1 to 2 tablespoons more all-purpose flour.

Lightly oil a large bowl and a piece of plastic wrap. Lightly flour your work surface. Turn out the dough and shape into a ball. Transfer to the oiled bowl. Cover with the oiled plastic wrap and let rise until doubled in size, about 1½ hours (see Note).

Turn out the dough onto your floured work surface and divide it into 8 pieces. Work with one piece at a time, keeping the remaining pieces covered with plastic wrap. Roll the dough into a thick rope, about 10 inches (25 cm) long. Join the ends around your fingers to form a bagel-like round with overlapping ends, leaving a small hole in the middle, and pinch to seal. Shape the other pieces in the same manner, then press them lightly to flatten and transfer to a parchment paper–lined baking sheet, about 1½ inches (4 cm) apart. Cover with plastic wrap and let rise for 30 minutes more.

At least 20 minutes before baking, preheat the oven to 400°F (205°C).

NOTE: *Instead of leaving the dough to rise on the counter, you can refrigerate it overnight. It will still rise, albeit very slowly. Let the dough come to room temperature (1½ to 2 hours) before dividing and shaping the* friselle. *After shaping, let rise for about 45 minutes, until almost doubled in size.*

Bake the *friselle* for 10 minutes, then reduce the oven temperature to 375°F (190°C) and bake for 10 to 15 minutes more, just until they start to color. Remove from the oven and let cool for 3 minutes. Reduce the oven temperature to 180°F (80°C). Using a piece of wire, halve the breads horizontally while still warm. Place the *friselle* halves, cut side up, directly on the rack in the middle of the oven, overlapping them a little if necessary. Bake for about 40 minutes or more, until completely dry.

Let cool completely on the oven rack and store in airtight containers. The *friselle* keep for at least 6 months.

Rosemary-Scented Cornmeal Biscotti with Nuts VEGAN

1 cup (140 g) hulled sunflower seeds

¼ cup (15 g) fresh rosemary leaves (see Note)

2 cups (320 g) yellow cornmeal

2 cups (240 g) whole-wheat flour

2 cups (250 g) all-purpose flour, plus more as needed

½ cup (50 g) ground flaxseeds (optional)

2 envelopes (4½ teaspoons/14 g) instant active-dry yeast

1½ tablespoons salt

½ to 1 teaspoon freshly ground black pepper

2 teaspoons ground turmeric

1 cup (240 ml) olive oil, plus more as needed

½ pound (225 g) shelled pistachios, walnuts, or pecans

These are another of my trademark biscotti, the savory snacks that fill and quickly disappear from my cookie jars. Nutritious and aromatic, these vivid-yellow, crunchy slices, dotted with green pistachios or whitish walnuts, are difficult to resist. After baking, the biscotti have to be sliced and baked again to dry; I am sure you will agree that they are well worth the extra effort. If you want to make stunning green biscotti, substitute nettle pulp for water (see Variation), and maybe change the herbs, adding oregano or dried basil instead of rosemary. I usually have different-colored biscotti in my large cookie jars: yellow, green, and dark, adding a few tablespoons of carob flour to the dough.

In a food processor, grind the sunflower seeds together with the rosemary to get a fine paste.

Add the cornmeal, flours, flaxseeds, yeast, salt, pepper, and turmeric and pulse to blend. With the motor running, pour in the olive oil and then slowly add enough water, about 2 cups (480 ml) or as needed, to form a soft dough. Process on medium-low for 5 minutes, or until the dough forms a ball that "cleans" the sides of the bowl.

Oil a large bowl and a piece of plastic wrap. Lightly flour your work surface. Turn out the dough and knead for 1 minute. Transfer the dough to the oiled bowl, cover with the oiled plastic wrap, and let rise until doubled in size, about 1½ hours.

Line a baking sheet with parchment paper.

Turn out the dough onto your floured work surface and divide it into 4 pieces. Flatten each piece and form 9-by-8-inch (23-by-20-cm) rectangles. Spread one-quarter of the pistachios on the first rectangle and dust lightly with flour. Press hard with your palms so that the nuts half sink into the dough, then roll tightly, like a jelly roll, pressing the seam with wet fingers to seal. Transfer to the baking sheet, seam side down. Then, by gently pressing and pulling, extend the roll into a 13-inch-long (33-cm-long) baguette. Shape the remaining rectangles in the same manner, using different nuts on each, if you like. Cover with the oiled plastic wrap and let rise for 35 to 40 minutes.

At least 20 minutes before baking, preheat the oven to 375°F (190°C).

Bake for 35 to 40 minutes, until the baguettes are a light golden color. Carefully, because the baguettes could break, transfer to a wire rack, cover with a clean kitchen towel, and let rest for 12 to 24 hours.

NETTLE-GREEN SAVORY BISCOTTI WITH NUTS

Instead of water, use 1 cup (240 ml) room temperature nettle pulp (see Freezing Nettles, page 24), mixed with 1 cup (240 ml) water, or as needed. Use walnuts or pecans, not pistachios, to contrast with the green color of the dough.

Using a good serrated knife, cut the baguettes into about ¼-inch (0.6-cm) slices and arrange in rows, on oven racks or baking sheets, overlapping them if necessary. Turn the oven to 180° to 190°F (82° to 88°C) and bake the slices for about 2 hours, rotating halfway through, until the biscotti are completely dry.

Let cool in the oven with the door open, and when completely cool, store in airtight containers. The biscotti will keep for at least 3 months.

NOTE: *If you like, substitute dried basil or oregano (2 to 3 tablespoons, depending on how aromatic your herbs are) for the rosemary.*

"Tomato Salad" Flat Bread Topped with Cheese and Tomatoes

MAKES 2 *LAGANES*
(FOCACCIA-LIKE FLAT BREADS)

2½ cups (310 g) all-purpose flour, plus more as needed

3½ cups (420 g) whole-wheat flour

1 cup (150 g) barley flour, or 1 more cup (120 g) whole-wheat flour

2 envelopes (4½ teaspoons/14 g) instant active-dry yeast

1 teaspoon salt

1 to 2 teaspoons Maraş pepper or a good pinch of crushed red pepper flakes (½ teaspoon freshly ground black pepper works well, too)

¼ cup (60 ml) olive oil, plus more as needed

2½ cups (300 g) tomato pulp (see Note)

FOR THE TOPPING:

2½ cups (250 g) coarsely grated or shaved *graviera*, pecorino, or aged cheddar

3 large beefsteak tomatoes, cut into very thin slices, or several cherry tomatoes, halved

Good, fruity olive oil, for drizzling

Good pinch of dried Greek oregano and/or freshly ground black pepper, for sprinkling

I invented this bread to make use of leftover tomato salad. The juices from the everyday summer salad—made with the garden's vine-ripened tomatoes, flavored with thinly sliced onions and capers, and drizzled with good, fruity olive oil, are so good that we often keep them for two days, simply adding fresh tomatoes to the half-wilted leftovers. I usually serve this bread warm with wine, whenever we have a crowd for lunch or dinner. In the winter, when vine-ripened tomatoes are not available, I use sun-dried tomatoes with some fresh cherry tomatoes (see Note). The leftover bread can be frozen and reheated before serving. I suggest you shape half the dough into *lagana* and the other half into individual buns (see Variation), which are ideal to serve with marinated sardines, cheese, or with any meze spread.

In the bowl of a stand mixer fitted with the dough hook attachment, combine the flours, yeast, salt, and Maraş pepper and pulse to mix well. With the motor running on low speed, add the olive oil and the tomato pulp and work for 1 to 2 minutes to blend. With the motor running on the lowest speed, add water, about ⅔ cup (160 ml) or as needed, and work the dough, increasing the speed to medium-low for 5 minutes, occasionally stopping to turn the dough over with a large spatula. The dough should still be wet and sticky, but should start to "clean" the sides of the bowl. If it is too dry, add a little more water; if too wet, add 1 to 2 tablespoons more all-purpose flour.

Lightly oil a large bowl and a piece of plastic wrap. Lightly flour your work surface. Turn out the dough and shape into a ball. Transfer to the oiled bowl. Cover with the oiled plastic wrap and let rise until doubled in size, about 1½ hours.

(When the dough has expanded to about 1½ times its size, you may transfer the bowl with the dough to the refrigerator, and leave it overnight or up to 24 hours. It will continue to rise slowly. Before proceeding further, bring to room temperature, about 2 hours.)

Turn out the dough onto your floured work surface and halve it with a spatula.

Line 2 baking sheets with parchment paper and place one piece of dough on each sheet. Wet your fingers and press the dough, making dimples with your fingers, expanding the dough out to fill the baking sheet. Oil 2 pieces of plastic wrap, cover the dough, and let the *laganes* rise for 30 minutes more—they won't rise much.

Preheat the oven to 450°F (230°C).

Spread the cheese over each of the breads to cover the surface. Press so that the cheese sticks to the dough, and top with tomato slices. Drizzle with a little fruity olive oil and sprinkle with oregano and/or black pepper.

Heat the broiler and place the first baking sheet 5 to 6 inches (12 to 15 cm) beneath the heat source, with the other baking sheet low in the oven. Broil for about 6 minutes, until the tomatoes on the top bread start to sizzle and the cheese melts. Move this bread to the bottom of the oven, and slide the other baking sheet into the vacated space, close to the heat. After 5 to 6 minutes, turn off the broiler, reduce the oven temperature to 375°F (190°C), and rotate the bread positions once more. Continue baking for 15 minutes more, then change the positions of the breads one final time and bake for 10 minutes more. Check to make sure that both breads are well browned on top and bottom; if not, bake them a bit longer.

When done, lift the breads using the parchment paper, transfer to a wire rack to cool, and slide the paper out from beneath the breads. Let cool a little, 5 to 10 minutes, and slice to serve.

NOTE: *To make the tomato pulp: Using summer vine-ripened tomatoes, puree in the blender 2 to 3 medium tomatoes, 1 small quartered onion, and 1 tablespoon rinsed and drained capers. Measure the pulp you need and use any leftover for sauces. In the winter I use organic sun-dried tomatoes, not those preserved in olive oil. Soak 5 good-quality sun-dried tomatoes in ⅓ cup (80 ml) warm water for about 20 minutes. Transfer the tomatoes and their liquid to the blender together with 8 to 10 large cherry tomatoes, 1 small quartered onion, and 1 tablespoon rinsed and drained capers. Puree to get the pulp. Measure the pulp you need and use any leftover for sauces.*

VARIATION

TOMATO BREAD BUNS

Instead of two flat breads, shape all or half of the dough into small buns—reduce the topping ingredients or omit them.

Halve the dough, and shape one piece—or both—into a 14-inch (35.5-cm) log. With a dough scraper, cut triangles and place them on a parchment paper–lined baking sheet, about 1½ inches (4 cm) apart. Cover with plastic, let rise, and bake in the middle of the oven for about 20 minutes, until light golden on top and bottom. Let cool on a rack before serving.

DESSERTS, JAMS, PRESERVES & DRINKS

The cornerstones of Greek and Balkan sweets are seasonal fruit preserves. Each home has several different jars of spoon-sweets, as these fruit preserves are called, in the pantry. Sour cherry and quince (opposite, bottom right) are the most common, but there are plenty of more exotic ones like tiny eggplants, tomatoes, or green, unripe almonds and walnuts. The walnuts are the most difficult to make: You have to dedicate more than five days of tedious preparation that involves peeling each nut meat and then soaking them for two days or more, changing the water often to get rid of excess bitterness. The green walnuts are then cooked in syrup, then repeatedly cooled and cooked again. Only the most passionate cooks, like the lady from Cyprus pictured on page 6, still make *karydaki*, as the walnut preserves are known.

Fruit preserves are now used as topping for yogurt or ice cream, but in the old days guests were offered a teaspoon of the sweet with a glass of water as a welcome to the house; in Turkey and the Middle East seasonal fruits are made into concentrated syrups—*shebets*—that are diluted with water to make refreshing drinks. *Shebets* are also drizzled over nut-filled sweet breads and cakes.

In my home, as in most Mediterranean households of yesteryear, sweets were not made every day, but only on special occasions. Desserts were served on Easter, Christmas, at family feasts, and sometimes on Sundays. And perhaps because they were made so rarely, sweets are among the very few foods for which written recipes exist, well-kept in kitchen ledgers. Even women who could barely write managed to record the procedure and the amount of sugar needed for each one of the various seasonal fruit preserves, and the instructions for the traditional sweet breads and desserts.

Cherry Cake from Bosnia (*Colaç od Trešanja*)

SERVES 6 TO 8

3 eggs

1 cup (200 g) granulated sugar, plus more for sprinkling

8 tablespoons (115 g) butter, softened, or ½ cup (120 ml) olive oil

Zest of 1 lemon, preferably organic

2 cups (250 g) all-purpose flour

2 teaspoons baking powder

½ teaspoon ground cinnamon

1 cup (120 g) coarsely chopped walnuts or almonds, with skins

Olive oil, for the pan

About 10 ounces (300 g) pitted fresh cherries (see Note)

This fruit cake is inspired by a recipe from *Journey through Herzegovina: Stories of Food and Farmers*, written by Andrea Semplici and Mario Boccia. I picked the booklet from the country's stand at the 2012 Slow Food Salone del Gusto in Torino. A few other recipes I tried were not memorable, but this simple and delicious cake from Mostar was an instant success and has become part of my select repertoire of sweets. I make it with olive oil and I often use canned sour cherries. My husband, a discerning judge of sweets, loves it!

Preheat the oven to 375°F (190°C).

In a medium bowl, use a handheld mixer to beat the eggs with the sugar until they are creamy and almost white. Add the butter and lemon zest and beat for 1 minute more.

In another bowl, stir together the flour, baking powder, and cinnamon. Gradually add the flour mixture to the eggs, stirring just to incorporate. Add the walnuts and stir briefly to mix.

Line a 9-inch (23-cm) square pan with parchment paper and oil it lightly.

Pour in the batter and knock the pan against your work surface to distribute it evenly. Top the batter with the pitted cherries and sprinkle with 1 teaspoon of sugar.

Bake for about 40 minutes, until golden brown. A knife inserted into the cake between the cherries should come out clean.

Let cool on a wire rack for 20 minutes before removing from the pan.

NOTE: *If fresh cherries are not available, use canned Oregon pitted tart cherries in water, drained. I much prefer Oregon cherries to sweeter varieties. Taste them—if you prefer a slightly sweeter taste, sprinkle the top with an additional tablespoon of sugar. Candied or dried cherries are not good for this recipe.*

Flourless Almond Cookies (*Amygdalota*) from Kea GLUTEN-FREE

MAKES ABOUT 60 COOKIES

2 pounds (1 kg) blanched almonds
(or unskinned, if you like), plus
60 whole blanched almonds

2 cups (400 g) granulated sugar

6 or 7 egg whites

¼ teaspoon salt

2 to 3 drops almond extract

5 tablespoons (75 ml) orange blossom water

2 to 3 tablespoons lemon liqueur

Amygdalota, the traditional cookies of the Cyclades, are a kind of rustic macaron that are the perfect kosher-for-Passover sweet. Most people use blanched almonds in their recipes, but I find that, although less attractive, *amygdalota* made with whole, unskinned nuts are more delicious, not to mention less labor-intensive—especially if you're starting from the harvest field, as we do here on Kea. Similar almond cookies are baked all over the eastern Mediterranean, with small variations—often scented with rosewater instead of citrus blossom, and sometimes made with a mixture of walnuts, pistachios, and hazelnuts in addition to almonds.

Preheat the oven to 325°F (165°C). Line 2 baking sheets with parchment paper.

In a food processor, finely grind the almonds, excluding the 60 whole almonds, with all but 1 tablespoon of the sugar. Depending on your food processor, you may have to do this in two equal batches.

In a bowl using a handheld mixer, beat the egg whites with the reserved 1 tablespoon sugar and the salt until they form soft peaks.

Transfer the almond mixture to a large bowl. Add the almond extract and gradually add enough egg whites to make a sticky, soft mixture that can just barely be shaped into cookies. Be careful at this stage, because you don't want to make a wet paste that will not hold its form. You may not need to use all the egg whites.

In a bowl, combine the orange blossom water and liqueur.

Wet your hands with the orange blossom water mixture. Take walnut-size pieces of the almond mixture and roll them on your palms to form balls. Flatten slightly, pushing your finger on top of each to make a dimple. Place 1 whole almond into each dimple. Place the cookies on the lined baking sheets.

Bake for about 20 minutes, until lightly golden on both top and bottom. Be very careful not to overbake and dry them out. *Amygdalota* must be hard on the outside and soft on the inside. They are soft as you take them out of the oven, but they harden as they cool.

Let the cookies cool completely, then store in airtight containers or freeze in zip-top bags. Bring to room temperature before serving.

Sweet Wheat Berry and Nut Pilaf (*Kollyva*) VEGAN

SERVES 12 TO 20

2½ cups (500 g) wheat berries

1 teaspoon sea salt

2 bay leaves

2 cinnamon sticks, each about 2 inches (5 cm) long

1 teaspoon whole cloves

1½ cups (150 g) coarsely chopped blanched almonds

1½ cups (180 g) coarsely chopped walnuts

¾ cup (105 g) toasted sesame seeds

1 cup (160 g) sultanas (golden raisins)

1 cup (140 g) dried black currants

1 cup (170 g) pomegranate seeds

1½ teaspoons ground cinnamon

1½ cups (150 g) confectioners' sugar, plus more for serving

½ to ⅔ cup (50 to 75 g) ground roasted chickpeas or fine dried bread crumbs, lightly toasted in a dry skillet over low heat

Whole blanched almonds and pomegranate seeds, for decorating (optional)

Some scholars say that *kollyva* was the Christian, vegetarian version of sacrificial food, a replacement for the pagan custom of slaughtering animals to please the gods. Others will tell you that *kollyva* is the continuation of *polysporia*, the mixture of grains symbolically offered by ancient Greeks to some of their gods, especially Demeter, goddess of agriculture.

Up until recently *kollyva* was strictly prepared at solemn occasions to commemorate the passing of loved relatives. Fortunately creative Athenian restaurants included the grain on their menus. We can now serve this delicious treat any time without the fear of being frowned upon by very traditional local guests.

Serve *kollyva* with ice cream as dessert or make it part of a wholesome breakfast, adding oranges or any seasonal fruit. And, of course, complement with creamy yogurt.

Rinse the wheat berries in a colander and place in a large pot. Cover with water by 2 inches (5 cm), adding the salt. Tie the bay leaves, cinnamon sticks, and cloves in a piece of cheesecloth and place in the pot. Bring to a boil over high heat, reduce the heat, and simmer, stirring occasionally, for about 30 minutes. Add a little water if necessary and continue to simmer until the grains are cooked but still somewhat chewy. Don't overcook them!

Drain the wheat berries and spread them on thick kitchen linen or cotton towels. Leave them to dry for at least 3 hours or overnight. Reserve the cooking liquid, discarding the cheesecloth sachet, to use as a broth for cooking. (The boiled and dried grains can be kept in a zip-top bag for up to 3 days in the refrigerator or frozen for at least 6 months. Bring to room temperature before finishing the sweet.)

In a large bowl, using your fingers, mix the cooked wheat berries with the chopped almonds, walnuts, sesame seeds, sultanas, currants, pomegranate seeds, and ground cinnamon. The mixture can be prepared up to this point and stored in the refrigerator in an airtight container for 1 day.

Just before serving, add the confectioners' sugar and roasted chickpeas or toasted bread crumbs to the wheat berry mixture, mixing well with your fingers. Arrange on a large plate or tray lined with a doily, if you like. Using your hands, shape the wheat berry mixture to form a smooth mound. Sprinkle with confectioners' sugar and decorate with whole almonds and pomegranate seeds.

Serve spoonfuls in individual bowls or, as is the custom in Greece, in small paper cones or bags. Leftovers can be stored in an airtight container in the fridge for at least 6 days.

Orange and Crumbled Phyllo Cake (*Portokalopita*)

A few years ago, *portokalopita* suddenly went viral, as the expression goes. It appeared in various forms in practically every bakery around Greece. Bakers I asked could not say where the recipe comes from. My husband offered a plausible, if slightly cynical, explanation: "A novice, probably frustrated cook who couldn't manage to make a decent pie and ended up with torn-up phyllo pieces decided to dump them into the batter," he said. And he is probably right!

In my recipe, I adopted the crimped phyllo base of the Turkish "poor people's börek," baked without filling and then doused in syrup. I added sugar, cinnamon, and almonds to the crimped phyllo to make it more crunchy. I also substitute olive oil for the margarine or butter used in common recipes. I serve the cake upside down, making for a more interesting presentation, I think. I glaze it with my bitter orange or lemon marmalade (page 238), but any marmalade will do.

FOR THE SYRUP:

2 oranges

1 cup (200 g) granulated sugar

FOR THE BASE:

3 tablespoons olive oil, plus more as needed

1 pound (500 g) frozen phyllo, thawed
according to package instructions

¼ cup (50 g) granulated sugar

2 teaspoons ground cinnamon

¼ cup (25 g) finely ground almonds

FOR THE BATTER:

5 eggs

½ cup (100 g) granulated sugar

1 cup (240 ml) olive oil

½ teaspoon salt

1½ teaspoons baking powder

⅓ cup (80 ml) brandy

1 cup (250 g) Greek-style yogurt

1 cup (140 g) black currants or raisins (optional)

½ cup (120 ml) citrus marmalade

3 to 4 tablespoons orange or lemon liqueur

Make the syrup: Zest and juice the oranges; place the juice in a small saucepan and reserve the zest in a small bowl to be used in the batter. Add the sugar to the saucepan along with 1 cup (240 ml) water and bring the mixture to a boil over medium-high heat. Reduce the heat to low and simmer for 8 minutes. Let cool to room temperature.

Make the base: Preheat the oven to 375°F (190°C). Brush a 9-inch (23-cm) springform pan with olive oil.

Unroll the thawed phyllo. Take 6 sheets for the base, and leave the other sheets on the counter uncovered to dry—contrary to what one usually does when using phyllo to make pies.

In a bowl, mix the sugar, cinnamon, and almonds.

Lightly brush 1 sheet of phyllo with olive oil and sprinkle with some of the sugar-cinnamon mixture. Using your fingers, crimp the phyllo, pinching and pleating to create a long, tight, accordionlike piece. Transfer to the baking dish. Repeat with the remaining 5 sheets, placing them one next to the other to cover the bottom of the dish.

Bake the phyllo for about 15 minutes, until it is a light golden color. Remove from the oven and let cool on a wire rack. Don't turn the oven off.

Make the batter: In a large bowl, whisk the eggs with the sugar until light yellow and creamy. Add the reserved orange zest, the olive oil, and the salt and whisk to incorporate. In a cup, dissolve the baking powder in the brandy and add it to the egg mixture, together with the yogurt and currants (if using), whisking to combine. Tear and crumble the remaining phyllo sheets and add them to the batter, just folding them in with a spatula. Pour the batter over the baked phyllo.

Bake in the middle of the oven for 35 to 40 minutes, until golden brown and set.

Transfer to a wire rack, prick the top with a toothpick, and pour the cooled syrup over the cake. Let cool and invert onto a serving platter.

Dilute the marmalade with the lemon or orange liqueur and spread it over the cake. If you like, just before cutting, sprinkle the cake with more orange or lemon liqueur.

Rustic Chocolates with Dried Figs, Pistachios, and Toasted Nuts GLUTEN-FREE

MAKES 40 TO 80 SQUARES

½ pound (225 g) dried figs, chopped with scissors and soaked overnight in ½ cup (120 ml) lemon-flavored liqueur

4 ounces (115 g) dried banana, chopped with scissors, or mixed dried cherries and raisins

1½ cups (180 g) shelled pistachios

2 cups (about 200 g) toasted and coarsely chopped mixed nuts: hazelnuts, walnuts, and almonds

½ teaspoon salt, or to taste

½ teaspoon freshly ground black pepper, or to taste

3 tablespoons olive oil

1½ pounds (680 g) bittersweet chocolate (65% cacao or higher), chopped and melted in a double boiler or in the microwave

My friend Vicki Snyder says that every cookbook, no matter what its subject matter, must include a chocolate dessert. Here is mine: a medley of dried figs, banana jerky, chopped toasted nuts, and pistachios—barely held together by bittersweet chocolate. I offer boxes to friends together with jars of my marmalade (page 238). All through the winter and spring, I have a jar of these chocolates next to a jar of savory biscotti (page 218). But when the weather gets hot I stop making them, because they melt and their taste isn't quite the same when kept in the fridge. Irresistibly crunchy, my rustic chocolates are a perfect, healthy snack; they can also accompany ice cream, sorbet, and creamy desserts.

In a large bowl, toss together the figs, bananas, pistachios, toasted nuts, salt, and pepper.

Stir the olive oil into the melted chocolate and pour the chocolate over the fruits and nuts. Toss well using two large spatulas, making sure all the fruits and nuts are well-coated with chocolate.

Line a baking sheet with parchment paper and pour the chocolate mixture on it. Lay another piece of parchment paper over the chocolate and press well with your palms to spread and even the chocolate on the baking sheet.

Refrigerate for 30 to 45 minutes, until hard.

Slide the paper with the hardened chocolate onto a large cutting board. Using a large knife, halve the block, then halve both pieces. Cut each piece into 10 to 20 squares or bars, depending on the size you prefer.

Store in airtight jars or boxes in a cool, dark place. Don't refrigerate, unless the temperature is high enough that the chocolate will melt.

Pumpkin Preserves VEGAN GLUTEN-FREE

MAKES ENOUGH TO FILL ABOUT
2 (1-PINT/480-ML) JARS

FOR THE CALCIUM BATH:

1 cup (220 g) pickling lime

2 pounds (1 kg) peeled and seeded
  pumpkin or squash, cut into 1-inch
  (2.5-cm) cubes (see Notes)

FOR THE SYRUP:

5 cups (1 kg) granulated sugar

2 (4-inch/10-cm) cinnamon sticks

¼ cup (60 ml) fresh lemon juice

The recipe for *kolokytha rossoli*, as this "spoon sweet" is called, is so easy you won't believe the stunning and mouthwatering results. You don't even need to use special, expensive pumpkins—the leftover flesh from your decorative Halloween pumpkin works wonderfully. I am sure you will love it as topping for yogurt or ice cream, but this sweet can stand on its own. At the center of a small plate, with some of its syrup, it is a unique homemade dessert to offer to your friends. If you happen to have a fancy cutter that makes fusilli-like chunks, the pumpkin preserves will be spectacular on the eyes. But don't worry: Simply dicing the bright-orange flesh into small pieces will result in equally irresistible crunchy chunks.

Dilute the pickling lime in 4 quarts (4 L) water and add the pumpkin pieces. Leave for at least 4 hours or overnight. Drain and rinse thoroughly under cold water. Lay the pieces on a double layer of paper towels to dry completely.

Make the syrup: In a large pot, bring the sugar and 1 quart (1 L) water to a boil. Add the cinnamon sticks and boil for 3 to 4 minutes. Add the pumpkin pieces, return to a boil, then reduce the heat. Simmer, stirring often, for 10 minutes. Add the lemon juice and cook for 5 minutes more, or until the pumpkin is crunchy and sweet.

Transfer to clean, sterilized hot jars (see Notes), filling almost to the top. Close the lids and let cool and seal on a rack. If the lids don't pop, store in the refrigerator and eat the preserves within a month or two.

NOTES: *You can also use a melon scoop to make pumpkin balls. If you have a special cutter that can make curls, dig it out of the kitchen drawer for this recipe!*

To sterilize the jars, place them (not the lids) on an oven rack and heat to 180°F (80°C) for about 20 minutes. Fill with the preserves while the jars are still hot.

Rose Petal and Yogurt Mousse GLUTEN-FREE

SERVES 6 (OR 8, IF USING SMALL GLASSES)

FOR THE ROSE PETAL JAM:

5 cups (300 g) packed fragrant rose petals,
   or ⅓ cup (40 g) crushed dried organic
   rose petals

1 to 1½ cups (200 to 300 g) granulated sugar

¼ cup (60 ml) fresh lemon juice

¼ to ⅓ cup (60 to 80 ml) rosewater, to taste

FOR THE MOUSSE:

1½ teaspoons unflavored gelatin

1 cup (240 ml) whole milk

½ cup (100 g) granulated sugar

¼ cup (60 ml) rosewater

1½ cups (375 g) full-fat Greek-style yogurt

¾ cup (180 ml) heavy cream, chilled

3 tablespoons coarsely chopped pistachios,
   for serving

Fresh or dried rose petals, for serving

For many years now, we have tried to cultivate heirloom fragrant roses in our garden on Kea—*Rosa damascena* and related varietals—but our dry climate and poor soil have made it very difficult to produce enough rose petals to make jam. Fortunately, good-quality organic dried rose petals, together with good rosewater (see Sources, page 244), have helped me make plenty of jam to flavor this light yogurt mousse that our guests love. High-quality jars of Bulgarian, French, or Turkish rose-petal jam are available online. If you manage to get your hands on one, there is no need to make your own.

Make the rose-petal jam: If using fresh rose petals, rinse and dry the petals with paper towels. Sprinkle with ½ cup (100 g) of the sugar and massage with your fingers to wilt and soften the petals. In a saucepan, bring 1½ cups (360 ml) water and the remaining 1 cup sugar to a boil, add the rose petals (wilted fresh and/or dried), and simmer for 15 minutes, or until the petals are tender. Add the lemon juice and ¼ cup (60 ml) rosewater and simmer, stirring often, for 10 minutes more. Remove from the heat, taste, and add more rosewater, if you like. Let cool completely. The result is not going to be a thick jam, but more like a fragrant sauce.

Make the mousse: In a small bowl, sprinkle the gelatin over ¼ cup (60 ml) of the milk and let stand for 2 to 3 minutes to soften.

In a saucepan, bring the remaining ¾ cup (180 ml) milk and the sugar to a boil over medium heat. Simmer and stir until the sugar dissolves. Add the gelatin mixture and turn off the heat. Stir vigorously until the gelatin dissolves completely. Pour the mixture into a metal bowl and place it over an ice-water bath to cool rapidly. Let cool for 15 to 20 minutes, stirring often, until cold. Add the yogurt and whisk to incorporate.

Using a handheld mixer, whip the heavy cream until it gets a good amount of body. Fold the cream into the yogurt mixture. It must be completely incorporated. Cover with plastic wrap and refrigerate for about 30 minutes, until it starts to set. You can let the cream set overnight in the bowl. Take out of the refrigerator and stir the cream a few times before assembling the mousse.

To assemble: Place 2 tablespoons rose-petal jam in the bottom of each serving glass and then divide the chilled mousse evenly among them. Cover with plastic wrap and refrigerate for 2 to 3 hours or preferably overnight.

Just before serving, top each glass with 1 to 2 teaspoons of rose-petal jam, if you like, and sprinkle with pistachios and rose petals.

Quince Preserves (*Kydoni Glyko*) VEGAN GLUTEN-FREE

MAKES 3½ PINTS (1.5 L) OR
6 (1-CUP/250 ML) JARS

4 medium-large quinces (about
   3 pounds/1.5 kg)

1 lemon, quartered

4½ to 6 cups (900 g to 1.2 kg)
   granulated sugar

½ cup (120 ml) honey

¼ cup (60 ml) lemon juice

4 rose geranium leaves (see Notes)

1 cup (125 g) blanched almonds

Quince is one of the most popular Greek spoon sweets. It is served as a dessert topping for yogurt in taverns all around the country. Tourists love it, though unfortunately most restaurants use cheap commercial preserves. By cooking down the peels and cores that contain most of the pectin, and adding their rich broth to the sweet, we can make our own quince preserves with less sugar and more fruity flavor and aroma. I prefer to fill small jars—once opened, the contents are difficult to resist. At least with small jars you might pause before breaking the seal, but then again, you might not! By adding spices, I turn some of the spoon sweet into an unusual relish (see Variation).

Wash and dry the quinces. Place 1 quart (1 L) water in a medium bowl, and squeeze the lemon quarters into the water, tossing in the squeezed lemon pieces.

Using a large knife and working on a sturdy cutting board, halve one quince crosswise, through the equator. Place one piece on the board, cut side down, and quarter it, then using a good paring knife, peel, core, and seed each piece. Drop the cleaned pieces into the lemon-water. Place the peels and cores in a saucepan and continue preparing the rest of the quinces the same way.

Add enough water (about 1 quart/1 L) to the saucepan to cover the peels and cores. Bring to a boil over medium-high heat, then reduce the heat and simmer, stirring occasionally. Add more water as needed to prevent burning while you finish cutting the quince.

Slice and cut each quince piece into *batonnets* (matchsticks) about ¼ inch (0.6 cm) thick or less—but not too thin. If you have a good mandoline cutter and a steel glove to protect your hand, you can cut thick quince into julienne quickly. Drop the cut pieces back into the lemon-water as you work.

Drain the quince pieces, transfer to a saucepan, and add 4½ cups (900 g) sugar. Discard the lemon peels and pass the water through a fine sieve. Measure 3 cups (720 ml), reserving the rest, and add it to the pot with the quince. Bring slowly to a boil over medium-high heat.

Drain the quince cores and peels through a fine-mesh sieve over a bowl to collect their juices, pressing hard to drain. You should have about 1 cup (240 ml) of juices. If it is less, fill the cup with the reserved lemony water. Add to the pot, discarding the solids.

Place two saucers in the freezer. Bring the quince to a boil and skim the surface as needed. Reduce the heat to medium and cook, stirring often, for 20 minutes, or until the quince is almost cooked—the precise time depends on the size of the pieces. Add the honey, lemon juice, rose geranium leaves, and almonds. Increase the heat and cook for 5 to 10 minutes more. Taste and add more sugar, if you like. Cook for 1 minute over high heat, until the syrup thickens. When it begins to look syrupy, take one of the saucers from the freezer and drop ½ teaspoon of syrup on the cold saucer. As it cools, push it with your finger. If it wrinkles, it is done. If not, continue cooking, stirring for a few minutes more, then repeat the test with the second saucer.

If the quince is soft but the syrup is still watery, use a slotted spoon to remove the fruit to a bowl, cook the syrup down to thicken, testing, as described above, then add the fruit back in. Bring to a boil, stir, and after 2 minutes transfer the quince preserves to sterilized jars (see Notes), filling almost to the top. Close the lids and let cool on a rack. The lids will seal—if they are metal, you will hear a pop. If the lids won't pop, store in the refrigerator and eat the preserves within a month or two.

Store the jars in a cool, dark place—they will keep for at least 1 year. Refrigerate after opening.

NOTES: *If you don't have rose geranium, I suggest you don't add anything else—like cinnamon stick, as some people do. I prefer the pure, unadulterated quince aroma, which is hardly tainted by the delicate rose geranium.*

To sterilize the jars, place them (not the lids) on an oven rack and heat to 180°F (80°C) for about 20 minutes. Fill with the preserves while the jars are still hot.

VARIATION

SPICY QUINCE PRESERVES
Spicy quince preserves make an excellent topping for yogurt and for creamy, soft cheeses, both sweet and spicy. Adding 1 to 2 teaspoons fresh lemon juice or cider vinegar makes a great relish for roast chicken and turkey.

In a small skillet, slowly heat 1½ cups (360 ml) quince preserves, adding 2 teaspoons grated fresh ginger, 1 teaspoon ground allspice, and a small pinch of cayenne pepper. Do not let the mixture boil—just heat it through so that the flavors and aromas mix. Transfer to a jar or bowl, let cool, cover, and refrigerate. Use within 1 month.

Bitter Seville Orange and Lemon Marmalade VEGAN GLUTEN-FREE

MAKES ABOUT 7 (8-OUNCE/225-G) JARS

6 untreated organic lemons, washed, stems discarded

5 to 7 bitter (Seville) oranges, washed, stems discarded

3 to 3½ pounds (1.5 to 1.6 kg) granulated sugar, depending on your sweet tooth

This marmalade is based on a traditional English recipe that has evolved in my kitchen over the years. I add it to cakes, puddings, creams, breads, and sauces, both sweet and savory. I make lots of it every year to use up our abundant supply of bitter oranges as well as lemons from our old, very productive lemon trees. Traditionally in Greece citrus peel is zested, cut into segments, rolled and coiled on a thread, then cooked in syrup to make bitter orange or lemon preserves, called *karoulakia* (as shown opposite). Besides marmalade, I juice my leftover Seville oranges and freeze the fragrant liquid to use year-round in place of lemon in dressings and in chickpea or bean soups, following a tradition from Crete. My marmalade is very fragrant and quite chunky—I don't cut the peels very fine. But you can add more sugar or spend more time finely cutting the peels, if you like.

Choose a pot that holds the fruit snugly in one layer. Add enough water to fully cover the fruit, about 2 quarts (2 L) or as needed, and place a heavy, heatproof plate directly on the fruit to keep it immersed. Bring to a boil and cook for 15 minutes. Using a large fork, pierce the lemons and oranges in several places; continue cooking until the skins are quite tender. With a slotted spoon, transfer the fruit to a colander set over a bowl and leave to cool a bit.

Place a double layer of wet cheesecloth in a medium bowl. Working over the cheesecloth-lined bowl, halve each fruit and scrape out the seeds, the pulp, and the membranes, dropping everything into the cheesecloth, but setting the scraped peels aside. Tie the cheesecloth with cotton string and place it in the pot, hanging the string over the side.

Place a cutting board inside a baking pan to catch any juices, and use a sharp knife to cut the peels into thin strips.

Stir the peels into the pot with the liquid and the cheesecloth sachet, together with the juices that have accumulated in the baking pan.

Place two saucers in the freezer.

Turn the heat to medium, bring the mixture to a boil, and simmer, stirring often, for about 10 minutes, until the peels are quite soft. Add 3 pounds (1.5 kg) sugar and bring the marmalade to a boil, stirring and pressing the cheesecloth to release the juices and pectin from the pulp and pips. Cook, stirring often, for 15 to 20 minutes, until the syrup sets. Taste, and if you prefer your marmalade sweeter, add a bit more sugar.

When the marmalade begins to look syrupy, take one of the saucers from the freezer and drop ½ teaspoon syrup on the cold saucer. As it cools, push it with your finger. If it wrinkles, the marmalade is done. If not, continue cooking, stirring a few minutes more, then repeat the test with the second saucer.

Pour immediately into hot sterilized jars (see Note), filling almost to the top. Close the lids and let cool on a rack. The lids will seal—if they are metal, you will hear them pop.

The marmalade can be stored in a cool, dark place for at least 1 year. Refrigerate once opened.

NOTE: *To sterilize the jars, place them (not the lids) on an oven rack and heat to 180°F (80°C) for about 20 minutes. Fill with the preserves while the jars are still hot.*

Bitter Orange Drink (*Vin Apéritif à l'Orange Amère*) VEGAN GLUTEN-FREE

MAKES 3 QUARTS (3 L), TO FILL
1 (4-QUART/4-L) GLASS JAR, OR
2 (2-QUART/2-L) GLASS JARS

5 bitter (Seville) oranges, preferably organic (see Note)

1 orange, preferably organic (see Note)

½ untreated lemon, preferably organic (see Note)

1 tablespoon whole cloves

1 cup (200 g) granulated sugar

2 bottles rosé wine from Provence or any good dry rosé wine

1 pint (480 ml) eau de vie, grappa, or 80-proof vodka

2 cinnamon sticks

2 cups (480 ml) good-quality dark rum

1 cup (240 ml) Simple Syrup (opposite), or more to taste

When our trees overwhelm us with Seville oranges and I have made enough marmalade to last me for the year, I make this fragrant aperitif. Inspired by a recipe from Provence, I macerate the fruit to get a citrusy, Campari-style drink that I serve in a tall glass with a splash of seltzer or tonic water, a fresh orange slice, and just a couple of ice cubes. The drink is extremely easy to make, but the fruit needs to macerate in wine for at least six weeks—so plan ahead. If you can't get Seville oranges, use grapefruit (see Note).

Wash all the citrus very well. Pat dry and quarter the oranges. Insert the cloves into some of the bitter orange pieces.

Place the sugar and the wine in a 3-quart (3-L) jar (or divide them evenly between two smaller jars) and stir briefly. It doesn't matter if all the sugar does not dissolve.

Add the oranges, eau de vie, and cinnamon sticks. Juice the lemon and add. Seal the jar or jars and carefully shake to mix the ingredients.

Leave at room temperature for at least 6 to 7 weeks—the longer you leave it, the better it gets. Shake the jar once a day the first week and then whenever you remember, at least once a week.

Pass the mixture through a very fine-mesh sieve lined with wet, double-layered cheesecloth into a bowl. Add the rum and syrup, stir, and taste. If you find it too bitter and sour, add more syrup, but keep in mind that the flavor should be quite strong, as it will be served with seltzer or tonic.

Transfer to bottles and refrigerate for 1 to 2 days before serving.

NOTE: *If you can't get bitter oranges, use 3 oranges and 2 grapefruits and omit the lemon juice. Choose somewhat unripe fruits. Quarter the oranges; halve the grapefruit and divide each half into 6 pieces. Proceed as described above.*

Simple Syrup VEGAN GLUTEN-FREE

MAKES ABOUT 3½ CUPS (750 ML)

2½ cups (500 g) granulated sugar

In a saucepan, combine the sugar and 2 cups (480 ml) water and bring to a simmer over medium heat. Simmer for 3 minutes. Let cool completely and use as needed. Keep the rest in a sealed jar in the refrigerator to use in cocktails or to pour over cakes.

Thyme Liqueur VEGAN GLUTEN-FREE

MAKES 1 PINT (480 ML)

⅓ cup (20 g) packed flowered thyme sprigs, or 3 tablespoons dried Mediterranean thyme

1 pint (480 ml) vodka or eau de vie

½ cup (100 g) granulated sugar, or to taste

Simple Syrup (above; optional), to taste

1 sprig fresh thyme (optional)

This fragrant thyme liqueur from the south of France is the ideal finale to a Mediterranean dinner. The French believe that thyme tisane is an excellent digestive and the perfect treatment for a hangover. But I suggest thyme not for its medicinal properties, but because its aroma, with a bit of help from the alcohol, will transport you to the rugged hills overlooking the dark-blue sea—and if that is not therapeutic, I don't know what is. I make this liqueur in June with our strongly aromatic wild thyme, but good-quality dried thyme makes an equally delicious version. Try it also with sage or with the hauntingly aromatic Greek mountain tea (see Variation).

Place the thyme in a bottle that holds more than 1 pint (480 ml). Add the vodka, seal, and let it stand for 3 weeks, shaking every 1 to 2 days. Add the sugar and shake well. Let stand for another week, shaking at least once every day. The sugar should dissolve within a week. Taste and see if you like the level of sweetness and the aroma. Let it macerate longer or add some Simple Syrup (see above), if you like.

Pass the liqueur through a double layer of moistened cheesecloth and transfer to a fresh bottle, adding the sprig of fresh thyme for decoration, if you like. Store in the refrigerator and serve in shot glasses after a meal.

VARIATION

To make sage or mountain-tea liqueur, substitute ⅓ cup (20 g) sage leaves or dried sprigs of mountain tea (see Sources, page 244) for the thyme. Both are delicious.

Lemon Liqueur VEGAN GLUTEN-FREE

MAKES ABOUT 2 QUARTS (2 L)

7 very fresh, thick-skinned organic lemons
1 quart (1 L) vodka, preferably 80-proof
3 cups (600 g) granulated sugar

What follows is an all-purpose homemade liqueur, loosely based on Italian *limoncello* from the Amalfi coast. It needs to infuse for four to six weeks, so plan accordingly, but do plan—it is worth that wait. I add this liqueur to fruit salads, drizzle it over cakes, and of course serve it ice-cold after a meal.

Following this recipe, you can also make tangerine and orange liqueurs if you find very fresh, aromatic fruit. I like to mix lemons and bergamots, the deeply fragrant citrus fruit used to make Earl Grey tea. Bergamots are not easy to get, but if you find one or two, add their peels together with the lemons; never use them by themselves because their aroma can be overpowering.

Wash and dry the lemons. Using a vegetable peeler, remove about two-thirds of the yellow part of the peel from each lemon. Make very thin strips, starting from the tip of the lemon and ending at the stem.

You will end up with a mostly white lemon with a few yellow stripes. Use the lemons for Bitter Seville Orange and Lemon Marmalade (page 238), or juice them.

Place the peels in a 1-quart (1-L) Mason jar and add the vodka. Seal and let stand at room temperature for 4 to 6 weeks, shaking every now and then.

In a saucepan, mix the sugar with 3½ cups (840 ml) water and cook over medium heat for 2 to 3 minutes, until the sugar dissolves completely. Reduce the heat and keep the mixture simmering.

Drain the vodka through a sieve into a clean jar and set aside. Keep the peels in the sieve and place the sieve over a large bowl. Pour the boiling syrup over the peels. Discard the peels and set the syrup aside to cool completely.

Mix the infused vodka with the cooled syrup. Pour the lemon liqueur into clean bottles, seal, and store in the refrigerator.

Tangy Mint Syrup VEGAN GLUTEN-FREE

MAKES ABOUT 1½ PINTS (720 ML)

1 cup (200 g) granulated sugar

1 cup (240 ml) distilled white vinegar

15 to 20 sprigs fresh mint

FOR SERVING:

Water or seltzer

Ice cubes

Mint sprigs

Lime or lemon slices

While looking through an 1862 Turkish cookbook compiled by Turabi Efendi, I came across a vinegar-sugar syrup scented with sweet marjoram called *oxymel*. *Oxymeli* (vinegar-honey) is an ancient Greek word that probably referred to similar sweet-sour drinks in antiquity. Sugar has replaced honey, and people continue to enjoy similar syrupy drinks today, especially in Muslim countries where alcoholic beverages are prohibited. Starting with the old book's basic recipe, I experimented with different quantities of sugar and vinegar, using marjoram, mint, and rose geranium as flavorings. By far my favorite was the mint-flavored *oxymel*; it is a truly refreshing sweet and tangy drink that probably became what we call a "shrub" today, and is certainly better than commercial sodas. You can try the recipe with other herbs as well.

In a nonreactive pan, combine the sugar with 1 quart (1 L) water and bring to a boil. Simmer for about 10 minutes, then add the vinegar. Continue simmering for 25 minutes more. Add the mint to the pan and return the liquid to a boil. Remove from the heat and let cool. Remove and discard the mint sprigs. Pass the syrup through a fine-mesh sieve and store in an airtight bottle in the refrigerator. The syrup will keep for at least 6 months.

To serve, place 2 to 3 tablespoons syrup in a glass. Pour in very cold water or seltzer and add ice cubes, a fresh mint sprig, and a thin slice of lime or lemon, if you like.

SOURCES

The majority of the ingredients for the recipes in this book can be found at your local farmer's market, in supermarkets, and in the various ethnic and Middle Eastern grocery stores across the United States and Europe. Here are some sources for the best-quality spices and other foods that may be difficult to find in your neighborhood.

Spices, Maraş and Other Peppers, Sauces, and Other Middle Eastern Ingredients

Alteya Organics
(312) 528-9161
Toll-free: (877) 425-8392
www.alteya.com
Bulgarian Rose Otto rose petal jam, rose water, and other USDA certified organic products.

Amazon Grocery
www.amazon.com
Authentic products from Lebanon: Cortas brand pomegranate molasses and their excellent orange blossom and rose waters; Alwadi Al Akhdar brand grape molasses; as well as tahini, dried apricot paste, and many other products.

Arabica Food & Spice Company
Arch 257 Grosvenor Court
Grosvenor Terrace
London SE5 0NP UK
+44 (0) 20 7708 5577
www.arabicafoodandspice.com
Online ordering and other retail locations throughout the UK and Europe. Orange blossom and rose waters, pomegranate molasses, aromatics and flavorings, herbs and spices, fruit preserves, pickles and pastes.

Buonitalia, Ltd.
75 Ninth Avenue
New York, NY 10011
(212) 633-9090
www.buonitalia.com
This store within New York's famed Chelsea Market has vincotto (grape molasses), shelled pistachios, and cheeses from various parts of Italy, as well as other Italian specialty items, also available for online ordering.

Buy Lebanese
www.buylebanese.com
+961 3 602405
Dried *kishk* (*keshek*), Sabe3 Bharat (seven spices mix), sumac, dried Lebanese thyme (*zatar yabes seda*) and za'atar spice blend, pomegranate molasses and many other Lebanese foods available for online ordering.

Daphnis and Chloe
11742 Acropolis
Athens, Greece
www.daphnisandchloe.com
Three different kinds of wild Greek oregano, as well as other herbs, mountain tea and other infusions, plain or in blends, available for online ordering.

Farm to People
New York, NY 10023
Toll-free: (877) 564-0367
www.farmtopeople.com
In addition to other local food products, good-quality Mina brand harissa—produced in three different types—is available for online ordering.

Formaggio Kitchen
244 Huron Avenue
Cambridge, MA 02138
(617) 354-4750
Toll-free: (888) 212–3224
www.formaggiokitchen.com
Aleppo, Maraş and urfa pepper, as well as Italian cheeses, olives, and olive oils, available for online ordering.

igourmet.com
508 Delaware Avenue
West Pittston, PA 18643
Toll-free: (877) 446-8763
www.igourmet.com
This internet grocery sells foodstuffs from around the world, including Greek and Middle Eastern products like Kimi dried figs from Greece, green wheat freekeh, Lebanese za'atar, organic preserved lemons, pomegranate molasses, shelled pistachios, and so on.

Kalustyan's
123 Lexington Avenue
New York, NY 10016
(212) 685–3451
www.kalustyans.com
This renowned store sells Maraş and Aleppo pepper, spices, coarse bulgur, barley couscous, *kishk*, and all kinds of spices and Middle Eastern ingredients, also available for online ordering.

Porto-Muiños
Polígono Industrial Acevedo
15185 Cerceda
A Coruña, Spain
(34) 981 688 030
Spanish seaweeds, fresh and dried, available for online ordering at www.cocinaparanavegantes.com

Qupia
The Pfizer Building
630 Flushing Ave.
Brooklyn, NY 11206
(855) 999-9150
www.qupiafoods.com
Grape molasses (*petimezi*) from Greece, giant white beans (*gigantes*), herbs, olives, olive oil, thyme-honey, and other selected Greek products are available for online ordering.

Spanish Table
1426 Western Ave
Seattle, WA 98101
(206) 682-2827
www.spanishtable.com
With retail stores in Seattle, WA; Berkeley and Mill Valley, CA; and Santa Fe, NM: ñora peppers and *pimenton* (smoked paprika), Piment d'Espelette, Judion white beans, chickpeas (garbanzos) from Astorga-Leon, and other items from Spain and Portugal are also available for online ordering.

Supermarket Italy
(201) 729-0739
www.supermarketitaly.com
This internet grocer has salt-cured capers, organic Italian beans, and many cheeses, all available for online ordering.

Taste of Crete
3775 Park Avenue
Edison, NJ 08820
(908) 685-2035
www.tasteofcrete.com
Excellent olive oil from Greece is available for online ordering.

Titan Foods
25-56 31st Street
Astoria, NY 11102
(718) 626-7771
www.titanfoods.net
Look for the Kyknos Greek tomato paste, To Manna barley rusks from Crete, giant white beans (*gigantes*), Kalamata dried figs, feta, and the creamy manouri cheese, all available for online ordering.

Tulumba
129 15th Street
Brooklyn, NY 11215
(718) 369-8904
Toll-free (866) 855-8622
www.tulumba.com
Turkish products, including hot and sweet pepper paste, tarhana both mild and spicy, pickled cabbage, pickled green plums, bulgur in various grades, grape molasses (*pekmez*), pomegranate molasses, mulberry and carob molasses are all available for online ordering.

World Spice Merchants
1509 Western Avenue
Seattle, WA 98101
(206) 682-7274
www.worldspice.com
Spices, herbs, and blends from all over the world, including both Syrian and Israeli za'atar, hazelnut dukka, Iranian advieh, and Arabic baharat are available for online ordering.

Zingerman's
422 Detroit Street
Ann Arbor, MI 48104
(734) 663-3354
Toll-free: (888) 636-8162
www.zingermans.com
The famous Michigan deli has salt-packed capers and caperberries, olive oils, olives from all over the Mediterranean, and artisanal Mediterranean cheeses available for online ordering.

Cheeses and Yogurt

Christos Marketplace
200 Massachusetts Avenue
Arlington, MA 02474
(781) 641-0695
www.christosmarket.com
Barrel-aged feta from Greece and other imported cheeses, also the creamy Skotidakis Greek yogurt made from goat and cow milk (from Canada). Available for online ordering.

Mount Vikos
(888) 534-0246
www.mtvikos.com
Imported Greek cheeses and other products. Visit the website to find a local retailer.

Grains and Flours

Anson Mills
1922 C Gervais Street
Columbia, SC 29201
(803) 467-4122
www.ansonmills.com
Farro and other heirloom grains and beans are available for online ordering.

Bob's Red Mill
Whole Grain Store:
5000 SE International Way
Milwaukie, OR 97222
(503) 607-6455
Toll-free (800) 349-2173
www.bobsredmill.com
Wheat berries, whole-grain bulgur, organic cracked wheat, barley flour and barley grits, and all kinds of organic flours, gluten-free rolled oats, peeled dried fava beans and other legumes, chickpea flour, and many other grain products. Widely distributed in retail stores and available for online ordering.

King Arthur Flour
135 US Route 5 South
Norwich, Vermont 05055
Toll-free: (800) 827-6836
www.kingarthurflour.com
Barley flour and all kinds of organic flours. Widely distributed in retail stores and available for online ordering.

Malted Barley Grains

Home brewing suppliers all over the United States and Europe sell various kinds of malted barley grains; any of them can be used for the recipe on page 214.

E.C. Kraus
733 S Northern Blvd.
Independence MO 64054
(816) 254-7051
www.eckraus.com/malt-barley-grains
I suggest you choose 2 to 3 different grains in small quantities (1 to 2 pounds) and experiment to see what you prefer to add to your barley rusks dough; I use any of the "caramel," or "Belgian Biscuit malts."

Garden Seeds for Herbs, Vegetables, and Greens

The Cook's Garden
P.O. Box C5030
Warminster, PA 18974-0574
(802) 824-5526
www.cooksgarden.com
Seeds for leaf celery (cutting celery), savory, and all kinds of vegetables and greens. Available for online ordering.

Seeds of Change
P.O. Box 4908
Rancho Dominguez, CA 90220
Toll-free (888) 762-7333
www.seedsofchange.com
Organic and heirloom seeds for herbs, vegetables, and chili peppers. Available for online ordering.

Seed Savers Exchange
3094 North Winn Road
Decorah, IA 52101
(563) 382-5990
www.seedsavers.org
Black cumin (herb), Greek oregano, many kinds of basil, savory, and various heirloom vegetables and greens. Available for online ordering.

Kitchen Utensils

Sassafras
1622 W. Carroll Avenue
Chicago, IL 60612
(312) 226-2000
www.sassafrasstore.com
Superstone Bread Dome and baking dishes for round and for long loaves. Available for online ordering.

Canning Pantry
Highland Brands, LLC
2406 Bristol Rd
Columbus, OH 43221
(614) 564-9817
www.canningpantry.com
Clay crocks for fermenting cabbage and other canning supplies. Available for online ordering.

Tulumba
(see page 245)
Earthenware dolma stones in various sizes to weigh down stuffed grape or chard leaves so that they cook submerged in the broth.

Weck Jars
450 E. Congress Pkwy #E
Crystal Lake, IL 60014
(815) 356-8440
Toll-free: (800) 345-7381
www.weckjars.com
Beautiful canning jars and bottles. Available for online ordering.

ACKNOWLEDGMENTS

More than two decades have passed since my very first book, *The Foods of Greece*, was published by Stewart, Tabori and Chang and won the Julia Child award. Leslie Stoker was my publisher then and it was she who chose to publish this book. I am immensely grateful to Leslie. I was fortunate to have Marisa Bulzone as my new editor; her wise and creative decisions were indispensable. Many thanks to Holly Dolce, the executive editor at Abrams, for her help and support, and also to senior production manager Tina Cameron, associate managing editor Emily Albarillo, and the designer, Sarah Gifford, who helped make the book beautiful.

My dear friend Seth Rosenbaum is my guardian angel: he shaped my far from perfect texts in the first edit of the manuscript. I couldn't be happier that the exceptionally talented Penny de Los Santos was the photographer. She came to Kea along with the amazing food stylist Liza Jernow; many thanks also to Hunter Lewis—now executive editor of *Southern Living*—who styled some of the pictures (pages 17 and 19) and to Lenio Margaritouli. I am indebted to my potter friends Vicki Snyder, Vasso Vernardaki, Christina Morali, and Hara Bahariou, who provided me with exquisite plates, bowls and casseroles.

I have been gathering recipes and ideas over the years, traveling, tasting, cooking with local chefs and home cooks, and researching ancient texts, old and new books; the unsurpassed works of Claudia Roden and Paula Wolfert showed me the way and helped me enormously when I decided to concentrate on food after working as journalist and editor for many years. Paula has been a true friend and mentor, sharing with me her vast knowledge and her contacts throughout the region; I can never thank her enough!

I am grateful to my friend Stamatia Stylou, a passionate cook and keeper of the old frugal traditions, and to my tireless assistant Ela Allamani and her mother Drita Aliay who shared their Albanian and Balkan recipes; many thanks to my dear friend Marilena Raouna who deciphered the secrets of Cypriot cuisine, especially the breads and sweets.

From Istanbul, my soul mate Marianna Gerasimos, an ardent cook, inspired author, and researcher of Ottoman Cuisine has answered my many questions and helped me converse with our mutual friend Musa Dağdeviren, one of the wisest chefs I know. Defne Koryürek, Burcu Gezeroğlu, and their lively Slow Food Istanbul group introduced me to some amazing Turkish cheeses. Semsa Denizsel's delicious, no-frills cooking and baking at Kantin Lokanta was a great inspiration. The journalist and author Aylin Öney Tan as well as Ayfer Ünsal and Filiz Hösukoglu from the Gaziantep led me through some of the region's most enticing foods.

Many thanks to Anissa Helou, the London-based Lebanese food writer and researcher for sharing her vast experience of Arab and Middle Eastern cuisine, and for introducing me to Syrian-born chef Mohammed Antabli, owner of *Al Waha* (the Oasis), one of London's top Lebanese restaurants. I am grateful to chef Antabli for generously sharing some of his wonderful recipes. Many thanks to Barbara Abdeni Massaad who taught me all about the regional varieties of *man'oushé,* the versatile Lebanese bread that has become one of our staples.

I will always be grateful to Dalia Lamdani for guiding me during my very first trip to Israel; she helped me discover authentic Sephardic foods. Thanks to Joan Nathan, I experienced the exciting pan-Mediterranean dishes of young Israeli chefs, especially Erez Komarovski's ingenious creations.

Last but not least, I would like to thank my husband for bearing with me, and above all thank Sarah Jane Freymann, my agent and beloved friend; her inspired guidance and support help me realize my full potential.

INDEX

NOTE: Page references in *italics* refer to photographs and captions

Published in 2014 by Stewart, Tabori & Chang
An imprint of ABRAMS

Page 1: Homemade fresh cheese and crunchy, twice baked leftover bread with cherry tomatoes.
Pages 2–3: Leftover meze, bread and spreads at the author's outdoor kitchen.
Page 4–5: Hora, Kea's main town, with the mainland in the back.
Page 6: Preparing green walnuts (*karydaki*) preserves (see page 218).

Library of Congress Control Number: 2014930935
ISBN: 978-1-61769-073-0

Editor: Leslie Stoker
Designer: Sarah Gifford
Production Manager: Tina Cameron

The text of this book was composed in Adobe Garamond Pro, Chronicle Display, Proxima Nova, and Verlag Two.

Printed and bound in China
10 9 8 7 6 5 4 3 2 1

Stewart, Tabori & Chang books are available at special discounts when purchased in quantity for premiums and promotions as well as fundraising or educational use. Special editions can also be created to specification. For details, contact specialsales@abramsbooks.com or the address below.

115 West 18th Street
New York, NY 10011
www.abramsbooks.com